Small Actions, Big Diffe

Despite dire warnings about global warming, carbon emissions by the world's largest companies are *increasing* and only a few companies have strategies for managing carbon emissions and water resources.

So what separates the best from the rest? In one word, the answer is *ownership*: companies that are winning at sustainability have created the conditions for their stakeholders to own sustainability and reap the benefits that come with deeper experience with and ownership of social and environmental issues: a happier, more productive workforce, increased customer loyalty, higher stock valuations, and greater long-term profits.

Based on interviews with 25 global multinational corporations as well as employees, middle managers, and senior leaders across multiple sectors, this is the first book to connect sustainability to the theory and principles of psychological ownership and to propose a succinct, easy-to-digest model for managerial use.

CB Bhattacharya is the H. J. Zoffer Chair in Sustainability and Ethics at the Katz Graduate School of Business, University of Pittsburgh, Pennsylvania. He is a world-renowned expert in business strategy innovation aimed at increasing both business and social value. He is co-author of *Leveraging Corporate Responsibility: The Stakeholder Route to Maximizing Business and Social Value* and co-editor of *Global Challenges in Responsible Business*.

"Everywhere we turn, we hear the word 'sustainability'. But what are companies actually doing? CB Bhattacharya's honest and bracing answer is simple: Not enough. But in this smart, actionable book, he shows how companies can change their ways. By making sustainability central to your purpose, he says, you can improve the health of communities and the planet—and build a better, more profitable business. *Small Actions, Big Difference* belongs on every leader's bookshelf."

Daniel H. Pink, *New York Times best-selling author of WHEN and DRIVE*

"When the world finally makes the turn to sustainable development, it will have been pioneers such as Professor CB Bhattacharya who will have made the difference. Professor Bhattacharya has long understood that sustainable development – combining economic progress with social inclusion and environmental sustainability – is not a gimmick or a pleasantry, but a vital need for the planet and therefore for each of us. He continues his great efforts in this new and important book, a very wise and clearly written guidebook to sustainability for business leaders."

Jeffrey Sachs, *New York Times best-selling author, University Professor, Columbia University*

"CB Bhattacharya's book *Small Actions, Big Difference* is a powerful rallying cry for business to take full ownership of delivering sustainable and equitable growth. As this book argues, business must re-double its efforts through new thinking and a values-based approach that puts people and the planet first."

Paul Polman, *CEO Unilever, 2009–2018*

"*Small Actions, Big Difference* is an important and timely book for businesses who are beyond the "why" and "what" phase of sustainability and firmly on to the "how". It is an important and practical contribution for those looking to drive sustainability through their organization. Based on the authors academic excellence and extensive work with practitioners over decades, it is backed up with relevant case studies and research on what works and what doesn't to drive sustainability impact AND business success. In an era, where business has never been under more pressure or more needed to lead on sustainability, it is a welcome contribution and recommended read for both generalist and specialist alike."

Peter Lacy, *Senior Managing Director, Accenture Strategy*

"The title and the cover picture of this book are a perfect synthesis of the book itself. Sustainability is often the sum of many apparently obvious thoughts and simple actions, resulting in a powerful and large positive impact on mankind. A fascinating discovery for the reader and a powerful call to action."

Francesco Starace, *CEO, Enel*

"There's lots said about the 'why' of sustainable business much less about the 'how' and that's what CB does here so effectively and succinctly, distil the theory into tough, practical action that's needed to make sustainable change stick!"

Mike Barry, *Chief Sustainability Officer, Marks and Spencer*

"In *Small Actions, Big Difference*, Professor Bhattacharya cogently brings into focus the inherent conflict between short-term goals and long-term deliberate corporate action around Sustainability. He challenges the somewhat myopic view of organizational success, compelling readers to re-think the very Purpose of business itself. Well researched and honest, CB's articulation is persuasive and relatable. He moves away from the usual finger-pointing and takes the bold stance of linking Profits to Sustainability. He thus elevates Sustainability to the top of the agenda; making it everybody's day job, especially that of the Leadership."

Vipin Sondhi, *CEO, JCB India*

"This book is an urgent, clear-eyed and eminently implementable clarion call to companies the world over to make a palpable and meaningful contribution to the battle against the environmental and social ills that threaten to destroy our planet and its inhabitants. Bhattacharya's research into the barriers companies face in being sustainable, rather than simply saying or wishing they are, is incisive both in breadth and depth. The framework Bhattacharya builds based on his insights to get every employee to take ownership of sustainability is sensible, practical and ultimately essential if companies are to truly transform themselves into stewards of the environment and society. Essential reading for anyone in the business world who wants to go beyond good sustainability intentions to actually making a real difference."

Joel Makower, *Chairman and Executive Editor, Greenbiz Group Inc.*

"This book does three key things ... a) creates a good conceptual frame around the issue b) develops a model for transformation and c) provides countless examples that help inform and motivate. For companies like DBS, who are relatively new on this journey, all of these are invaluable. One of my best reads this year!"

Piyush Gupta, *CEO, DBS Bank*

Small Actions, Big Difference

Leveraging Corporate Sustainability
to Drive Business and Societal Value

CB Bhattacharya

Routledge
Taylor & Francis Group

LONDON AND NEW YORK

First published 2020
by Routledge
.2 Park Square, Milton Park, Abingdon, Oxon OX14 4RN

and by Routledge
52 Vanderbilt Avenue, New York, NY 10017

Routledge is an imprint of the Taylor & Francis Group, an informa business

British Library Cataloguing-in-Publication Data
A catalogue record for this book is available from the British Library

Library of Congress Cataloging-in-Publication Data
A catalog record has been requested for this book

ISBN: 978-0-367-33755-1 (hbk)
ISBN: 978-0-367-33756-8 (pbk)
ISBN: 978-0-429-32169-6 (ebk)

Typeset in Bembo
by Deanta Global Publishing Services, Chennai, India

Fritzi and Felix

Contents

PART IV
Entrench: demystify, enliven, and expand ownership   123

About the author

CB Bhattacharya is H. J. Zoffer Chair in Sustainability and Ethics at the Katz Graduate School of Business, University of Pittsburgh, Pennsylvania. He is co-author of *Leveraging Corporate Responsibility: The Stakeholder Route to Maximizing Business and Social Value* and co-editor of *Global Challenges in Responsible Business*, both published by Cambridge University Press. He has been named twice on *Business Week*'s Outstanding Faculty list and has been recognized by Thomson Reuters and Google Scholar as one of the top-cited scholars in his field. He received his PhD in Marketing from the Wharton School of the University of Pennsylvania, his MBA from the Indian Institute of Management, Ahmedabad, and his bachelor degree from St. Stephens College, Delhi. Prior to his PhD, he worked as a brand manager at Reckitt Benkiser, during which time he launched the now best-selling toilet-cleaning brand *Harpic* in the Indian market. He consults for several large companies and is often interviewed and quoted in top media outlets.

Foreword by Jeffrey D. Sachs

When the world finally makes the turn to sustainable development, it will have been pioneers such as Professor CB Bhattacharya who will have made the difference. Professor Bhattacharya has long understood that sustainable development – combining economic progress with social inclusion and environmental sustainability – is not a gimmick or a pleasantry, but a vital need for the planet and therefore for each of us. He continues his great efforts in this new and important book, a very wise and clearly written guidebook to sustainability for business leaders.

Sustainable development presents a paradox, one that Professor Bhattacharya powerfully articulates and that motivates his thinking. On the one hand, the idea of sustainability is talked about incessantly, not only at UN gatherings but at business conferences, university lectures, and now even in corporate boardrooms. On the other hand, not much seems to change. The earth continues to warm, species continue to face extinction, and the oceans continue to fill with plastics and other pollutants. Inequalities and social stresses continue to mount even as the gross domestic product (GDP) rises.

We have, in short, a basic breakdown between a concept and its implementation. In the meantime, the global economy continues to push us toward widening inequalities and harrowing threats to the earth's life-support systems. As the recent 1.5-°C report of the Intergovernmental Panel on Climate Change makes clear, we just have a few years left to change course globally if we are to avoid very dangerous and potentially runaway climate disasters in the future. Our goal must be to reach net-zero greenhouse emissions by mid-century, an enormous task that will require the active engagement and leadership of the business community. How to achieve that active engagement is the key question addressed in this book.

Businesses should address four fundamental questions regarding sustainable development. First, are the business's products beneficial for society? Companies producing fossil fuels, unhealthy foods, or dangerous and addictive products, should reconsider the very core of their operations. As Professor Bhattacharya emphasizes, the core products should also contribute to society, not merely make money at the expense of society. Second, are the business's production processes socially and environmentally sustainable? Third, are the business's value chains, including its upstream suppliers and downstream customers, sustainable? Professor Bhattacharya rightly emphasizes that every company is part of a broader ecosystem and each business must be co-responsible for that ecosystem. Fourth, is the company a good citizen of the community, the nation, and the world? Does it pay its fair share of taxes, obey the law, promote gender equality, respect its workers, and engage with its stakeholders? As Professor Bhattacharya stresses, a company must think and act beyond itself, even beyond its own, to find its rightful place in the world.

The great power of Professor Bhattacharya's analysis is to go beyond mere diagnostics, indeed far beyond, to real solutions. As he powerfully notes, "Corporate sustainability has become unsustainable – the understanding and the willingness exist, but companies are stranded about how to become sustainable." In his words, "Now is the time to turn well-worn sentiments into planet-saving deeds."

The book provides a clear, cogent, and bracing approach that is oriented toward the real lives and activities of business leaders. And leadership is key. Leaders should have a clear sense of purpose in order to inspire the entire workforce. Leaders must lead by example, explaining how and why the business contributes to society beyond its mere bottom line, and aligning corporate activities with the values of the employees and of people around the world seeking a safer, healthier, fairer, and more prosperous world.

Professor Bhattacharya emphasizes real stakeholder engagement, not merely platitudes, and calls for a deep conversation with stakeholders about the company's purpose and direction. As he notes, such a conversation requires "a deep knowledge of the course of the world" and of the "company's place within it." In other words, sustainability is not about checking boxes on an annual sustainability report. It requires a careful and detailed analysis to understand how global sustainable development challenges such as climate change should shape the company's core strategy and operational plans.

A key refrain of this book is the need for corporate leaders to inspire all stakeholders – customers, suppliers, workers, corporate boards, competitors, and governments – to "own" sustainability by aligning global concerns such as climate change, biodiversity, and poverty reduction with the personal values and purposes of the stakeholders. Sustainability practices depend on true commitment, and true commitment depends on the alignment of a company's practices with those personal values of the stakeholders.

To endure for the long haul, sustainability practices must be integrated into the very fabric of company activities, and this book suggests several ways to accomplish this, including through the measurement and reporting of key performance indicators for sustainability, regular communications of corporate sustainability decisions and practices, measurement of the company's social impacts, and assigning monetary values to social profits and losses.

Ultimately, a deep and long-lasting culture of corporate sustainability should be based on the philosophy of "co-creation" by the company and its workers. Co-creation means that the company's workers participate in working toward goals that are bigger than the job or the company itself. Workers will find inspiration in that "self-transcendence," that will encourage them to innovate, share, and build upon the company's commitments.

Professor Bhattacharya is wise to note that companies must take up this challenge "because they have the means and the expertise to do so, while governments are all too often paralyzed by politics." Our challenges in meeting the Sustainable Development Goals and the Paris Climate Agreement are too big, too difficult, and too complex to leave to the politicians. Companies have an indispensable and irreplaceable role: they have the technologies, global scale, management capacity, and organizational skills to make critical breakthroughs.

NASA flight director Gene Kranz summed up NASA's can-do attitude in the title of his memoirs, *Failure is Not an Option*. Professor Bhattacharya knows that the same is true when it comes to sustainability. We must get the job done, all of us, including the business sector. By adopting the wise advice of this book, we will be much further along the path to success.

Jeffrey D. Sachs
Director of the UN Sustainable
Development Solutions Network
University Professor, Columbia University

Foreword by Paul Polman

CB Bhattacharya's book *Small Actions, Big Difference* is a powerful rallying cry for business to take full ownership of delivering sustainable and equitable growth.

For too long business has sat on the sidelines, either unable or unwilling to be part of the solution to our systemic environmental and social challenges. But this is now rapidly changing – as the limitations of governments and international bodies become ever more apparent, as consumers, employees and the young increasingly demand change, and as the cost of inaction starts to exceed the cost of action.

Action that is now greatly needed, given the unprecedented strain we have put on our planet; from increased air pollution and degradation of our forests to plastics in our seas. No wonder the Intergovernmental Panel on Climate Change has warned that if we do not change our economic model and consumption patterns, we will reach irreversible tipping points that do permanent damage to our plants, animals, and habitats.

The moral impetus for urgent change is therefore pronounced. We simply cannot afford to delay our response. Not least, as any failure to do so will lead to even more inequality, poverty, disease, and human rights abuses.

Fortunately, we have a north star to plot our recovery. The United Nations Sustainable Development Goals (SDGs), which provide an ambitious blueprint for a better world. Spanning key areas from climate action to life below water, from ending poverty to gender equality, and from zero hunger to fairer institutions and peace, the SDGs have as their ultimate objective the mission of rebalancing economic growth with protecting our planet.

This is the most pressing challenge of our time. But, regrettably, we are not moving anywhere near fast enough to implement the UN's plan by 2030. We now have less than 12 years to alter our trajectory and ensure we live within our planetary boundaries.

As this book sets out, there is one group that can make an outsized contribution in helping to put the world back on track; and that is the business community. Indeed, the resources, scale, expertise, and innovation of business make it ideally placed to have an enormous impact.

And it's in business's interest to do so. A world where systemic environmental and social challenges persist is not a world in which business can thrive and prosper over the long term. That's why a growing number of companies are embedding the SDGs in their strategies – whether larger corporates, entrepreneurs, or start-ups, where we see some of the boldest action being taken.

Business can best contribute to this agenda by deploying sustainable business models and activating the circular economy to drive the system changes needed. And those that do so will be rewarded.

There is now increasing evidence that this approach enables companies to drive innovation and growth, better manage risks, access new markets, anticipate regulatory action, and recruit and retain talent – all of which have a strong bearing on corporate reputation, which is a critical part of any company's value.

The commercial imperative for investing in sustainable and equitable growth is therefore fast becoming a matter of corporate self-interest. In fact, it's a huge economic opportunity. Worth up to $12 trillion a year with the potential to generate at least 380 million jobs. As BlackRock Chairman, Larry Fink, has said: "Purpose is not the sole pursuit of profits but the animating force for achieving them. Profits are in no way inconsistent with purpose – in fact, profits and purpose are inextricably linked."

We must however recognize there will always be limitations in the ability of any one company to act alone. Corporates need to look beyond their own operations and take a share of responsibility across the total value chain. They also need to work in deep partnership with a broad coalition of actors – developed and developing countries, non-governmental organizations (NGOs) and charities, academia and civil society groups, among others – to move at speed and deliver maximum impact.

Financial markets also need to move to the long term. Primarily recognizing the risks of failing to invest in the SDGs right now, they are starting to act. Environmental, social, and governance (ESG) assets under management have grown to $22 trillion; $32 trillion of assets under management is asking for a price on carbon; and $82 trillion has been signed up to the "Principles for Responsible Investment."

It's clear however that the financial community can do even more. A key to unlocking progress will be moving to more open and transparent reporting and the building in of externalities. If you "measure what you treasure" you automatically drive greater accountability for the system changes that are needed to shift, for example, to a low carbon economy. Ultimately, this will help companies to better calculate the risks and opportunities of climate change and make it easier for investors to direct capital to more sustainable businesses.

It's very encouraging that more and more companies are comprehensively embracing the SDGs and the Paris Agreement on climate change as a powerful roadmap for long-term success.

But, as this book argues, business must redouble its efforts in support of driving sustainable and equitable growth, through new thinking and a values-based approach that puts people and the planet first.

Paul Polman
CEO, Unilever, 2009–2019

Acknowledgments

This book would not have seen the light of day without the help, guidance, and support of many. First, I thank the several companies and managers – too numerous to name individually – for opening their doors and talking to me. Thanks also to the managers that attended the Sustainable Business Roundtable meetings at the European School of Management and Technology (ESMT), Berlin, the discussions at which provided the initial spark for writing this book and then provided rich fodder for the text.

I have been very fortunate to receive research support first from ESMT, and then from the Katz Graduate School of Business at the University of Pittsburgh, Pennsylvania. I would not have been able to travel to my research sites, transcribe my interviews, and analyze my data without such support.

I am nothing without my research assistants who have helped me every bit of the way. In order of appearance for this project, they are Nicola Meyer, Sezen Aksin Sivrikaya, Joanna Radeke, Samantha Plummer, Leslie Marshall, John Cuda and Michael Neureiter. Thanks are also due to Seth Schulman for his help with the proposal and to Gerrit Wiesmann for making my writing more colorful and accessible. My excellent administrative staff over the years – Silvana Pophal, Claudia Bierschenk, Jennifer Buchko, and Jill Morris – thank you so much for all your support.

This book has benefited tremendously from the feedback I received at various conferences and seminars worldwide. I am grateful to the many academics and practitioners who have provided feedback over the years. My longtime friend and collaborator Sankar Sen deserves a big shout out for everything he has taught me over the years. A big thank-you to my students – in MBA, Executive MBA, and non-degree executive education settings – for their encouragement and feedback. I hope you find the book to be of use as you change the world for the better.

This project would not have come to fruition without the faith and guidance of the good folks at Routledge. For this, I owe Rebecca Marsh, Sophie Peoples, and their entire team, a big debt of gratitude. Big thanks also to Áine and the entire team at Deanta. A ton of thanks to the dynamic design duo, Margot Perman and Jurgen Riehle of RDA, Real Design Associates, for developing such a striking book cover.

I have learned a lot over the years from the two stellar individuals who wrote the Forewords for this book. Paul Polman, thank you for your wisdom and for everything you do for the cause of sustainability. You will always be a "CEO's CEO" to me. Jeffrey Sachs, thank you for your indefatigable energy and for everything you do to bring environmental and social concerns to the forefront. It has been fun collaborating with you both, and I hope we have more opportunities in the future.

Finally, my deepest gratitude goes to my family and friends, without whose love, support, and enthusiasm there would be no book. My parents and family back in India and my family in Germany patiently endured my thumping on the laptop rather than chatting with them on my precious visits. My dear partner Elfriede Fursich has been my inspiration for three decades now and held the fort steady for many days and nights when I was traveling for my interviews. Finally, my son Felix, who makes a cameo in the conclusion of this book, brightens up every day of my life and serves a daily reminder of how desperately things need to change in our world if his generation is to enjoy the same quality of life as ours. I love you all.

Introduction

I was visiting a large European financial services firm to learn more about its efforts to tackle global issues such as climate change, water scarcity, and inequality. This firm managed large pensions and insurance assets, touching the lives of millions. It was 2015, and if any company needed to address the big issues, it was this one. The firm touted itself as a model corporate citizen: hundreds of millions of euros invested in renewable energy, a reduced carbon dioxide footprint, micro-insurance policies written for people and businesses in developing countries. But all was not what it seemed. In many important areas – such as the amount of corporate funds invested in renewable energy, or the number of "green solutions" rolled out by the company – the company wasn't improving much year over year. It was becoming marginally more sustainable, but it wasn't positioning itself for future success or making strides on behalf of humanity – not even close.

I met with a C-level executive, hoping to shed some light on these subpar results. I had worked for months to get this interview and was excited to meet with such a senior executive. But I knew something was wrong the minute I sat down in his plush, wood-paneled office. Although cordial, he seemed distant and a bit diffident. When I asked if I might videotape a more formal interview with him for my research, he refused. After some cajoling on my part, he did finally agree to my recording the conversation. But I still couldn't videotape him and would have to make do with an audio file.

After I turned on my recording device, I asked him to detail how his company was transforming itself to serve the common good and to secure its position in an unstable world. For the next 45 minutes, the executive spoke eloquently about the financial services firm's desire to deliver both profit and purpose. His company, he told me, knew that it could only do well by doing good. It wanted to be a "responsible corporate citizen" that looked out for different "stakeholder groups."

When I asked about the accomplishments listed in his firm's sustainability report, he said by way of explanation, "Employees today don't just work for the money or the title. They want to be able to have pride in the company they work for." For that reason, the company was actively engaging with public interest groups, he said. It was taking action on environmental and social issues, and it was measuring the impact of these actions. It was also paying close attention to values when hiring new employees. "I think the whole board is really pretty much aligned in terms of what we want to do," he told me. He noted that he and the company's chairman had given speeches about rising to meet big global challenges. Both were posted online, he added with some pride.

I found myself wondering whether the executive was giving me the whole truth or merely feeding me the company line. He sounded very impressive. He was saying all the right things. The company as a whole seemed to "get it." But then why was the company making only mediocre progress in investing in renewable energy, say, or coming up with green solutions? And why had the executive been so awkward or disengaged and not want to be videotaped talking about this issue?

The answer would reveal itself during my next conversation. After wrapping up my conversation with the executive, I was led down a hallway and into a much smaller, more austere office. There, a middle manager stood waiting for me. As we sat down, I asked once again if I could videotape our session. "Sure, why not," he said with a broad smile. Quite a contrast to his boss, I thought. I asked the manager, who worked in human resources, to offer his assessment of how progressive his company was and how quickly it was transforming. At first, he praised his company's employee-oriented policies, which included social responsibility programs, volunteerism, and waste recycling.

But as I probed a bit deeper, he confided that the company had been struggling for some time to get ahead of emerging changes in markets and societies. "We have too many different approaches," he said. "The messages from the top are mixed, and as a result, my colleagues and I are confused. We certainly don't feel all that responsible to actually do our part." Although the senior executive had earlier claimed that the board and company leadership were aligned with a single message, this manager felt lost and saw himself as a bystander. He said he did not consider himself "all that responsible" for making the company sustainable. It was clear that the company had failed to create the conditions for all its stakeholders to take ownership of sustainability.

This manager seemed relieved about finally being able to communicate what he had long felt but couldn't openly express. He was frustrated that his everyday reality on the job didn't measure up with the company's professed ideals, and he assured me that others in the company felt the same.

> Look, just trying to engineer eco-friendly travel between our campuses is difficult [he said]. My direct boss was pretty critical. You know what he told me? "All this stuff – why do we do it? Is it just for reputational purposes, to look good to outsiders? Why are we doing this?"

Somewhat incredulously, the manager pointed out that this had been a pretty small project. "If we had executed it well, it could have created some momentum. But we didn't." This employee was clearly primed to take ownership of sustainable business, but his direct boss and colleagues around him failed to connect the well-being of the planet to the well-being of the company. The company had failed to make sustainability prestigious and enhance the status of those who pursued it.

Now I understood why the senior executive had been so nervous about speaking with me. The company had a glossy sustainability report and website, but not much else to show for itself. Leadership didn't regard enlightened, forward-looking policies as key to the company's own future success. They didn't push employees to recognize the interdependence of the planet's, society's, and the company's well-being, and didn't galvanize them to take ownership of sustainability. Those employees who *did* recognize their responsibility to act sustainably, even in minor ways, were denied a deep experience of ownership because of dysfunctional and disingenuous leadership.

I wish I could say that this company was unique, but it wasn't. Over the past five years, I've visited dozens of large, publicly listed companies and spoken with hundreds of employees, middle managers, and senior leaders. I've been to branch offices, mines, stores, and factories. I've traveled from Madagascar to the heartland of India to the streets of London to the outskirts of Shanghai to Chile's Atacama Desert. I've solicited the observations of top-level executives, senior managers, and a host of regular employees. In addition to this research, I've engaged with 25 multinational corporations as part of the Sustainable Business Roundtable, a unique, peer-to-peer learning network I founded in Berlin. For seven years, it offered companies intent on future-proofing their business models and taking the lead on global challenges a place to exchange ideas and experiences (www.esmt.org/sbrt). What I heard from them about the difficulties of spreading sustainability thinking across and beyond their sectors left me every bit as frustrated as that middle manager.

The word "sustainability" entered the English language as late as 1972. According to the *Oxford English Dictionary* (*OED*), the US economist Thomas Sowell first used the term in his book *Say's Law*, which traced the evolution of the idea that supply creates demand from the early nineteenth-century work of Jean-Baptiste Say: "An increase beyond limits of sustainability existing at any given time would lead only to reduced earnings and subsequent contraction of the quantity supplied," Sowell wrote to explain one of the Frenchman's dictums.

But, as Martin Geissdoerfer and his colleagues explain in their essay "The Circular Economy," the verb "to sustain" in the sense of "to hold up or support" comes from the French verb "soutenir" and the codification of forestry rules in the early seventeenth century. Foresters very probably knew long before that the wood they harvested should not exceed the amount of wood that could grow to replace it. This idea was used to define the broader ecological principle of respecting nature's ability to regenerate itself, and then to help furnish the modern *OED*-definition of being "able to be maintained at a certain rate or level."

A big step in broadening our conceptual understanding of sustainability came in 1987. That year, the United Nation's Brundtland Commission declared our human development and our natural and social environments as "inseparable," defining "sustainable development" as that which meets the needs of the present without compromising the ability of future generations to meet theirs. Environmental sustainability became linked to social and economic sustainability in what became a powerful and defining public narrative.

This inspired entrepreneur and corporate thinker John Elkington to demand that companies shift focus from their traditional bottom line to what he called the "triple bottom line." Instead of just computing profits that accrued within corporate systems, companies needed to measure their external social and environmental impacts along with the financial one. As Elkington put it in his 1997 classic *Cannibals With Forks*, sustainable business is about "people, planet, profit." And this is where my inclusive vision of sustainability starts.

Conducting business with due regard for the environment is important, but it is only one aspect of the kind of sustainability I believe the corporate world must attain. If you agree with the logic of acting in an environmentally sustainable way, you'll find it easy to apply that thinking to Elkington's additions, people and profit. It is logical for a company not to pollute its environment, because a ruined environment will soon impinge upon – and possibly endanger – the company's operating environment. In the same way, it is logical for a company to help ensure social cohesion, as a ruined society will soon make itself felt within the factory gates.

Lastly and perhaps most surprisingly, this logic has to apply to making money, too. It is logical for a company to operate in a way that does not endanger its financial stability because a ruined balance sheet puts an end to all future profits. Short-term gains might be what many shareholders still crave, but corporate leaders have to balance their demands with the financial needs of the company – to only extract as much profit as the company can sustainably deliver, year in, year out. Next to ensuring the sustainability of people and planet, the sustainability of profit is an absolutely essential element of my thinking. A company that cannot rely on the existence of people, planet, and profit over the long term is an unsustainable company.

So, when I talk about sustainability in business, my definition and my ambition is necessarily broad. Income inequality, human rights abuse, and legal or forced immigration flows can be as important to doing business in a sustainable way as the paying out of reasonable profits, or decent waste recycling, or cutting emissions. The inclusiveness of my vision is as exciting as it can be terrifying. There really is an awful lot at stake, for companies and for the people on this planet. But I hope this perspective will prove more of a spur than a deterrent – the magnitude of our multiple problems demands that we act, and that we strive to make a difference.

Sadly, my research led me to conclude that the current corporate sustainability movement is unsustainable. One example says it all: Despite dire warnings about global warming, carbon emissions by the world's largest companies are still *increasing*. Only a few companies have strategies for managing carbon emissions and water resources, and only a third of the 600 largest public companies in the US have any kind of sustainability oversight at the board level. Meanwhile, environmental and social challenges are getting increasingly dire, and the United States' exit from the Paris Agreement that is a key element of the United Nations Framework Convention on Climate Change has dimmed the prospect of swift and effective governmental action.

The good news is that the sustainability movement is failing not because companies are pursuing the wrong goals. Companies have never been more conscious of the need to do business in an environmentally, socially, and economically responsible fashion. But the bad news is that they are pursuing the right goals in the wrong way. When it comes to practicing and not just preaching sustainability – when companies have to develop and implement a sustainable business model for themselves – many struggle and most founder. Rather than taking ownership of sustainability, they remain paralyzed and incapable of addressing the urgent issues facing our planet and the opportunity to create change.

Why is it that something as important as *sustainability* is given short shrift through the inaction of so many? Through my research, I've found that companies' lack of interest in the social and environmental impact of their practices reflects a disturbing trend: most companies treat sustainability as "someone else's problem." Employees and managers pawn it off on the sustainability department; senior executives of large companies view it as the government's problem; and leaders of small companies say it is something for large companies to worry about. The truth is that creating the conditions for a healthy, successful future is *everyone's problem*. When an entire organization thinks "it's someone else's problem," nothing changes. And when many organizations fail to change, our species inches closer toward extinction.

Yet, the situation is not entirely hopeless. Not all companies are waiting for someone else to take charge. A handful of companies around the world *are* taking ownership of sustainability and getting it right, even if they themselves remain works-in-progress. At consumer goods colossus Unilever, for example, employees see sustainability as integral to their work. At the company's sites all over the world, shop-floor workers have of their own accord come up with a raft of innovations – such as smaller paper seals for tea bags – to cut down on waste and increase profit. The company's belief in the power of small actions to make a big difference helped inspire this book and its title.

While Unilever has been widely lauded for its embrace of sustainable practices, companies like Enel (Italy), Marks & Spencer, BASF, IBM, ING, Coca-Cola European Partners, Nestlé, Siemens, and a few others are also resolutely pushing sustainability much further than most of their peers. Not only are these businesses taking the lead in protecting humanity from environmental disaster and social upheaval. In preparing for the future, they are also positioning themselves to reap the enormous business benefits that come from sustainability ownership – increased profitability, revenue growth, reputational gains, higher workforce engagement, lower employee turnover, and easier access to capital.

Based on my groundbreaking research, *Small Actions, Big Difference* is the first book to explain the key challenges that companies face in embracing and implementing sustainability and to detail what they should do to transform their stakeholders from bystanders to owners. Writing for the current and future leadership of companies large and small, I have developed a model that shows leaders how to push meaningful progress on global issues by galvanizing stakeholders, getting them to take ownership of sustainability, and making it everyone's job – even when governments aren't.

So, what does ownership mean and why would we want to take ownership of sustainability? Psychological ownership refers to feelings of possessiveness and connection that we develop toward people, companies, things, or even ideas like sustainability. Research has shown that feelings of ownership lead to greater job satisfaction, engagement, productivity, and profits. It is an especially helpful concept for companies seeking to align their ideals and practices and galvanize their stakeholders around sustainability. Confronted daily with media reports about climate change and human rights abuses, most of us yearn to do something, but don't know how to assert control and shape our environments. Taking ownership of sustainability helps create meaningful solutions to the problems that surround us. That's because taking ownership of sustainability drives *all* stakeholders – both internal and external, from the mail room to the boardroom – to contribute to coming up with sustainable solutions to business problems.

My research has identified a three-phase development of sustainable ownership. Depicted in Figure 0.1, I like to describe the schema using a brief analogy: like prospective buyers deciding what kind of house is appropriate for them,

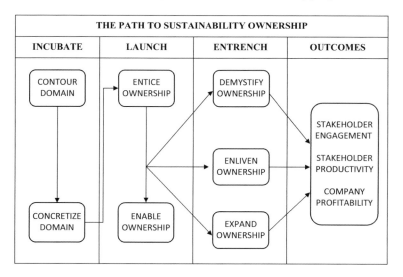

Figure 0.1 The path to sustainability ownership

how much house they can afford now and in the future, company leaders first incubate their idea of ownership by developing and contouring the purpose of their business. They then make a list of concrete issues their organization must address to be sustainable.

Then, just as banks persuade future homeowners to take loans and secure the tools necessary to make consistent payments, leaders entice their stakeholders to buy into their plan and enable them to act sustainably. Finally, like home buyers moving in and making the house a home by establishing routines, decorating, and giving all family members a sense of belonging, companies entrench feelings of ownership by demystifying stakeholders' contributions, enlivening the experience of ownership, and expanding the sense of ownership to new groups of stakeholders.

Each of these phases includes key steps to taking ownership of sustainability. Put together, they give you the power to move your stakeholders from the sidelines to the front lines of addressing your company's and our world's biggest challenges.

Incubate: In the incubation phase, you must develop the domain of sustainability you want to own by marking the contours of your company's specific purpose in the world. Then make this purpose concrete by translating it into measurable goals.

- **Contour**: Contour the sustainability domain by deciding what your company is taking ownership of. Answer fundamental questions about the purpose of your business. Who are we? Why do we do what we do? Why should we take ownership of sustainability now? Articulate how the firm adds or creates value beyond shareholders' pockets; define your company in terms of the society it both emanates from and serves.
- **Concretize**: Concretize your goals by answering the following questions. Where is growth likely to come from in the future? How will mega trends like climate change come to affect our business? How big is our ecological footprint and what are its main contributors? What do our stakeholders want? Generate a list of material issues across your entire value chain and prioritize them by biggest potential impact.

Launch: In the launch phase, entice and enable stakeholders to take ownership of your plan by giving them the opportunity to participate in, understand, and identify with sustainability.

- **Entice**: Entice stakeholders to own sustainability by selling it as an opportunity to contribute to the future well-being of the company. Figure out how and why your stakeholders respond to change. Sometimes you will need to appeal to the head, other times to the heart, and often both. Entice your employees, and other internal and external stakeholders, including board members, your supply chain, your community members, and even consumers, to get off the sidelines and become owners.

- **Enable**: Enable ownership by putting systems, structures, and training in place that lower the costs and increase the benefits of acting sustainably. Give your stakeholders the tools, confidence, and freedom they need to contribute to sustainability goals. Set strict requirements but give your stakeholders the flexibility to decide how they go about solving problems. In a word, make sustainability everybody's job.

Entrench: To entrench sustainability, you must maintain its momentum and integrity by demystifying stakeholders' contributions and enlivening and expanding the ownership experience. When sustainability is entrenched in a company, it is so firmly established in its ethos that it is difficult if not impossible to act unsustainably.

- **Demystify**: Demystify stakeholders' contributions to the achievement of sustainability targets and show the connections between these goals and the purpose of their jobs and the company. Measure key performance indicators and provide ongoing feedback on sustainability targets. This gives stakeholders the opportunity to learn how sustainability works and how they contribute to achieving goals.
- **Enliven**: Enliven sustainability ownership by developing initiatives, events, and practices that keep it fresh and relevant and maintain the initial excitement and belief. Nip entropic tendencies in the bud; create a strong and vibrant sustainability culture by committing to "the three Cs": co-creation, communication, celebration.
- **Expand**: Expand feelings of ownership by building broader industry collaborations. These are required to solve complex supply chain and distribution challenges and drive systemic change. This step is necessary to create the really big changes that our planet and its people need – and that businesses need, too.

Companies reap benefits from taking ownership of sustainability. My research reveals that sustainability ownership not only increases profit margins through improved resource management, increased revenues, and lower cost of capital. It also amplifies employee engagement, which is tied to business performance. Companies that take ownership of sustainability engage employees by enabling them to express their personal values and to help solve environmental and social problems at work. Employees' engagement grows as they come to discover their colleagues' self-investment in sustainability. As one employee told me:

> One of the reasons I have stayed at my company for thirty years is that I have enjoyed working with the people I have been working with. I feel that they are fundamentally trying to the do the right things for the company and for the long term.

Gallup (2018) has declared a "worldwide employment engagement crisis," finding that only 15 percent of employees worldwide are engaged at work.

But companies that take ownership of sustainability see remarkable levels of engagement. By increasing employee engagement, sustainability ownership not only bolsters employee retention, but also enhances productivity, and thus profits. At Unilever, where engagement scores are consistently among the highest, CEO Paul Polman explained to me: "When you have that level of employee engagement, you'll still find a way to overcome most challenges and be successful." With this model, after decades of failure and false promises, you'll have the tools you need to position your companies, yourselves, and humanity for long-term success.

Previous books on sustainability and corporate responsibility have explained why it makes sense for companies to change society and our environment for the better. But relatively few have shown *how* companies can switch from traditional, profit-driven business models to business models that honor people and planet alongside profit. And only one book – this one – identifies a crisis in corporate transformation efforts, analyzes the root causes of this failure, and provides research-based prescriptions for rendering a company's approach to sustainability that is more enlightened, forward-looking, and effective. Drawing on well over a hundred interviews with executives, managers, and employees, and mustering an extensive arsenal of academic research in the social sciences, I've developed a robust model of sustainability ownership. I explain how you can use the model and make it work through the inspiring stories that I gathered during my research.

Small Actions, Big Difference begins by making the case that existing sustainability efforts are unsustainable, and that virtually all companies have failed to secure their and humanity's future. I argue that governments alone won't save human societies – companies, business communities, and individuals have to. I explain what sustainability ownership is and why it is the best concept for understanding what companies should do to become truly sustainable.

The remaining chapters detail my research-based model for transforming your stakeholders from bystanders to owners. Each chapter lays out a key step your company must take to move beyond the talk and take ownership of sustainability. Collectively, these steps enable executives in any company regardless of its size to transform their business models and create progressive, dynamic cultures of engagement. Preparing for the future thus becomes an important part of *everyone's* job within the company and beyond, engaging managers and employees in all parts of the company, from marketing to operations, strategy to finance, as well as stakeholders in the ecosystem.

As the Zoffer Chair of Sustainability and Ethics at the University of Pittsburgh's Katz School of Business, Pennsylvania, I am a leading global expert on corporate sustainability and responsible leadership. But I have a confession to make. At one time, I also considered a broader concern for our common welfare as "someone else's problem." Early in my career, I dedicated myself to researching an entirely unrelated topic, statistical models for marketing. It was only in the mid-1990s that my world shifted. I met Ben Cohen, the co-founder of Ben and Jerry's ice cream, and became intrigued by the idea that environmental and social concerns could drive people to do business with particularly environmentally and socially engaged companies. Over the next decade, I completely reoriented my research efforts, devoting myself to establishing the business case for investing in forward-looking policies that safeguard the environment and address social ills.

Studying companies such as Procter and Gamble, General Mills, Eli Lilly, Timberland, Green Mountain Coffee, and Stonyfield Farm, I was able to demonstrate that under certain conditions, consumers and employees really do reward companies for considering more than just their profit margins. This led to my first book, *Leveraging Corporate Responsibility: The Stakeholder Route to Maximizing Business and Social Value,* co-authored with Sankar Sen and Daniel Korschun. But in doing this research and continuing it over the years, I noticed something else – sustainability or corporate social responsibility was hopelessly marginalized inside companies. At almost every company I visited, the person in charge of these initiatives wielded little influence over his or her organization's decision-making process. In my teaching, I likewise noticed that executives tended to regard concern for our common welfare as "someone else's job," and that most didn't even know what their *own* company was really doing to secure their organization's and humanity's future. This disconnect struck me as terrible for people and planet – and, by extension, for profit.

I wrote *Small Actions, Big Difference* because I was deeply shocked by the political dysfunction in the US and elsewhere. I became more determined than ever to set companies on the right course so that they, at last, can secure our future. Think of what the world would be like if the ten largest global companies took ownership of sustainability. Now think of what the world would be like if *half* of all companies on the planet took that ownership. It's almost mind-boggling to contemplate. In the latter scenario, most people would love their jobs, and devote their full energies to making their companies successful. Organizations would be far more efficient and productive, building better reputations, and enjoying easier access to capital. Societies would be more equitable, peaceful, and prosperous. Our planet would make real headway in the fight against global warming and other environmental problems. Ultimately, the business community would succeed in securing the continued existence of human civilization for future generations.

After decades spent establishing *what* companies have to do to secure their and our collective future, it's high time they finally mastered *how* to do it.

Bibliography

T. Sowell (1972). *Say's Law: An Historical Analysis.* Princeton University Press.

M. Geissdoerfer (2017). The circular economy – A new sustainability paradigm?, *Journal of Cleaner Production,* 143, 757–768.

United Nations (1987). *Report of the World Commission on Environment and Development Our Common Future.* NGO Committee on Education of the Conference of NGOs.

J. Elkington (1997). *Cannibals With Forks: Triple Bottom Line of 21st Century Business.* John Wiley & Son Ltd.

J. Harter and Gallup (2018). *Employee Engagement on the Rise in the U.S.* Gallup Press.

CB Bhattacharya, S. Sen, and D. Korschun (2011). *Leveraging Corporate Responsibility: The Stakeholder Route to Maximizing Business and Social Value.* Cambridge University Press.

Part I

From bystanders to owners

In Part I, I present evidence that companies have failed to engage properly in sustainability despite boasts to the contrary. Based on my research, I argue that most corporate sustainability endeavors fail because companies are either (a) unwilling to take action because they view sustainability as a costly add-on and a hindrance to short-term performance, or (b) unable to engage employees and integrate sustainability into their operations and stakeholders' lives. I then explain what ownership is and why it is a useful concept for companies seeking not just to talk the talk, but truly to walk the walk of sustainability.

1 The unsustainability of "sustainability"

1.1 Lots of talk and no action

"Fishbanks" is a business simulation exercise I like to run with executives who attend my continuing education programs. I think of it as "Monopoly" for sustainability, with one crucial difference. Dividing the executives into small teams, I ask them to compete against one another to become the most profitable commercial fishing company. I create a display that shows the teams' running profits and set them loose to borrow money, build their fishing fleets, and outperform the competition. These executives, who hail from corporate stalwarts such as Accenture, Allianz, L'Oréal, Rio Tinto, or Siemens, are highly educated and enlightened. They know they're taking part in a session about sustainability, and yet, without fail, as they compete against one another, they build up their fleets by a factor of six or more to extract more fish from the sea than their competitors. But guess what happens – the ocean runs out of fish.

As the game progresses, the players do become aware of the dangers of overfishing. Yet they continue to buy more ships and send them out to sea to fish. "We're okay now," some executives always say about the fish stocks. "We'll start cutting back soon." But of course, they don't. And other executives don't even see fish stocks as a problem. They make excuses for dwindling stocks, attributing the dip to cyclical factors like bad weather. As the fish run out, executives desperately try to sell boats nobody wants anymore. "Damn nature," one player will say. "I can't believe how greedy I was," says another. These executives don't even play for real money, but everybody loses every time. That's the one crucial difference to "Monopoly," because in that game someone always has to win.

This fishing simulation is not an idle game. It is a stark demonstration of a phenomenon called the "tragedy of the commons," an idea popularized by the American ecologist Garrett Hardin in a 1968 *Science* article about common pasture ruined by overgrazing. "Fishbanks" illustrates that the overriding business mindset hasn't changed in the half century since Hardin's groundbreaking article. Many existing business practices are unaffected by 50 years of public debate and corporate pledges about "sustainability." Most managers blissfully continue to maximize the private gains of their companies without regard for the collective losses borne by society. They continue to externalize the costs of pollution and the healthcare of their workers.

Yes, a few small companies – outdoor-clothing maker Patagonia, for example, or organic yoghurt producer Stonyfield – have made substantial progress on environmental and social issues. But the vast majority of companies, including the world's biggest, have done little or nothing to avoid the disasters that follow resource degradation and depletion. They have not adopted sustainable business models. They still have not prepared their businesses – and with that an important part of society – for a future free of the tragedy of the commons and its follow-on disasters.

Sustainability means saving the planet and its people from irreparable harm. It is a task for politicians and business people, but, sadly, politics has so far failed to do its part – there are even signs its efforts have slackened in recent years. Toward the end of 2018, the United Nations Intergovernmental Panel on Climate Change (IPCC) warned that "rapid, far-reaching and unprecedented changes in all aspects of society" would still be needed if the world wanted to cap global warming at 1.5 degrees above preindustrial levels. With global mean surface temperatures already roughly one degree higher than in the period from 1850 to 1900, the IPCC said that by 2030 man-made CO_2 emissions would have to fall by around 45 percent from 2010 levels and to "net zero" emissions by 2050 to reach that goal. Only weeks later, the International Energy Agency said that CO_2-emissions in advanced economies had risen in 2018, the first annual rise in five years. Politicians seem to have their heads in the sand.

I think we should heed the warnings of large groups of learned scientists, not their evidence-free rejection by political populists. If we consider the natural ability of our planet to continually replenish key resources such as air and water, humanity today is consuming resources worth 1.5 planets. By 2050, assuming business as usual, we'll be consuming three planets' worth of resources. As Sowell said of Say: supply has increased beyond the limits of sustainability. We are chopping more trees down than can be replaced in time by new ones growing. Sustainability as it's currently being practiced isn't sustainable. Fixing it is an urgent human imperative. Politicians and business people should tackle this problem together. But there has been much talk and little action. And if politicians continue with their refusal to engage wholeheartedly, the imperative for businesses to act becomes even greater – not least because stakeholder pressure and environmental emergencies will soon hit untenable levels.

But companies are also failing to prepare and protect society at large because, on a fundamental level, they have not allowed the concept of planning for the future to take root in practice. Top executives often wax eloquent about sustainability. They tell us about their policies and programs, their key performance indicators used to keep track of corporate virtue. They describe their sustainability departments, compliance programs, and risk management procedures. A few more broad-minded executives even tout their sustainability initiatives as an exciting business opportunity. But the further you move away from the C-suite and its ideals into the many lower levels of a company, the more sustainability becomes mired in the day-to-day of mixed messages and confusion, demoralization and inertia.

Sustainability is "someone else's job" – this attitude is still prevalent among too many employees and managers. They don't understand the business relevance of sustainability, so they don't put it into practice. As one executive told me, too many people "are talking about the problem, and reiterating and reiterating the problem, but not actually doing anything."

Recounting his dealings with middle managers, a sustainability director at a large retailer said, "The conversation in the business is always positive about the need to change. But there's always a question about pace. 'Can we just wait another six or twelve months before we start [the sustainability] part of the journey? I've got other things I've got to deliver in the short term.'" He related what a hard time stores had had accepting greater autonomy to engage with their local communities. There was a "whole load of work that [needed] to change internally" before it happened, he said.

In most large organizations, attitudes and internal work processes haven't evolved to allow individuals at every level of the business to practice sustainability, for example, by participating in sustainability initiatives however large or small. As a result, little of any importance gets done to avoid the tragedy of the commons, to end the unsustainability of sustainability.

Procrastination rules. As I argue in this chapter, companies have failed to integrate sustainability into their operations for four reasons. Firstly, many executives still operate in a business world in which the short-term extraction of profit is deemed more important than the long-term creation of value. Even those who know better still defer to the demands of owners or investors steeped in the lore of shareholder value.

Secondly, corporate leaders often still view sustainability as the next phase of "corporate responsibility," something optional that companies *can* do out of the goodness of their hearts. They don't recognize it as a strategic imperative, something they *must* do in order to prepare for the future. Both these failures lead to failure three – too many corporate executives still view sustainability as a cost and not as an investment, a drag on, rather than a catalyst for profit.

Lastly, and perhaps most importantly, even well-intentioned and enlightened executives fail to practice sustainability within their organizations because they don't understand how to implement it so that the whole company buys in. They believe sustainability can be embedded via "change management," which is fallacious because sustainability touches upon profound questions about business purpose and business philosophy in a way change management doesn't.

In particular, these executives don't understand how to engage and motivate employees and other stakeholders by lowering the costs of acting sustainability and increasing the benefits for all involved. This leads to a misalignment of values – as members of society, people see the need for acting sustainably, as corporate employees, they feel they can or must forego such thinking. It is no less than companies forcing their employees to be idealists and cynics both at the same time. But such split personalities are unsustainable over the long term.

Instead, companies need to imbue their employees and other stakeholders with a new sense of purpose around sustainability. That will encourage stakeholders to identify with sustainability, so that they come to recognize a personal stake in preparing their organization for the future. That, in turn, will give them ownership of sustainability, which is nothing less than a sense of personal responsibility for the well-being of the people and the planet.

The chapters that follow provide a framework for mobilizing an organization around sustainability. Stakeholders at all levels become engaged, both rationally and emotionally, and move from being bystanders to owners of that process. In the pages that follow, I will discuss why companies remain unwilling or unable to implement sustainable business models. But I also look beyond the gloom and detail positive sustainability-related changes taking place on the edges of the corporate world. There are many reasons to despair, but also many that offer hope. I am a believer in the corporate stakeholders of the world.

1.2 Companies are unwilling or unable to engage

Too many companies continue to place profit before people and planet – very possibly the company you work for, too. You might find that hard to accept, as you and your colleagues are probably aware of the need to factor environmental and social costs into the overall cost of doing business. But, as I said in the introduction, the steps from insight to effective implementation are hard, and often difficult to judge in their effectiveness. Thinking and talking about doing business sustainably is one thing. But actually putting concepts into practice is an entirely different proposition – the leap is too large for many companies.

Recall my students' behavior in the "Fishbanks" exercise. These are usually relatively young people, well educated, and aware of their responsibility toward the planet. But when they play the fishing simulation at the start of their course, the same thing always happens. Some do come to see disaster looming, but disaster always unfolds, regardless.

I have watched young executives play this game for many years and I'm still startled by its uncanny, unwavering ability to lead astray people who quite obviously know better. After all, my seminars are about *sustainability*, so it should be obvious where the exercise is headed. But, sadly, "Fishbanks" is a gloomy demonstration of the problems companies face when trying to implement policies to save the planet. It shows how easy it is to focus on profit – and make people and planet someone else's problem. Half a century after Hardin's observation about the tragedy of the commons, nothing has changed. Without fail, these young managers hone in on their team's profit – and the profits other teams are making – and quite naturally fall into a way of thinking and acting that lends business a rapacious and self-serving quality.

When the sizes of their catches start to plummet, most players begin to notice that their revenue problems are structural, not cyclical. Much of their wisdom about environment and society starts flooding back. Teams reach out to each other, self-appointed spokesmen or spokeswomen try to get their class-mates to agree on moratoria or quotas. In the end, all teams understand what they've done, and they do finally react. But they always discover that all solutions are fraught in different ways – and being presented too late.

What happens, year in, year out, in my seminars is still happening ten thousand-fold in companies across the globe. Executives, middle managers, shop-floor workers are more sensitized to the fragility of the planet than any generation before them. But short-termism, profit focus, conservative corporate cultures, and human timidity mean that theory isn't being transformed into action. They know that overfishing is a classic example of the tragedy of the commons, of externalizing the social and environmental costs of doing business until everything collapses under the strain. And yet they keep on fishing. Why? Because they are both unwilling to engage properly in doing business sustainably, and they're unable to.

a. Short-termism still rules in the boardroom

Short-term financial targets and the bonuses in pay they determine do more to undermine employees' willingness to do business sustainably than any other fact of corporate life. Investment in sustainability almost by definition takes longer to bring forth dividends than the three-month gap between the quarterly financial results so many companies now publish. This mismatch between the time-horizon needed for sustainability initiatives and the time-horizon for financial returns demanded by investors is a grave problem for executives.

One CEO I interviewed was very candid about the "enormous pressure" on company leaders to deliver fast and ongoing improvements in financial performance. "The [financial] markets put enormous pressure on you ... and if it's not the markets, it might be your own board." He noted that "the tenure of the CEO is now less than four years in many places" and sketched the bind many corporate bosses are in. Even if they believe in sustainability, they might not have the time – and therefore the incentive – to show that investments in people and planet can bear fruit. "Unfortunately," he said, "We still live in a fairly short-term life-cycle environment, and that can sometimes mean that the right decisions take longer to make – or are not made at all."

In circumstances like this, pursuing short-term profit is the safest course for many executives. Indeed, many managers continue to assume that sustainability is not a priority among the majority of investors. "Investors would hate that," the finance manager of a large electronics company said when asked about emphasizing more longer-term corporate metrics. "They are very clear about the fact they would be unhappy if they saw us replace cash flow or top-line growth with (a metric showing) the percentage of products sustainably procured."

Sustainability and short-term financial targets are not natural friends. Their mismatch is compounded by the reticence of institutional investors – actual as much as perceived – to accept trade-offs between short-term profit and sustainability. "Mainstream investors focus on current trading and latest financial results, they don't talk about sustainability at all," said one investor relations officer at a big industrial corporation. I'll be taking a closer look at investor attitudes later in the chapter. For now, it's important to note that corporate perceptions of financial-market demands lead to a bias toward short-term thinking.

The main reason for this is that short-term profits are easier to quantify than longer-term increases in value. The vice president (VP) of investor relations at a large food manufacturer spoke openly about the temptations of short-termism: "Costs in the short term are relatively easy to capture and codify and quantify. But the benefits are often out in the future and highly uncertain." Preparing a company's supply chain for the impact of climate change was no doubt a valuable thing to do, he noted. But the managers would probably have a tough time funding their initiative should they admit that they knew neither exactly when nor where a water crisis, say, might hit the supply chain.

Recognizing the possibility of longer-term value creation over short-term profit often required experience, individual or collective, this manager went on to say. He explained that during the early years of television, shareholders were unconvinced about the potential benefits of TV advertising, seeing it as pure cost rather than marketing investment. Trying to get stakeholders to buy into the value-creating effects of sustainability was "in many ways [...] no different from trying to work out the return from a TV advert," the latter being a "difficult" proposition that "everyone got used to" as experience built up. "Everyone now has years of dealing with the uncertainties and costs of [...] TV advertising." In a similar way, he said, passing time and accreting experience would allow managers to observe the long-term costs of not acting. This would eventually allow them to quantify the extent to which long-term benefits would outweigh short-term costs as new sustainability-linked projects arose. But sadly, the dire straits humanity is in currently, do not allow us the luxury of such nuanced calibration.

Importantly, short-termism is not just a problem that affects the top of every company. Indeed, my interviews with people on the front lines of sustainability suggested that the pressure to meet short-term financial targets deeply influenced mindsets in the operational belly of many companies. Short-term pressures across large parts of any organization can be as heavy as those on corporate leadership.

Indeed, as a sustainability officer noted, the commitment of middle management is key to doing business more sustainably: "We have senior management very much committed to [sustainability ...] and we have young people coming in with equal degrees of commitment and fire in their bellies. But it's the people in the middle who have actually got to deliver the results. They have actually got to deliver this week's sales. They have to build factories and make them work. If that does not happen there are of course serious consequences for the business and for them."

Sustainability champions must overcome a significant hurdle. They must demonstrate the long-term value of sustainability to stakeholders who mainly still think short-term. This includes consumers, as one retail industry manager told me. "One of the biggest problems is that the people who buy our products so far have not shown any great willingness to pay more for a sustainable product," he said with an undertone of frustration. "In many cases they say in consumer research that they like sustainable products and will buy them. But when they get into the store they tend to buy a product that is on offer or cheaper, whatever it might be."

b. Sustainability is seen as a traditional "add-on" initiative

The second reason why company executives are unwilling to engage with sustainability is its legacy as an "add-on" component of normal business, not one that should be integrated into all levels and all ways of doing business. Executives that fall prey to this thinking see sustainability as part of old-style "corporate social responsibility" (CSR) activities – traditionally under the charge of specific employees who are usually responsible for nothing else other than these programs.

The sustainability writer Henk Campher traces holistic modern sustainability thinking back to the corporate philanthropy that began with the Industrial Revolution and reached a peak with the mass industrialization of the late nineteenth and early twentieth centuries. As "strategic" as this type of corporate spending came to be seen, it was still a cost that was accounted for outside of the company's normal activity of economic value creation. It was an add-on, an expense accepted as a license to continue doing business.

Out of corporate philanthropy grew CSR, which was a step toward the simultaneous creation of economic, social, and environmental value. Where corporate philanthropists had invested in causes beyond the factory gates, CSR experts started looking at their company's value chain and at ways of reaping benefits for people and planet while still making profits. But even these initiatives were often "offset" models, by which a company did good in one field to make up for bad deeds like emissions in another area – as if pollution could be offset by social benevolence.

Unfortunately, these past efforts at "doing good" were by modern standards badly coordinated – a small initiative here, a symbolic one there, and perhaps a bit of marketing-driven "greenwashing" to amplify the effect. As I mentioned in the Introduction, I heard of one mid-level manager's boss asking of an inexpensive sustainability initiative: "All this stuff – why do we do it?" One reason sustainability has a bad name is that it's been done badly for too long. By design or accident, too many employees came to see sustainability as being about doing good in a scattershot way, or about looking rather than truly being good.

As a result, many sustainability efforts were at best ignored and at worst became suspect within their own organizations. "Everybody knows it's a bit of a charade," said a sustainability project manager at a large beverage maker.

"It's ambiguous. So it's about personal commitment and turning that personal commitment … into action and real-life things happening." Without that transition, as the managers at a large financial services company noticed, those charged with spreading the word about sustainability would be largely ignored. In many companies, there is still no shared understanding of what sustainability means to them. "We report [our initiatives] once a year in our sustainability report," one person said. "The problem, of course, is that I'm not sure all the employees actually read it."

Sustainability for some employees has become a cosmetic exercise – "finding the right photo for the annual report," as one manager put it. For others, it has turned into a calculating search for trade-offs, doing good in one place to make up for unsustainable activity in another. One sustainability officer at a large consumer goods company said: "I think the established corporate social responsibility (CSR) programs are one of the biggest problems we have in this area – it somehow allows you to do something good in CSR to negate something bad you're doing elsewhere. That's not sustainable."

Sustainability also has to be more than just an add-on because add-ons can come to be viewed as fads, as trends that will inevitably fade. An executive at a large food manufacturer suggested his employees still see sustainability "as a bit of a blip, they see it as a fad that will pass." It might have already proved to be a long fad, he conceded. "But they see it as a fad that will pass and they want to go back to their core ways of working." So part of the challenge is to address these skeptics and those resistant to change, and to get them to change the way they think about and go about their day-to-day business.

c. Sustainability is seen as fixable by change management

Globalization and technological advance have made change and the need to adapt to it a constant in any organization. It has become so constant, in fact, that many companies use "change management" and "change managers" to help the workforce adapt to and adopt new working methods through digitization, big data, artificial intelligence, or new organizational models, with simpler structures or fewer hierarchies, for example.

Change-management initiatives are usually driven by external factors that are a drag on internal performance. They have over the past generation usually been aimed at short-term goals such as increasing profitability and shareholder value. On top of that, many change-management initiatives succeed in captivating only certain parts of an organization, and many fail because too few employees truly embrace them – if they miss this one, another one will be along soon.

Many companies see embedding a sustainable business model as yet another change-management initiative. They fail to grasp that implementing a sustainable business model is different not only in the degree but also in the nature of the task. It is about people and planet, about long-term value creation not just short-term profit. It is about finding and practicing a business philosophy.

It is about creating value for all stakeholders in the corporate ecosystem, and about viewing profits as a consequence of such value creation. Implementing a sustainable business model requires executives to engage with the entire organization and with stakeholders – consumers, employees, suppliers, regulators, competitors, non-governmental organizations (NGOs), in addition to shareholders – to balance out different and even conflicting goals. That's much harder than traditional change management.

d. Sustainability is still not seen as a source of profit

Short-termism and the add-on models lead to a regrettable knock-on effect – sustainability and profit are still widely regarded as mutually exclusive. Funds that flow into sustainability initiatives are defined as costs rather than investments that will bring returns. Just as corporate ethics are seen as distinguishable from personal ethics, saving people and planet, and making money, are still widely seen as separate courses of action.

In spring 2017, for example, a Forbes.com guest writer lambasted Unilever's then-CEO Paul Polman for his pioneering sustainability work. Business commentator Tom Borelli accused Polman of putting his "personal political agenda" – making the consumer goods producer a sustainability leader – ahead of the – presumably impersonal – corporate agenda of making money. "In a *Fortune* magazine interview last month, Polman expressed more interest in supporting the United Nations Sustainable Development Goals than Unilever's 2016 financial results" said Borelli. In the same vein, a *Financial Times* article about Polman's retirement described his tenure as failing to deliver shareholder returns, and his sustainability passion as an eccentricity: "Mr. Polman lost sight of his main mission, namely to grow sales and profits at one of the world's biggest consumer goods companies, and succumbed to the siren song of being a regular on the UN-to-Davos circuit." Never mind that shareholder returns in Polman's time hit a very impressive 282 percent, while the UK's FTSE index racked up only 131 percent.

The risk to profits – as well as to people and planet – of this kind of myopic thinking was shown starkly in 2015 by the think tank Carbon Tracker. In a report issued ahead of the United Nations Climate Change Conference in Paris in December of that year, the think tank warned that energy companies could end up wasting $2.2 trillion in fossil fuel investments. Why? Because coordinated efforts by governments to restrict global warming to well below 2 degrees looked set to make extraction projects too expensive.

Indeed, the *Financial Times* at the time reported about a separate study by think tank Critical Resource:

> Overseen by, among others, Sir Mark Moody-Stuart, ex-chairman of Shell, and Lord Browne, BP's former chief executive, [it] has pointed out the "significant disconnect" between the fundamental rethink required to meet that goal (of fighting climate change), and the efforts of companies themselves.

Critical Resource had polled 13 natural-resources companies and found that only 3 of them thought global warming was not a material business issue – but only 1 of the other 10 had drawn up a scenario for the 2-degree limit.

Nero, the epitome of ineffectual leadership, is said to have played the fiddle while Rome burned.

e. These failings lead to a misalignment of corporate and personal values

The four failings outlined above lead companies to act as if sustainability is not integral to everyday business. This, in turn, skews corporate values and the values of each employee. The add-on model involving sustainability officers or change managers encourages employees to differentiate between isolated pockets of corporate sustainability and business as usual everywhere else. As a result, employees also measure ethical failures and successes differently: they accept that a company is really there to make money and treat its sustainability efforts as a welcome sign of guilt-driven "making good" – even if these actions are largely symbolic.

Short-termism, the add-on model of sustainability, and the belief that it is not a source of profit institutionalize two contradictions: firstly, that companies can carry on "doing bad" as long as they implicitly recognize this shortfall by "doing good" somewhere else; and, secondly, that employees have split personalities, being both corporate employees who accept the "logic" of corporate externalizing of social and environmental costs, and members of society who know that this type of action will eventually prove ruinous to people and planet – and the companies they work for. Cynicism and idealism are forced to co-exist – both in official corporate policy and in the head of each employee.

Put bluntly, too many people, corporate employees front and center, still accept that companies are here just to make money, not to serve the planet and its people as well. They fail to see that doing good for our world and doing good business are mutually supportive goals. Corporate thinking about sustainability isn't integrated, but neither is that of employees.

A survey by the management consultancy McKinsey in 2011 provided some heart-warming headline numbers about sustainability trends. Some 67 percent of executives polled said sustainability had been "completely or mostly" integrated into corporate mission and values. But other answers undermined that claim. As many as 50 percent of those polled said sustainability had not been integrated into employee engagement, and some 59 percent said sustainability had not been integrated into supply chain management – both essential, early steps, as I will demonstrate. Three years later, only 45 percent of companies questioned described their sustainability efforts as aligning "extremely well" or "very well" with "core business strategy." Over half the sample – some 53 percent – said this took place only "somewhat" or even "not at all." By 2017, as many as 66 percent said sustainability had not been integrated into human resources and 74 percent said that sustainability had not been integrated into supply chain management.

These trends are moving in the wrong direction. A lot more has to be done to embed sustainability into corporate DNA. Only this will enable corporate values to align with social values, and employees to heal their split personalities.

1.3 But there are glimmers of hope

Today's unsustainability of sustainability is the result of huge economic forces that also feed unwillingness and even inability to think anew about business. But I do not want my necessarily bleak taking stock to drive despondency and inertia. That's because there are underlying corporate and social forces at work that make it possible to significantly increase the chances for true sustainability in the coming years. As bleak as the moment might appear, the world is on the cusp of a big change – one in which many people will have a role.

Taking concrete steps away from corporate short-termism and toward integrating sustainability, rather than keeping it as an add-on feature, can create a new willingness to view business through the sustainability lens. And turning change initiatives into more fundamental transformations, involving corporate values and purpose, can foster a new ability to engage with sustainability. This will help companies align their values with those of their employees and other stakeholders in the value chain. They, in turn, will no longer have to split their personal values between those of a corporate employee or supplier or customer, and a member of society. Such reconciliation will enable them to assume full ownership of sustainability – it will not be "someone else's problem" anymore.

There are huge opportunities to be reaped – if we seize the moment to create a new way of doing business. I see signs in every problem area described above that indicate we can rejig every executive's and every employee's cost-benefit analysis, that often subconscious weighing-up people do at work almost continuously. When you're asked to do something new, to adopt a new way of doing things, you weigh up the potential benefits against the cost of doing it. If a new method promises trouble with superiors and no discernible advantage in terms of your pay, position, or self-esteem – what's the point?

To push sustainability, we finally need to tip the scales in favor of people and planet.

a. Even short-termist stakeholders are showing new willingness and ability

Above, I minced no words about the blame short-termism carries for companies' unwillingness or inability to engage fully with sustainability. But it is useful to remember that the problem of short-termism and faulty financial incentives has been on academics' minds since the 1980s. The theory of creating only shareholder value has long been under fire.

As Beale and Fernando argue, the beginning of the corporate world's focus on short-term financial returns a generation ago led to "the emergence of the archetypal management cadres who, benefiting from the short term bottom line increases, are share-market driven, hard-nosed and hard-driving." The authors go on to note that "at its worst, this process has resulted in corporate pathology and managers who maximize short run value and capitalize their options gains and quit before the crash" – an incentive-induced pattern that "has been counterproductive for long-run economic growth as well as social cohesion and environmental sustainability."

"The shareholder value theory thus failed even on its own narrow terms: making money," as the management writer Steve Denning put it on Forbes. com. He says the inventors of shareholder value and stock-based executive compensation hoped they would get executives to improve corporate performance and increase shareholder value. "Yet, precisely the opposite occurred. In the period of shareholder capitalism since 1976, executive compensation has exploded while corporate performance declined."

In 2015, MIT Sloan Management Review and Boston Consulting Group (BCG) polled 3,000 managers and investors from all over the world. They found that three-quarters of senior executives at investment houses said a company's sustainability performance was something they considered when making investment decisions. Interestingly, only 60 percent of company executives said investors thought that way, showing a marked and unsettling disconnect between the worlds of investment and corporations.

In 2017, a stunning 90 percent of executives said they saw sustainability as important, but only 60 percent of companies had a sustainability strategy. Moreover, 86 percent of respondents agreed that boards should play a strong role in their company's sustainability efforts, but only 48 percent said their CEOs were engaged, and fewer (30 percent) agreed that their sustainability efforts had strong board-level oversight. And while 60 percent of companies had a sustainability strategy, only 25 percent had developed a clear business case for their sustainability efforts.

Stakeholders are waking up to the problems of short-term profits and the possible benefits of long-term value. There are many examples of the differences this is beginning to make. Unilever, for example, stopped reporting quarterly profits shortly after Paul Polman took over as CEO in 2009. And in 2016, the insurance company AXA Group sold all its tobacco-industry assets in a deliberate attempt to burnish its image as a "responsible health insurer and investor." Step by step, financially driven short-termism is being pushed into retreat.

One reason for this is that more and more executives are coming to realize the financial benefits of sustainability – companies are coming to see it as an investment, not a cost. In fact, sustainability drives profits in two ways, directly and indirectly. Direct bottom-line effects are usually seen quickly through savings, be it in the form of lower electricity consumption, fewer raw material purchases, or less waste accumulation. These are often low-hanging fruits that can't be picked forever. But the savings they produce are real and ongoing, and their effect is an important encouragement to any employee still skeptical about sustainability.

The indirect effects are no less real. Done right, sustainability can increase brand value – and brand value, in consequence, can drive sales. Employees and other stakeholder groups reward sustainability with increased loyalty. My research with Daniel Korschun and Scott Swain has also shown tangible effects on sales if both frontline salespeople and customers believe in sustainability, allowing them to connect over the company's efforts. This bonding with customers drives sales – especially if customers and salespeople also know management is behind and fully committed to sustainability.

As Andrew Savitz and Karl Weber noted in 2014, the companies in the Dow Jones Sustainability Index and the FTSE4Good indexes saw better share-price performance than their counterparts in broader indexes; and the companies that had signed up as members to the World Business Council for Sustainable Development outperformed the stock exchanges on which they were listed by 15–25 percent over the previous three years. Moreover, a recent survey of business leaders by *The Economist* found that less than four percent of managers surveyed considered being socially and environmentally responsible to be a "waste of time and money." You better believe it – sustainability helps the bottom line.

Similarly, in 2016, *The Guardian* reported about the sustainability efforts of the retailer Marks & Spencer. The article said that at the time of the plan's launch in 2007, the company expected it to cost £40m. "Five years later, the company published a report detailing the key lessons from executing that plan and found that, instead of suffering losses, the changes it made, such as reducing packaging materials and food waste, resulted in a GBP 105 million net business benefit in 2012, which climbed to GBP 160 million in 2015."

Investors too are beginning to take note of long-term value creation. Pension funds, sovereign wealth funds, and other asset owners with longer-term horizons have for a number of years been pressing companies to better manage environmental and social issues. And the shorter-term investors recently started to join in. Blackrock, with over $6 trillion in asset management, has pushed the investment community to get serious about climate change. Larry Fink, Blackrock's CEO, in April 2018 sent a letter to S&P 500 CEOs suggesting they invest more for the long term and stop putting so much money into stock buybacks and dividends – a $1 trillion payout for investors that year.

Blackrock also created a new mutual fund that takes companies' environmental, social, and governance criteria – so-called ESG-criteria – into view. And there is other evidence from other organizations in the financial services arena. At Morgan Stanley, an analyst raised the stock price target for companies – in this case of three apparel giants, Nike, Hanesbrands, and VF Corporation – based on how well they were managing ESG issues. Around the same time, the fossil fuel divestment movement started growing quickly, bringing together universities, cities, and other institutions. Lastly, Bill Gates persuaded some friends to create the largest clean energy fund in history to invest in R&D. So-called "impact investing" is moving out of the niche world and into the mainstream.

Signs of social and environmental awareness are also becoming apparent among consumers who finally seem to be showing interest in sustainable products. Blackrock's new fund was specifically aimed at millennials, the group of workers and consumers who are demanding more environmental and socially sound products. A Morgan Stanley report found that millennials are twice as likely as other consumers to buy from brands with good management of environmental and social issues, and twice as likely to check product packaging for sustainability performance. For packaged goods and food in particular, it's the era of what many call the "clean label."

More and more people want to know how the things they buy are sourced, made, and delivered. There's real money to be made by companies who respond to this craving for value. Mega retailer Target, for example, assesses thousands of products it sells and scores them on sustainability performance. For a segment of Target's highest-ranked products, sold under the "Made to Matter" banner, sales are growing much faster than regular products – they are expected to have totaled $1 billion in sales in 2018. And Walmart took a fascinating step, trying to help choosy online customers by labeling thousands of its more sustainable products "Made by a Sustainability Leader."

"I think that many of the investments that we do make, or we have made, also make good business sense," an executive at a large drinks manufacturer told me. "If you were using less electricity, if you are using less water, if you are managing to send less waste to landfill, if you are lightweight in your bottles – there is a strong economic business case for doing that." But even big investments in things like renewable energy could pay off remarkably quickly, he added.

> Certainly we've had investments that have had longer pay back periods, that have had lower rates of return. Traditionally we may have not even got them through the first hurdle of the investment process. But because we've added reputation on, we've been able to look at them slightly differently – investments in solar panels for example. We know that they're the right thing to do reputationally.

There are more details about the financial upsides of sustainability throughout this book and particularly in Chapter 7. For the moment, I just want to underline that there is a discernible shift in business toward appreciating these financial benefits, be it through cost reduction, sales boosts, reputation boosts, risk reduction, sustainable innovation, or employee retention or attraction.

b. Employees want their work driven by purpose, not profit

Lastly, companies are beginning to realize their employees want to find more meaning in their work. Consequently, companies are transitioning from promoting change for change's sake to fostering values. Why do we do what we do? Because it helps make the world a better place. Because it helps save the planet. Companies are encouraging employees to think and act more according to personal values. All of this is done with an eye on making people identify with what they do at work. If done successfully, this can bridge the values divide described above. This is the key to inspiring individuals to take ownership of sustainability goals.

"I think when people look at it on a personal basis and try to understand it on a personal basis – so suppose you discuss it over drink in the pub after work – they completely get it," one executive told me. "When you contextualize it with their family, their children, the future their children will have, the kind of world they'll grow up in and what they will have and what they won't have. They understand it. So personalizing it really helps." The danger was that when people get to work they "don the corporate mask and have a hundred and one other priorities and pressures on them." So the trick, he said, was to encourage people to "bring through those personal thoughts into the workplace."

Paul Polman, the ex–CEO of Unilever, told me he saw sustainability as both "a heart and brain thing." He said:

> You have to get the people convinced that it's important. One could say that a strong sense of purpose comes from the heart and that helps you to be a trailblazer, while the increasingly clear economic case is something for the brain.

In his experience, people postponed taking a view on sustainability when they first encountered it. But when they personalized it – when talking about passing on a healthy world to their children, say – they suddenly understood. On top of that, he noted, younger people, especially millennials, responded to this kind of framing as it gave their work a wider meaning or "purpose."

Purpose is very important for Unilever in the whole sustainability journey. Polman described it this way:

> It's [sustainability] totally driven by purpose because it starts on a macro level, with the overall firm belief that you are here to serve society, that you're not here for yourself nor for your shareholders. The first thing I made very clear is that we focus on the citizens out there, and our multiple stakeholders, our employees, suppliers etc. Only by doing well for them will our shareholders benefit long-term.

After six years of spreading this "credo," he said it was now "well-ingrained in the company." His employees had come to recognize that they could find higher purpose in what they do by "serving others" and "working for the common good." "And the more you give – it's the same with your families, your marriage, your friendships – the better environment you create" for each individual and for the community they make up.

Employees, particularly the younger generation, are catching on that profit flows from the pursuit of a broader social purpose and increasingly looking to work for purpose-driven companies.

c. More and more stakeholder groups see the need for a new business model

As the last two sections have shown, different stakeholder groups are moving toward making sustainability sustainable because more and more of them are beginning to appreciate the cost of doing nothing. As one chief executive put it:

> We are getting to a point that the cost of not acting is going to be higher than the cost of acting. So even people who have not fully grasped the issues in this world – or [do] not care about them because they happen to live in the right part of the world, or because their business isn't global – they start to see that the cost of not acting is going to be higher than the cost of acting.

The cost of inaction is higher than that of taking action.

Put simply, sustainability amounts to long-term economic survival. Companies are becoming increasingly aware of the need to keep up with social and environmental changes to avoid costs later on. A food company executive speaking of the current economic climate suggested that companies are beginning to see this,

> They see that Nestlé and Procter and everyone are doing this stuff. So the easiest course of action is to assume it's a table stake. All companies will have to do this stuff otherwise they will all lose their ability to operate. And therefore it [not acting] will not be a source of competitive advantage, it will simply be a cost on the business of adapting business models to make them less reliant on resources or more socially compliant or acceptable or whatever.

You may have heard of phrases such as new capitalism, conscious capitalism, enlightened capitalism, or multi-stakeholder capitalism. These are attempts to reinvent our current economic system, to make it more inclusive, one that favors that firms work on the triple bottom line of people, planet, and profit over shareholder revenue maximization at all costs. While this more holistic, environmentally friendly form of capitalism may still be considered a fringe pipe dream by some, vast segments of our society are waking up to the fact that we cannot continue as we have in the past. What is needed, and what is now occurring in many forward-thinking companies, is a shift in the way that we think about doing business.

As crises mount, we will as a culture, perhaps out of a sense of enlightened self-interest, inevitably move from the dominant investor's short-term mindset to one that is environmentally sustainable. Many companies are beginning to see the writing on the wall, that we cannot simply continue extracting resources from the earth's crust and replacing them with poisons indefinitely. Sooner or later the costs of doing business in this shortsighted manner will come to bear.

But shaking off hundreds of years of individualist profit-oriented conduct is not easy. Acquiring a new perspective often requires a shift in one's perception and thought. Copernicus revolutionized our perception of the world by showing us that we inhabit a globe and not a flat surface. Just as our models of the cosmos required a makeover, our business models will also need to be rewritten. Today, environmental crises, collapsing ecosystems, water shortages, disappearing species, and rampant deforestation are forcing us to realize that "doing business" will very soon have to become synonymous with being ecologically sustainable.

As has become clear, the world is now entering a historic period of environmental and socioeconomic change, and business leaders should all be at the forefront of that change. Evolutionary change in a species alters the way an organism functions. Similarly, the paradigm changes currently happening in the business world are shifting our understanding of costs and what it means to be profitable. Having a healthy and abundant planet that we can share peacefully, that we can pass along to our children and their children, is a far more valuable asset than dividends paid out to shareholders.

To switch successfully to the new paradigm we will need to encode sustainability into our companies' DNA. As a chief sustainability officer of a food company put it:

> For me, it's really about understanding what it means to reconcile our species on this planet with planetary boundaries and our own social benefit. How do we make sure that we have viable, functioning societies that provide dignity and respect to people and grow in ways that don't violate natural ecosystem boundaries, that sustain us all, the social and environmental peace?

Sooner or later, capitalism will have to undergo the belated but necessary transformation from an exploitative and aggressive system of profit making to a more planet-friendly form of global stewardship. In the list below, I have highlighted some of the main paradigm shifts that will have to occur in the world of business. People, planet, and profit can only be saved if we shift the emphasis of doing business from:

- Shareholder primacy to stakeholder primacy.
- Focusing on the costs of acting to looking at the costs of not acting.
- An egocentric to an ecocentric perspective.
- Working to secure short-term profit to working to fulfill purpose and value.
- Being defenders of the old ways to becoming agents of change.

Chief among these is the shift from defending the status quo to working to actively change it. But as a food company executive reminded me: "How many in the financial sector are truly willing now to stand up and speak for changing versus defending?" The transformation to sustainable business models will take hard work and time from all of us.

As long as sustainability is seen as a largely symbolic and unprofitable add-on, it will continue to be very hard to get employees to identify with it. To really galvanize a company, to get every employee to see the need to and the advantage of doing business sustainably, corporate leadership has to align corporate values with all those personal values. Leaders need to inspire those under them to step up and take ownership of not only their own work, but of company sustainability initiatives as well. They must also help them to see that by doing so, they are contributing to something greater than either personal or shareholder profits.

Rather than seeing sustainability as a threat to their livelihoods, employees will be empowered to recognize their interconnectedness. By claiming the mantle of change for themselves, employees will realize that by protecting the earth and its people, they are insuring the viability of both their companies and those who depend on them. Sustainability is about creating a new purpose for doing business. It is about creating a new philosophy of business that explains why a company does what it does in human terms. A company exists not only to make money. It is there primarily to improve our human lot.

1.4 Turning words into deeds

I am an optimist. The majority of this chapter described why sustainability is in such bad shape. But I spent a good part of the last section also demonstrating that there's hope. On any number of fronts, personal and corporate attitudes are changing for the better. They're changing because there is good reason to do so. And they're changing because ever more people appreciate that things will only get worse — even worse — if they don't.

That's why I believe it is not only high time for a book like this — it is the right time for recommendations to initiate and implement change. In the following chapters, I'm going to be outlining *how* to do business more sustainably, both as an individual, and as an employee, a manager, or as the boss of a company.

I'm going to give very practical advice about developing a new sense of purpose in what you and your company do, how to prioritize the things that need to be done, and how to sell these new ideas internally and externally. I'm going to show you how to build sustainability ownership in your company so as to make sustainability everybody's job (not someone else's), how to track progress along this path, how to sustain momentum. Lastly, I'm going to show you how businesses can and should be opened up to explore new types of collaboration and cooperation. This last stage is often the most transformative of all.

Chapter 1 in summary

- Corporate sustainability has become unsustainable – the understanding and the willingness exist, but companies are stranded about how to become sustainable.
- Sustainability leaders need to assert themselves against the short-termism of investors, and a whole set of received ideas – like sustainability being someone else's job.
- Shareholder value theory is a powerful myth that can encourage corporate leaders to adopt financially unsustainable strategies – no more profits mean no more company.
- Investors and employees increasingly want to engage with ideas that go beyond short-termism, most stakeholders see there is no alternative to sustainable business models.
- However much evidence there is for the unsustainability of sustainability, there are signs the world is on the cusp of big, positive changes as a result of stakeholder attitudes.
- Now is the time to turn well-worn sentiments into planet-saving deeds – this book shows you and your company *how* to attain the goals you know you need to attain.

Bibliography

G. Hardin (1968). The tragedy of the commons, *Science*, 162(3859), 1243–1248.

United Nations Intergovernmental Panel on Climate Change (IPCC) (October, 2018). *Special Report on Global Warming of 1.5°C.*

IEA (2019). *Global Energy & CO2 Status Report: The Latest Trends in Energy and Emissions in 2018.* International Energy Agency.

A. Singh (2011). *Why CSR Is Not a Revolutionary Concept: Interview with Henk Campher.* The CSR Blog, Forbes.

T. Borelli (2017). *Unilever And The Failure Of Corporate Social Responsibility.* Forbes. Available at: https://www.forbes.com/sites/econostats/2017/03/15/unilever-and-the-failure-of-corporate-social-responsibility/#1b1ab5ea498d.

Financial Times (2017). Paul Polman: In his own words, *Financial Times.*

L. Abboud (November 29, 2018). High-flying Dutchman Polman divided opinion but leaves positive legacy, *Financial Times.*

Carbon Tracker Report (November, 2015). *The $2 Trillion Stranded Assets Danger Zone: How Fossil Fuel Firms Risk Destroying Investor Returns.* Carbon Tracker Initiative. Available at: https://www.carbontracker.org/reports/stranded-assets-danger-zone/.

P. Clark (November, 2015). Energy groups accused of inadequate action on carbon emissions, *Financial Times.* Available at: https://www.ft.com/content/fb0c70dc-9515-11e5-ac15-0f7f7945adba.

McKinsey & Company (2011). *The Business Of Sustainability.* Available at: https://www.mckinsey.com/business-functions/sustainability/our-insights/the-business-of-sustainability-mckinsey-global-survey-results.

McKinsey & Company (2014). *Sustainability's Strategic Worth.* Available at: https://www.mckinsey.com/business-functions/sustainability-and-resource-productivity/our-insights/sustainabilitys-strategic-worth-mckinsey-global-survey-results.

McKinsey & Company (2017). *Sustainability's Deepening Imprint*. Available at: https://www.mckinsey.com/business-functions/sustainability-and-resource-productivity/our-insights/sustainabilitys-deepening-imprint.

McKinsey & Company Global Survey (2018). *Economic Conditions Snapshot*. Available at: https://www.mckinsey.com/business-functions/strategy-and-corporate-finance/our-insights/economic-conditions-snapshot-june-2018-mckinsey-global-survey-results.

F. Beale and M. Fernando (2009). *Short-termism and genuineness in environmental initiatives: A comparative case study of two oil companies*, European Management Journal, 27, 26–35.

S. Denning (July 17, 2017). *Making Sense of Shareholder Value: 'The World's Dumbest Idea'*. Forbes. Available at: https://www.forbes.com/sites/stevedenning/2017/07/17/making-sense-of-shareholder-value-the-worlds-dumbest-idea/#df5aa3e2a7ed.

K. Haanaes (BCG) and D. Kiron (MIT Sloan Management Review) (February 16, 2015). *How Collaboration Advances Your Sustainability Efforts: Big Idea: Leading Sustainable Organizations Research Highlight*. Available at: https://sloanreview.mit.edu/article/webinar-how-collaboration-advances-your-sustainability-efforts/.

D. Kiron, G. Unruh, N. Kruschwitz, M. Reeves, H. Rubel, and A.M. Zum Felde (MIT Sloan Management Review) (May 23, 2017). *Corporate Sustainability at a Crossroads: Progress Toward Our Common Future in Uncertain Times*. Available at: https://sloanreview.mit.edu/projects/corporate-sustainability-at-a-crossroads/.

AXA Press Release (2016). *AXA Group Divests Tobacco Industry Assets*.

R. Larsen and F.B. Valentini (May 23, 2016). *AXA to Divest Its Tobacco Industry Assets Worth $2 Billion*. Bloomberg.

D. Korschun, CB Bhattacharya, and S.D. Swain (May, 2014). Corporate social responsibility, customer orientation, and the job performance of Frontline employees. *Journal of Marketing*, 78(3), 20–37.

A. Savitz and K. Weber (2014). *The Triple Bottom Line: How Today's Best-Run Companies Are Achieving Economic, Social, and Environmental Success—and How You Can Too*. San Francisco, CA: Jossey-Bass.

The Economist (2008). The next question: does CSR work?. Available at: https://www.economist.com/special-report/2008/01/19/the-next-question.

M. Wheeland (February, 2016). The new bottom Line: money is no longer a dirty word in sustainability, *The Guardian*. Available at: https://www.theguardian.com/sustainable-business/2016/feb/23/corporate-social-responsibility-sustainability-general-mills-patagonia-ben-and-jerrys.

A. Choi (2018). *How Younger Investors Could Reshape the World*. Morgan Stanley.

2 The power of ownership

2.1 Winning over stakeholders

In May 2016, I boarded an overnight train in Mumbai, India, and traveled 300 miles northeastward to a remote town called Khamgaon. Like many parts of India, the Khamgaon region lacked modern infrastructure as well as access to sufficient freshwater supplies. The economy was largely agricultural, with locals subsisting on livestock as well as what meager harvest they could scratch from the region's soil. Yet Khamgaon had an economic asset that was making quite a difference for people living there and nearby – a factory run by the multinational consumer goods company Unilever. I had come to see with my own eyes what a sustainability pioneer like Unilever was accomplishing for its workers, their communities, and itself. I learned that a company could simultaneously achieve successes for people, planet, and profit – if it managed to inspire a sense of ownership in its workforce.

My hosts from Unilever met me at the train station. They ushered me into a car that took us to the tiny farming village of Mandka. As soon as we got close, the villagers spotted us and flocked around the car, eager to show us the rest of the way. After walking for about ten minutes, we arrived in a shady part of a field where matting had been laid. More villagers had gathered there to speak with me. As Unilever employees passed out drinks and sweets, I asked the villagers about their lives and their experiences with the company. With great enthusiasm, one village elder told me how Unilever had helped the community build small, concrete "check dams" that held water in small ponds. With better irrigation for their fields, the villagers had been able to double their annual crop yields, better wash their clothing, and give their cows, sheep, and goats more water to drink. The quality of village life had dramatically improved.

The villagers emphasized that they had paid for the dams themselves, with Unilever providing only technical expertise and project management. As my Unilever hosts explained, the company had not wanted to give handouts or do charity. Rather, it had sought to empower the villagers as owners, to give them control and enable them to use it through training. The aim was to foster sustainable economic gains for the village and engender in each villager a deep sense of possession – Mandka's success was their success. The villagers seemed happy with this level of support, and they seemed particularly proud of the outcome. If they could make one more request of the company, I asked them, what would it be? Their answer stunned me. I expected them to say that they wanted a school for their village, or perhaps a medical clinic. But they didn't ask for anything more for their village. Instead, one village elder said: "We would like the company to help the next village build these dams, just as they helped us to build ours." When I asked why, he said, "Our lives have changed so much thanks to these dams. But our neighbors see this, too, and now they're looking at us with envy. We would like their lives to improve the way that our lives have." Unilever's support had inspired the villagers. They now wanted to spread the sense of ownership Unilever had helped them achieve to the surrounding villages. In a very concrete way, Unilever's mission had become their mission, too.

As we finally made our way into Khamgaon to tour the factory, I asked the factory's manager why Unilever had done so much for Mandka. Did it really make sound business sense? He nodded and assured me that it did. "The factory is nothing without a strong community," he said. Unilever relied on the villagers to provide the labor it needed – and in a rural area like this, far away from India's huge metropolises, reliable, competent workers were hard to find. Rising farm yields and incomes would allow local families to send more youngsters to college or to vocational schools, increasing the company's talent pipeline, the manager continued. "And public works also build goodwill in the community." He related how Unilever had just had to fire an under-performing local worker – and how the villagers had reacted with equanimity, not voicing any complaints. Because the villagers had taken ownership of the company's local environmental improvement mission, it seemed to me they were much more willing to trust other decisions by Unilever – including the one to fire a person many locals knew personally.

On top of that, the manager reported, the factory was meeting its targets and achieving high levels of productivity. As I toured the facility and spoke with the employees, I understood why. By taking ownership of Unilever's local sustainability drive, these workers had come to take ownership of the company's global sustainability mission. A real-life project, actions not words, had shown them how Unilever's values aligned with their personal commitments. As a result, they were incredibly engaged employees, proud of their affiliation with the company. Almost to a person, they showed a strong desire to tackle larger social and environmental problems and help solve them. The workers were happy to speak about the things they were doing to make the factory both ecologically sustainable and more profitable. One group of employees had come up with a way to harvest rainwater to help the factory's operations. One worker told me how he had been inspired by this new rainwater-harvesting scheme and that he was using the technique to increase freshwater supplies for his family at home.

As I further discovered during visits to other Unilever facilities and through interviews with managers worldwide, the company's way of operating in this tiny Indian village was not an isolated feel-good story. In November 2010, the company had adopted a Sustainable Living Plan that sought by 2020 to help at least a billion people "to take action to improve their health and well-being," and halve the environmental footprint of making and using Unilever products, by cutting greenhouse gas emissions, water use, waste and packaging, and sourcing all its raw materials in sustainable ways. (With exemplary transparency, it later pushed back this latter goal to 2030.) To implement this plan, the company did what it did in Mandka many times over and across the globe. It changed many elements of its operations by encouraging thousands of employees, suppliers, and community members to develop a sense of ownership about sustainability. Like in Mandka, Unilever's emphatic sense of purpose about sustainability became almost every employee's purpose, too. This sense of purpose drove employees' engagement and led them almost without fail to claim ownership of the company's sustainability goals.

Unilever's marketing managers, for instance, started work on lending "purpose" to several of their brands, developing "brand purpose statements" rather than the traditional positioning statements. For example, they made detergent brands Omo and Persil encourage parents to see the huge advantages of letting their children learn through play, even at the risk of getting dirty. Unilever's innovation team, meanwhile, introduced radical product and process improvements, including a compressed aerosol deodorant that cut aluminum use by half. To emphasize its long-term orientation, the company also stopped reporting quarterly results to financial markets. Savvy about digital developments, workers and managers used social media to communicate transparently with their internal and external stakeholders. Starting with initiatives like the one in Mandka, the company was able to transform its culture step by step. Instigating and implementing sustainability became a primary daily focus for the vast majority of Unilever's 160,000 employees. Only this buy-in made Unilever's sustainability plan a reality.

And this reality has been impressive, almost revolutionary. By 2014, the company had improved the hygiene of almost 400 million impoverished people, reduced carbon emissions by 8 percent over a 3-year period and slashed the amount of waste it produced by almost 80 percent. By 2016, the company was on track to meet a full 80 percent of its ambitious 2020 sustainability goals. In 2018, Unilever said it had reached more than 600 million people worldwide through its programs encouraging handwashing, sanitation, oral health, self-esteem, and safe drinking water, given 716,000 smallholder farmers help to improve their farming output, and now sourced 56 percent of its raw materials in a sustainable manner.

At the same time, Unilever's revenues and profits soared, fueled by brands in its portfolio designated as "Sustainable Living Brands," that is, brands that contributed to at least one goal in Unilever's Sustainability Plan. In 2016, these brands — household names such as Dove, Hellmann's, and Lifebuoy — accounted for 60 percent of the company's growth and were growing much faster than Unilever's other brands. A year later, these brands were delivering 70 percent of the company's profits. Shareholders have benefited enormously. Since 1986, the company has delivered almost four times the return on investment compared with the average Financial Times Stock Exchange listed company. Between 2008 and 2018, Unilever's dividend payouts and share-price increase outperformed the FTSE share-price index and rivals such as Nestlé.

Behind the scenes, Unilever's sustainability efforts have fired up its workforce. One survey found a remarkable 80 percent of employees at Unilever claiming to be highly engaged in their jobs, compared with only 15 percent of people in employment worldwide. In recent years, Unilever ranked as the preferred employer in most of the countries in which it operated, and as the third most searched company in the world on the online business network LinkedIn. Roughly half of the new recruits point to the company's sustainability culture and performance as their primary attraction to the company. "I think we're getting more energy out of the organization — the extra mile which often makes the difference between being a good company and a great company," Polman said.

My experiences in Khamgaon and Mandka offer a sketch of how Unilever, unlike so many other companies, moved beyond merely preaching sustainability to actually practicing it. But what detailed decisions and concrete steps did Unilever take to achieve this? How exactly did it manage to make sustainability everybody's job? How did it galvanize managers, employees, and entire communities around sustainability? And how did it do all of this and also increase shareholder returns? As I discovered, employees and other stakeholders at Unilever and at a handful of other large companies have taken ownership of sustainability. Taking ownership means viewing every business decision — from the mailroom to the boardroom — through the sustainability lens. Every company must do this to be truly sustainable.

In the remainder of this chapter, I explain the conceptual underpinnings of ownership and its connections to sustainability. I then briefly introduce my model of sustainability ownership and explain how each step contributes to transforming a company's different stakeholder groups from bystanders to owners, giving the business real competitive advantage.

a. How to define ownership and put it to use

The philosopher Jean-Paul Sartre once said: "The totality of my possessions reflects the totality of my being. I am what I have … what is mine is myself." He meant that a sense of ownership is part of the human condition and is accessible to everyone — even in the context of sustainability. Psychologists today define ownership as the feelings of possessiveness and connection that we have toward people, companies, things, and even *ideas*. We express these feelings, which we begin to develop in infancy and early childhood, through terms like "my," "mine," and "our." When we have a deep sense of ownership over something, we experience it as an extension of ourselves and as an expression of our identities.

As a result, the feeling of ownership engenders in every person a favorable behavior toward the thing that they claim as theirs. Companies seeking to transform their business and gain competitive advantage can tap into ownership to encourage this favorable behavior. In experimental studies, the behavioral scientist and Harvard Business School professor Francesca Gino has found that small initiatives that raise employees' sense of owning their jobs – the opportunity, say, to hang a poster on their cubicle wall – can improve engagement, happiness, and productivity. What's more, ownership activates what Gino calls a "mindset of possession" that endures across different contexts and shapes future decisions. Through their positive feelings toward Unilever and its sustainability plan, the villagers of Mandka came to trust the company in other fields of action, and this inspired them to share their good fortune with neighboring villages. Sustainability ownership can become contagious when people who have understood its purpose seek to spread the news. Feelings of ownership can be shared to foster a sense of collective ownership, a powerful concept that can even lead traditional competitors to collaborate as we shall see in Chapter 9.

There is a large body of research that posits that psychological ownership fulfills the three basic human needs of efficacy, or the need to feel competent and capable, of self-identity, or the need to define ourselves and express our identities to others, and of the need to belong somewhere or the need for personal meaning, security, and comfort in our surroundings. As the psychological ownership of sustainability does indeed fulfill each of these powerful needs, there is obvious scope to hardwire sustainability into each individual.

Efficacy

We are confronted daily with evidence of the devastation caused by climate change, environmental disasters, and human rights abuses. They leave most of us yearning to do something, to take control of and shape our environments, but without knowing exactly how or what. The immensity of the environmental and social issues facing our planet lead many of us to feel ineffectual, to see ourselves as unable to make a difference.

But taking ownership of sustainability helps create meaningful solutions to the problems that surround us, and all stakeholders, both internal and external, can contribute to the creation of sustainable solutions to business problems. As one senior executive from a beverage manufacturer told me, "Someone changes a valve ... or redirects the water flow ... it all adds up." Feeling useful cures despondent inertia.

In his book *Self-Efficacy: The Exercise of Control* the renowned psychologist Albert Bandura writes: "Unless they are externally coerced, [people] avoid transactions with those aspects of their environment that they perceive exceed their coping abilities." In other words, what matters is not merely whether we are able to address an issue, but also that we *perceive* that we are able to do something. Seeing that we can usefully contribute to solving a problem is the precondition to taking action against that problem. The problem then becomes ours. According to Bandura, perceived self-efficacy – a precondition for psychological ownership – is influenced by four factors: mastery experience, vicarious experience, verbal persuasion, and emotional state.

Mastery experiences occur when we are successful at doing something. These experiences influence behavior because we are more likely to believe we can accomplish something if it is close to something we have mastered. Studies show that women with babysitting experience, for example, are more likely to believe in their own maternal abilities than women without such experience. Analogously, those who receive sustainability training – or are successful even in related arenas such as volunteering or community service – will perceive themselves to be efficacious in integrating sustainability into their daily activities.

Vicarious experience refers to the process of watching someone similar to oneself accomplish a task that one would like to attempt. When leaders at companies similar to Unilever see Unilever's success in meeting sustainability targets, for example, it may increase their perceived self-efficacy in endeavoring to achieve similar goals. If they can do it, we can do it!

Verbal persuasion, a technique used nowhere more clearly than in the "you got this!" chant common in athletics, refers to the support of others while one is attempting to master or accomplish a task. Best-in-class companies use "sustainability ambassadors" at all levels of the organization and several other techniques to spur on their colleagues, as I discuss in later chapters. Company leaders should not underestimate the power of something as simple as verbal persuasion to suggest and entrench feelings of ownership among employees.

Finally, emotional states affect perceived self-efficacy by signaling to us our likelihood of success at the task we are about to perform. When we feel anxious or nervous, this lowers our perceived self-efficacy and, in turn, the likelihood that we will develop feelings of ownership. This is why companies like Enel, the Italian electric utility behemoth, show a tolerance for failure thereby giving its employees the sense of psychological safety that Amy Edmondson has written about. Chapter 8 has more details about Enel's coveted in-house "best failure awards," an annual event which is meant to heighten employees' perceived self-efficacy.

Self-identity

Self-identity is a complex idea. At the most basic level, it refers to how we define ourselves. "Who am I?" "Why am I here?" "What is my purpose in life?" Our self-identity is made up of answers to questions like these. And when we come to define ourselves, we make social comparisons – so our self-identities almost always depend on a societal context. Social identity theory posits that we define ourselves by the social categories to which we feel we belong. These include our workplaces and the companies that employ us.

Millennials are striving to "work for purpose, not paycheck," according to a *Forbes* magazine article. But this wish is not restricted to a company's youngest employees. More and more employees of all ages want more from their employers than a weekly or monthly pay packet. They want to identify with their workplaces, they want to work for organizations that allow them to express their values and identities. As I mentioned before, a 2017 Gallup poll, *State of the Global Workplace*, shows that only 15 percent of employees worldwide are engaged at work – a stark reminder that most companies espouse no purpose other than shareholder value maximization. Most employees cannot relate to that sort of purpose – but they can relate to others. Companies that define their purpose in terms of societal betterment – "making sustainable living commonplace," as Unilever phrases it – find that employee engagement shoots up to 80 percent, and that even consumers and investors take notice. The drive for self-identity motivates people to work for, contribute to, and buy from certain companies and not others. This is a huge opportunity.

In addition to social categories, we also use our possessions to define and convey our identities to the outside world. The things that we own are symbols of self-identity, a means of communicating our core values and achieving recognition and social prestige. Companies that demonstrate an authentic commitment to sustainability make it something stakeholders want to own and use to express who they are.

Belonging

The need to belong, the need to form social attachments through consistent interpersonal interactions and relationships, is a fundamental human motivation. Dr. Abraham Maslow, the celebrated social psychologist, ranks "belonging" third in his famous hierarchy of needs for human satisfaction and fulfillment. In Maslow's view, the need to belong is basic and fundamental to the formation of self-esteem – and preceded only by physiological and safety needs. For people to feel respected and important, they must first feel that they belong. For this reason, feelings of "belongingness" are associated with health and well-being. Belongingness gives meaning to life because being a member of a group or organization implies being part of something larger than the self. In the same way, as explained above, our self-identity almost always draws on the social context in which we live.

In an organizational context, a sense of belonging comes from having the time and opportunity to get to know, invest in, and take control of decisions that affect the organization or community. A company that values an individual's input and initiative not only creates opportunities for employees' sense of self-efficacy and belonging to develop, but also finds that these employees produce actual material benefits. Employees are more likely to take ownership of a situation when they feel free to exercise their professional judgment.

Employees who are empowered to take responsibility in this way often drive local innovations, for example, by tweaking and modifying business practices to make the office or factory in which they work more sustainable. As one executive told me about a recent visit he made to some factories: "Employees continue to probably be the biggest driver […] Site directors continue to point to small-scale, local innovation that is driven by employees." Examples like these show it is in every company's best interest to encourage employees to take ownership of their work by allowing them the freedom to innovate and make improvements.

As noted above, an employee's need to belong can only be fulfilled if his or her needs for physical and psychological safety are met first. Companies have to make their stakeholders feel safe through training and support and show them that they can have an impact on a larger enterprise. Only by doing this can companies create the conditions that allow feelings of belongingness and, in turn, a sense of ownership to emerge. Empirical research shows that people who have a sense of belonging to an organization are in consequence more likely to remain there than people who do not feel as though they belong.

b. How to encourage employees to develop a sense of ownership

The three basic human motivations described above – efficacy, self-identity, and belonging – are the roots of psychological ownership. They fuel the desire to target something and drive the willingness to own it. These three basic human motivations are satisfied by feelings of ownership and are essential factors in the development of psychological ownership. In short, these motivations explain why feelings of ownership exist. But how exactly can a company make its employees feel like owners? How does the desire to own arise?

Organizational psychologists have identified several pathways to ownership. One begins with having control over the target of ownership, another with developing deep knowledge about it, and a third with investing time, effort, attention, and creative energy in it.

Control

As any parent or anyone who has played with children knows, the ability to control something almost always leads to feelings of ownership toward it: every child loves its toys with sometimes fierce possessiveness. The noted psychologist David McClelland theorized that the more control and power we exercise over external objects, the more we view them as extensions of ourselves. Conversely, as empirical research has proven, we are less likely to view objects that we cannot control or influence as extensions of ourselves. Control implies a degree of freedom – a degree of autonomy – in one's interactions with the ownership target.

In Khamgaon and Mandka, Unilever ceded control after training the villagers to effectively help themselves. As a result, the villagers powerfully experienced their own usefulness or efficacy in the face of problems and a sense of belonging. Because they knew they had control of how to build the dam, the villagers experienced the ability to effectively transform their environments. Taking control in this way also enabled each villager to experience being an integral part of a larger, sustainable solution to water and food scarcity. So powerful was this feeling that they wanted the nearby villages to experience it, too.

Deep knowledge

Individuals develop feelings of ownership toward objects and ideas through close association with them. We are more likely to develop a sense of ownership toward a car we drive every day, or a house we have lived in for years, rather than a rental car or hotel room used on vacation. Through a living relationship with an object, we come to develop deep knowledge about and understanding of it. As well-known theorists of psychological ownership wrote in the *Academy of Management Review*: "The more information and the better knowledge an individual has about an object, the deeper the relationship between the self and the object and, hence, the stronger the feeling of ownership toward it" (p. 301). The better we know something, the more likely it is we will feel attached to it and identify with it – feel like we belong to it and it to us. Deep understanding in this way satisfies the basic human need for having a self-identity and a place to belong. In the same way, a company that gives employees and other stakeholders concrete sustainability goals and enables them to integrate sustainability into their day jobs encourages deep understanding and a sense of ownership.

Self-investment

As we invest our time, effort, and energy into creating or shaping objects, we come to see them as extensions of ourselves – economists and philosophers have long posited that. Creative self-investment in an object satisfies all three basic human motivations. Creating or affecting an object fulfills our need for efficacy, for feeling useful. Leaving our own mark on an object enables us to see ourselves in it and to self-identify with it. And viewing our efforts with regard to this object as part of a larger project satisfies our need to belong. In the same way, the more time, effort, and energy stakeholders expend on integrating sustainability into both their professional and their personal lives, the more their sense of ownership will blossom.

c. Why sustainability is a prime candidate for ownership

People develop feelings of ownership toward something only if this object – or job, goal, organization, or idea – has properties and characteristics that satisfy their basic human motivations and allow them to control it, know it, and self-invest in it. As I discuss briefly here and demonstrate throughout the rest of the book, the properties and characteristics of sustainability make it uniquely well suited to being a target for ownership.

Table 2.1 shows how sustainability provides many, many opportunities for the fulfillment of the three basic human motivations. We are constantly bombarded with news of horrendous environmental devastation and gargantuan social problems that leave us wanting to do something but feeling incapable of doing anything. Our efficacy motivation is constantly aroused, but then denied fulfillment. It is always an uncomfortable, numbing experience – we are "uncomfortably numb." In contrast, companies that embed sustainability offer stakeholders the opportunity to make meaningful, measurable contributions to solving the problems that surround them. Sustainability allows the efficacy motivation to find fulfillment.

Sustainability also offers a unique opportunity for people to satisfy their self-identity needs at and through work. The Gallup poll that shows only 15 percent of all employees are engaged at work is a warning: people are more likely to disengage and experience burnout when their values, goals, and identities do not align with those of their workplaces. Companies that value people and planet alongside profit, on the other hand, are more likely to engender engagement and feelings of ownership in their employees, especially in the younger ones.

Finally, sustainability provides stakeholders with the chance to be part of something larger than the individual. Helping to find solutions to the world's most pressing problems can stir strong feelings of belonging. By engaging in sustainability initiatives, stakeholders feel that they are doing their part to help. People are helping themselves and future generations – which for many means their children and grandchildren – to lower the risk of climate change or water scarcity. And, with that, they are giving their lives new personal meaning.

"For me it's all about being a responsible business, [about] making sure that we are growing our business responsibly," the director of corporate

Table 2.1 Sustainability and the motivation to own

	Efficacy	*Self-Identity*	*Belonging*
Motivations	The need to feel competent and capable of affecting our environments	The need to define ourselves and express our identities	The need for personal meaning, security, and comfort in our surroundings
The Pathway to Ownership	Control, creative self-investment	Creative self-investment, deep understanding	Control, deep understanding, self-investment
Why Sustainability Prime Candidate for Ownership	The chance to contribute to meaningful solutions with measurable effects	The opportunity to express personal values and identities through work	The chance to be a part of something larger than oneself and one's organization

responsibility and sustainability at Coca-Cola European Partners said of the company's water-stewardship policy. It encourages employees to take responsible ownership of the natural resources used in production. "Water is our number one ingredient, we know that every time we put any product into a bottle whether it's Coca-Cola, or whether it's a bottle of Glaceau smart water." Encouraging employees to be "responsible stewards" of water use has helped the company to better protect its water resources. Water use in factories has fallen, recycling rates have gone up, and new technology has, for example, allowed the substitution of air for water for some cleaning functions. Similar efforts have subsequently been applied to reducing packaging.

This example demonstrates an essential point. Companies that encourage employees to claim ownership of sustainability help them fill the need gap between their *desire for meaning* and their *ability to find it.* By transforming their stakeholders from bystanders to sustainability owners, companies can gain competitive advantage. Research has shown clearly that feelings of organizational ownership lead to greater job satisfaction, engagement, productivity, and profits.

d. Guiding employees from individual to collective ownership

Ownership typically implies that the target is of interest to the individual. But today's environmental problems, and issues involving human rights, transcend the individual. Even when the source of a problem is a specific country or industry, we all share the consequences. As a result public initiatives – preventing climate change and deforestation, say, or protecting endangered species – demand that we take a collective approach toward ownership.

Indeed, individual ownership could well be nothing more than a cultural construct. Biology has genetically programmed humans and other organisms to survive by looking after themselves. In some instances, this will lead humans to maximize the means of their own survival, for example, by exerting their dominance over competitors in the race for food and other necessary resources. But beyond this simple material level, individual ownership may not be the only or the best instrument to champion.

Rather than individuals serially taking individual possession of the fruits of the earth, they might decide to share nature with others and care for it as one would care for children. This would turn the concept of individual ownership into one of collective stewardship – an excellent basis for thinking about environmental protection and its implementation. Indeed, the United Nations Sustainable Development Goals require a similar sense of collective purpose to pervade attempts to end poverty and hunger, or to provide sanitation for all. These collective schemes help the underprivileged segments of society, and more of them are needed to tackle more societal and environmental problems. We need to shift fully from the *egocentric* paradigm to a collective, *ecocentric* one.

By shifting from an egocentric idea of ownership to a more ecocentric notion of stewardship and articulating a higher purpose, best-in-class companies are already making sustainable solutions possible. "I think if you want to make progress you do need to force the organization to do things differently," one executive told me. "And I think it is hard to do that without a bit of a shake from somewhere in most organizations." A shake from those who lead by example – an executive who makes a commitment to his or her personal sustainability goals will encourage others to take ownership in a similar manner.

Lastly, the actions of the executive and his or her colleagues do not need to be driven solely by material considerations. Actualizing an environmental and social conscience in this way is also driven by abstract ideals. After all, Abraham Maslow defined his fifth level of basic human needs as self-actualization, which includes the capacity to appreciate beauty and harmony. In doing so, Maslow said every individual also has an aesthetic view of the world that can be satisfied by achieving a state of equilibrium with one's surroundings. Establishing a sustainable relationship with nature and society is one way of finding this balance.

e. The "Million Man Effect": solving problems collectively begins with the individual

Paul Polman clearly sees the need for collective action. He told me:

> At the end of the day, the issues that we need to solve, such as climate change and poverty, are so big that no one can do it alone. But at the end, action helps at the individual level. Most of the environmental footprint that we have out there is caused by individuals and that's obviously where we have the biggest challenge to get traction.

His insight was both simple and vexedly complex. If all individuals could reorient their lives and think and act in sustainable ways, their impact on the planet would be enormous. They would form a collective of independently operating individuals sharing resources through sustainable practices. Swathes of people taking ownership of sustainability and becoming environmentally responsible holds the potential of the "Million Man Effect" – small changes made by huge numbers of individuals add up to one big change. Whether we are talking about individual consumers or company employees, if each person contributes, the end results can be sizeable. Small actions can lead to big differences. As one executive told me, "A local line engineer might just choose to tweak something, a local valve. But add all of those [local engineers and local valves] up and you make a very big difference."

As the example shows, enabling individuals to think and act sustainably will ultimately help the collective. Indeed, progressive companies are beginning to realize that the sustainability of the company is predicated on the thinking and actions of each individual employee. Polman continued

> You cannot have a sustainable company and a sustainable model that we're putting out there if the individuals themselves are not sustainable. So we

spent a disproportional amount of time on physical, emotional, mental, and spiritual well-being. All our [Unilever] buildings have gyms, for example, and we encourage flexible and inclusive working environments. We also have extensive global mental health programs. Individuals with purpose thrive, that's the spiritual part.

Remember Maslow described appreciating beauty and harmony as a facet of one of our basic human needs.

Every forward-thinking company should be striving to create the conditions that engender ownership in the workplace. Tapping the innate skills of employees not only boosts their confidence by giving them opportunities for increasing self-efficacy. It is also cost effective, because employee inputs often have tangible yields. Employees will find new meaning in their jobs, be happier, and be more productive and creative in their work. This combination of employees' self-efficacy, identity, and belonging will generate real dividends – for the companies they work for and for the environment, especially when their energies are channeled toward sustainability goals. Consider this quote from the chief sustainability officer of a large retailer:

> Some of the great leaps and breakthroughs with sustainability have happened because good people across the organization have been inspired to change things themselves without coming to me to ask for permission or talk through the details. They know their part of the business better than me.

This is sustainability ownership in action.

As human beings, we are all motivated to leave our mark on our environments, express our identities, and find meaning and a sense of belonging in our activities. Ownership of sustainability can help satisfy all those motivations. By studying companies that have succeeded in – and failed in – embedding sustainability throughout their organizations, I have learned what it takes for companies to take ownership of sustainability. I have developed a seven-step model that shows you how to transform your stakeholders from bystanders to owners. There follows a short preview of the model that I shall describe in detail over the next seven chapters.

2.2 Harnessing employees' ownership

How is a sense of ownership harnessed in the organizational setting? As described in conceptual terms above, stakeholders are more likely to take ownership of sustainability when they have many opportunities to make tangible and creative contributions, and when they can try out different techniques to achieve sustainability goals without fear of sanction. Also, feelings of ownership are more likely to emerge when stakeholders have ongoing opportunities to develop a deep understanding of the different facets of sustainability, the connections between them, and their relationship to the larger purpose of the organization, their industry, and our planet and people.

In practice, however, setting out to adopt a sustainable business model is somewhat like buying a house, as I mentioned in the introduction. Prospective buyers first need to decide what kind of dwelling – house or apartment – is appropriate for them and then analyze their financial status and future plans to figure out how much house they can afford. In the same way, you first have to incubate the idea of ownership by defining and contouring the purpose of your business – you have to give it meaning. Then, you need to concretize a list of key issues your organization must address to become sustainable – enabling focus and deep knowledge will become key issues here.

Then, just like banks persuading house buyers to take loans and secure the tools necessary to make consistent payments, you entice your stakeholders to buy into your plan – in no small part by fostering value alignment between the organization and each employee. Next, you must enable employees to act sustainably – by training, management systems, and psychological empower-ment. Finally, just like home buyers making the house a home by identifying with it and caring about the neighborhood, companies entrench or routinize feelings of ownership to make business through the sustainability lens feel like second nature. You do this by demystifying stakeholders' contributions showcasing progress, enlivening or keeping fresh the experience of ownership, and expanding the sense of ownership to new groups of stakeholders – even including traditional competitors. Table 2.2 provides a summary of the steps.

Taking ownership of sustainability involves giving stakeholders a sense of meaning and comfort. Your company has to create the right conditions to encourage stakeholders' esteem in themselves, their work, and their organiza-tions, and to foster in stakeholders an awareness of the risks that come with being unsustainable. Taking ownership of sustainability helps companies fill the need gap between their stakeholders' desire for meaning and their ability to find it. In turn, by transforming their stakeholders from bystanders to owners, companies advance their sustainability agenda and gain competitive advantage. I cannot emphasize enough that feelings of organizational ownership lead to greater job satisfaction, engagement, productivity, and profits. In the chapters

Table 2.2 Phases of sustainability ownership development

Incubate	Contour	Define the company's purpose
	Concretize	Specify sustainability goals
Launch	Entice	Get buy-in from stakeholders
	Enable	Invest in training and management systems; mainstream in all departments
Entrench	Demystify	Provide ongoing measures of progress
	Enliven	Keep fresh; communicate, co-create, celebrate
	Expand	Build industry collaborations including with traditional competitors

that follow, you will learn how your company can follow these steps to transform your stakeholders from bystanders to owners.

Chapter 2 in summary

- Ownership is a feeling of possessiveness and connection that we have toward people, companies, things, and even ideas.
- As symbols of self-identity and a means of communicating our core values, ownership targets are powerful ways to personalize one's workplace.
- Autonomy in the workplace creates opportunities for employees to experience mastery and to build self-confidence.
- As leaders cultivate a climate of employees' control, deep knowledge, and self-investment into sustainability, a sense of ownership will flourish among the workforce.
- Structuring work so that employees can express their identities addresses their need for belonging – for personal meaning, security, and comfort in their surroundings.
- Collective ownership and action offer employees a chance to be a part of something larger than themselves and their organization.
- The crucial shift from *egocentric to ecocentric* paradigm is driven by cultivating the values of stewardship – sharing nature and caring for it with others.
- Taking ownership of sustainability turns the exploiters of the environment to planetary stewards.

Bibliography

R. Donnell (2015). Unilever finds that shrinking its footprint is a giant task, *The New York Times*.

Unilever Sustainability Report (2018). *How Are We Doing Against Our Sustainable Living Plan Targets?* Unilever.

Vikas Vij in Corporate Social Responsibility (December 16, 2016). *Corporate Sustainability Helps Improve Employee Engagement*. JustMeans Business. Better.

J.-P. Sartre (1957). *Being and Nothingness: An Essay on Phenomenological Ontology*. New York: Methuen & Co.

F. Gino (2015). How to make employees feel like they own their work, *Harvard Business Review*, December 07. Available at: https://hbr.org/2015/12/how-to-make-employees-feel-like-they-own-their-work.

S. Dawkins, A.W. Tian, A. Newman, and A. Martin (2017). Psychological ownership: A review and research agenda, *Journal of Organizational Behavior*, 38(2), 163–183.

A. Bandura (1997). *Self-Efficacy: The Exercise of Control*. New York: WH Freeman and Company.

J. Pierce, T. Kostova and K. Dirks (2001). Toward a theory of psychological ownership in organizations, *The Academy of Management Review*, 26(2), 298–310.

F. Montigny and C. Lacharité (2005). Perceived parental efficacy: Concept analysis, *Journal of Advanced Nursing*, 49, 387–396.

A. Edmondson (1999). Psychological safety and learning behavior in work teams, *Administrative Science Quarterly*, 44(2), 350–383.

H. Tajfel and J.C. Turner (1985). The social identity theory of intergroup behavior, In: W.G. Austin and S. Worchel eds. *Psychology of Intergroup Relations*, 2nd edn. Chicago, IL: Nelson-Hall, pp. 7–24.

K. Moore (October 02, 2014). *Millennials Work For Purpose, Not Paycheck.* Forbes. Available at: https://www.forbes.com/sites/karlmoore/2014/10/02/millennials-work-for-purpose-not-paycheck/#263fac256a51.

S. Crabtree and Gallup (2013). *Worldwide, 13% of Employees Are Engaged at Work: Low Workplace Engagement Offers Opportunities To Improve Business Outcomes.* Gallup Press.

Gallup (2017). *State of the Global Workplace.* Gallup Press.

J. Harter and Gallup (2018). *Employee Engagement on the Rise in the U.S.* Gallup Press.

CB Bhattacharya and S. Sen (2003). Consumer-company identification: A framework for understanding consumers' relationships with companies, *Journal of Marketing*, 67(2), 76–88.

R.W. Belk (1988). Possessions and the extended self, *Journal of Consumer Research*, 15(2), 139–168.

A.H. Maslow (1943). A theory of human motivation, *Psychological Review*, 50, 370–396.

R.F. Baumeister and M.R. Leary (1995). The need to belong: Desire for interpersonal attachments as a fundamental human motivation, *Psychological Bulletin*, 117(3), 497–529. Available at: http://dx.doi.org/10.1037/0033-2909.117.3.497.

C. Olckers and Y.D. Plessis (2015). Psychological ownership as a requisite for talent retention: The voice of highly skilled employees, *European Journal of International Management*, 9(1), 52–73.

J.L. Pierce and I. Jussila (2011). *Psychological Ownership and the Organizational Context.* Cheltenham, UK: Edward Elgar.

D. McClelland (1951). *Personality.* New York: Holt, Rinehart & Winston.

M.E.P. Seligman (1975). *Helplessness.* San Francisco, CA: Freeman.

S. Apte and J. Sheth (2016). *The Sustainability Edge: How to Drive Top-Line Growth with Triple-Bottom-Line Thinking.* Toronto, ON: University of Toronto Press.

R. Bullock (September 25, 2014). *Motivating Employees Has Everything To Do With Giving Them Feelings Of Ownership.* Forbes. Available at: https://www.forbes.com/sites/datafreaks/2014/09/25/motivating-employees-has-almost-nothing-to-do-with-their-attitude-and-almost-everything-to-do-with-feelings-of-ownership/#6e5500971140.

A.A. Buchko (1992). Employee ownership, attitudes, and turnover: An empirical assessment, *Human Relations*, 45(7), 711–733.

M.P. O'Driscoll, J.L. Pierce, and A.-M. Coghlan (2006). The psychology of ownership: Work environment structure, organizational commitment, and citizenship behaviors, *Group & Organization Management*, 31(3), 388–416.

S.T. Hannah, B. Avolio, and D. May (2011). Moral maturation and moral conation: A capacity approach to explaining moral thought and action, *Academy of Management Review*, 36(4), 663–685.

Part II

Incubate
Contour and concretize your sustainability domain

In Part II, I introduce the first phase of my sustainability ownership model – incubation – which is comprised of two steps – contour and concretize. In this phase, decide the domain of sustainability your company wants to own. First, *contour*, or mark the specific shape, of your company's purpose, which will guide your decision about the facet of sustainability that is most important and relevant to your company. Second, *concretize*, or make real and definite, your purpose into a prioritized set of measurable and achievable goals. These two steps are imperative for generating feelings of ownership because together they enable stakeholders to connect to and understand sustainability as integral to the company.

3 Contour

3.1 Corporate leaders need to define purpose

Francesco Starace, chief executive of Enel, has driven his company to transform itself proactively from a large, traditional electricity company into a renewable energy powerhouse. When I first met him in 2016, I expected him to tell me about his corporate achievements. But he surprised me by telling me a story from the 1980s, when he was still a middle manager at another company. He was on a team of engineers building a power plant in a remote corner of the Middle East. The company was transporting crude oil to power the plant, one truck at a time. This had the executive scratching his head. "You had all the trucks coming down, unloading the oil to fuel the plant. And there was a transmission line from the plant – but with no load to feed," Starace recalled.

Instead of simply ticking his corporate boxes, this middle manager in the desert wondered about the context of the project, its place in the world. "We were puzzled," he said. "Why did these guys build this power plant at all?" Doing some digging, he discovered that the power plant was actually the cornerstone of a dubious piece of social engineering.

> The idea was that the whole area needed to be electrified. Houses needed to be built, air-conditioning needed to be put in these houses, so that the nomad tribes living in the area would finally stop moving around and sit in these air-conditioned homes and watch TV.

None of it made any sense to him, and he could see the plan wasn't sustainable.

Decades later, he remembers this experience as the first time he had thought about sustainability – and the spur to his efforts in this area. Whereas his bosses saw profit as their corporate purpose, he took a broader view, weighing narrow financial interest against its social and environmental effects. An energy company's business could not be about foisting new habits on social groups in order to boost electricity consumption. It had to be about asking these groups what use they could make of electricity. It was about enabling customers, not dictating to them. It was about rethinking why a company does what it does. It was about purpose before profit. Starace saw purpose could drive profit.

Purpose is "the statement of a company's moral response to its broadly defined responsibilities," according to Christopher Bartlett and Sumantra Ghoshal. Rebecca Henderson and Eric Van den Steen define it more broadly as "a concrete goal or objective for the firm that reaches beyond profit maximization." It is, they stress, "the meaning of a firm's work beyond quantitative measures of financial performance." Harvard Business Review Analytics proffers the broadest definition of all, purpose being "an aspirational reason for being which inspires and provides a call to action for an organization and its partners and stakeholders and provides benefit to local and global society." It is all about viewing profit as a consequence of value creation for all stakeholders.

Regardless of the scope of definition, purpose goes beyond strategy to ask almost philosophically about the role of business. When done well, it allows companies to define themselves and contour their purpose in terms of the societies they both belong to and serve. The cereal maker Kellogg's sees its purpose as "nourishing families so they can flourish and thrive"; drug maker Pfizer says its "purpose is grounded in our belief that all people deserve to live healthy lives"; chemicals manufacturer BASF says "we create chemistry for a sustainable future." These are all perspectives that go well beyond strategy.

In a 2014 article for *Harvard Business Review*, Graham Kenny described how the CEO of property group REA came to define its purpose as being "to make the property process simple, efficient, and stress-free for people buying and selling a property." As Kenny commented: "This takes outward focus to a whole new level, not just emphasizing the importance of serving customers or understanding their needs but also putting managers and employees in customers' shoes." It is precisely this "outwardness," this ability to consider and respond to the needs of customers, investors, and workers that sets purpose apart from other corporate tools.

Corporate mission, vision, or value statements, for example, are tried and tested instruments in the motivational toolbox of many companies. Mission, as Kenny notes, describes where the business is now and where it wants to be in a not-too-distant future; vision takes the scope of the company a few years beyond that – where does the company want to be in a few years? Values, lastly, describe the kind of culture corporate leaders would like to see in their company, like being "passionate about our customers."

All of these tools address how a company, and its employees, should view and comport themselves – a fairly rational process. Purpose, on the other hand, combines reason and passion, head and heart – both as an exercise in empathy (putting your workers in your customers' shoes), and as a motivational tool (I want to help our customers). Kenny says the executive he spoke to called it "the company's 'philosophical heartbeat.'" As can be seen, the switch from shareholder to stakeholder primacy automatically leads to a more sustainable way of doing business. A company isn't just looking for profit, it's looking out for "everyone," which includes the all-important natural and social environments. Purpose is all about sustainability. And sustainability all about purpose.

At the best-in-class companies I studied, the transformation of a company into a powerhouse of sustainability begins in a way very similar to this. Executives need to outline the organization's purpose and clearly articulate it. I like to call it contouring – giving more shape to existing principles and practices, or to entirely new approaches. In most companies, leaders don't ask the vital question: "Why do we do what we do?" And the few leaders who do, often don't come to a consensus with their teams. Short-term profit maximization reigns supreme. Consequently, business transformation initiatives with an eye on the future remain small and scattered – and appear meaningless to employees.

Before they can embed a sustainable business model, leaders need to commit themselves to a purpose that goes beyond considerations of profit. As Unilever's Paul Polman told me: "Sustainability is totally driven by purpose. It starts on a macro level, with the firm belief that you are here to serve society – that you're not here just for yourself, or just for your shareholders."

In this chapter, I'll examine the role that leaders play in contouring purpose and discuss why purpose is critical to sustainability ownership. I'll also present a number of strategies that companies such as Enel, Marks & Spencer, and Unilever use to broadcast purpose far and wide, including direct exposure to stakeholders and their needs, training and development, co-creation activities, and personalized, after-work conversations at pubs around the future of employees' children. Finally, I'll describe how purpose rebounds to the company's benefit. As the last two chapters have already touched upon, purpose provides the foundation for developing sustainability ownership among stakeholders. Companies that commit to a purpose will not only find they have a strong reputational advantage compared with companies that don't. They will also find themselves in a strong position to align corporate values with their employees' personal values, giving employees new meaning in their professional lives. As employees identify more with the company, they become more engaged and productive, not merely in sustainability but in all the work they do.

In this chapter, I'll be asking how and why the absence of a broader purpose prevents sustainability initiatives from gaining traction. I'll also be looking at why profit needs to be an outcome of value creation for all stakeholders, and not a starting point. To put corporate leaders in this position, I'll describe how best to communicate purpose to the organization, aligning corporate values with the personal ones of individual workers. Lastly, I'll consider how companies can create opportunities for employees to have their own epiphanies about purpose. Frank Starace's experience in the desert is too important not to be shared.

a. Why purpose is the star to follow

Starace became a chief executive who in recent years shepherded his company along a path of reinvention as renewable energy sources began to replace fossil fuels. To do this, he had to find and contour the purpose of that company. Having purpose is the result of rethinking why a company does what it does.

A company has to serve its surroundings, not the other way around. "You have to face up to the facts about why you do what you do," as Starace told me. His company produced electricity, an energy form that was not an end in itself, but a means to do other things.

> You need energy because you want to do things – you want to be cool, be warm, light up something, use it to produce things [he said]. It's basically an enabler for other stuff. So you say, "What are we going to be enabling people to do?"

All businesses are about helping their customers achieve something, they are not primarily about profit. Look at things from this point of view and inspiring new things can come into view.

Each business, whether it's energy, food, or pharmaceuticals must contour its own purpose and ask that all-important question of why it does what it does. It is a necessary first step, often a tough one. But once you get through this struggle, you will find that this process of contouring your business purpose has led you somewhere new. You will have redefined your business to be economically viable and also sustainable from a people and planet standpoint.

Sadly, still too few people in the world of business are ready to take that first step and ask: why do I do what I do? Have you ever asked yourself that as you go about your daily business? If you haven't, that's probably because you're stuck in the old world – the world in which executives believed their main job was to please shareholders by maximizing shareholder value.

In 2014, the Aspen Institute's Business and Society Program asked US executives about the purpose of corporations. It found that "the vast majority of respondents, regardless of their own opinions on the matter, believe that the conventional wisdom in American business today is that businesses are either legally or ethically obliged to maximize shareholder value." More than half of all respondents very much or vehemently supported the claim that serving shareholders – as opposed to customers, employees, the local community, or society as a whole – is the primary purpose of any company.

A study by Jeff H. Smith published in the *MIT Sloan Management Review* in 2003 found that this attitude was particularly prevalent in the US. Over eight years, Smith polled some 15,000 managers from various countries about their fellow citizen's views about corporate purpose. In the US, 40 percent of managers said the public considered making money a company's main goal, not taking responsibility for the well-being of all stakeholder groups. Australia came second, with 35 percent of executives saying society prized profit over attending to all stakeholders, while in Japan only 8 percent of those polled thought their society ticked like that – a revealing difference.

In her book *The Shareholder Value Myth*, Lynn Stout opined that the end of the twentieth century had seen "a broad consensus" established in "the

Anglo–American business world" that the shareholder called the shots. This attitude was enshrined as "shareholder primacy theory," which

> taught that corporations were owned by their shareholders; that directors and executives should do what the company's owners/shareholders wanted them to do; and that what shareholders generally wanted managers to do was to maximize "shareholder value," measured by share price.

Stout was looking at the high point of a development that started before World War II. For almost a century, the primacy of shareholder value has been able to insinuate itself into more than just corporate thinking – society as a whole has learned to go along with it, as the above poll showed. As R. Edward Freeman notes in *Stakeholder Theory of the Modern Corporation*: "Sanctions, in the form of 'law of corporations,' and other protective mechanisms in the form of social custom, accepted management practice, myth, and ritual, are thought to reinforce the assumption of the primacy of the stockholder."

But all the way up to the mid-twentieth century, you will find that companies served – and clearly saw themselves as serving – other purposes. As Stout notes, many companies in the eighteenth and nineteenth centuries were created to develop vital business infrastructure like roads and railways – and banks. Investors in these companies were often also customers, so they prioritized good service at reasonable price over pure profit maximization. Even just a cursory historical lookbook reveals shareholder primacy to be a myth – one created in the twentieth century by free-market economists.

In 1970 their high priest, the Chicago-based economist Milton Friedman, famously declared in a think piece for the *New York Times* that companies could not be expected to display social responsibility because they were not people. Meanwhile, the people in charge had "to conduct the business in accordance with their desires, which generally will be to make as much money as possible," he said. Six years later came Michael Jensen and William Meckling's article "The Theory of the Firm." As Stout noted in her book: "This article (...) repeated Friedman's mistake by assuming that shareholders owned corporations and were corporation's residual claimants." This assumption, she argued, erroneously led Jensen and Meckling to see getting wayward directors and executives to focus on maximizing the wealth of the company's shareholders as a key problem in corporations.

The twenty-first century has seen a shift away from this late-twentieth-century consensus. The recent work of Stout, Freeman, and other academics has done much to undermine the idea of shareholder primacy. In its place, "stakeholder primacy" is being debated in the media – and in companies themselves. Workers, managers, and business leaders have come to focus more and more on the question of purpose – just like Francesco Starace had come to do after his epiphany in the desert. There is mounting evidence that "purposeful" companies – companies that do what they do for reasons that transcend profit – perform better in the long term. As the accounting firm Deloitte noted in a 2013 survey called "The Culture of Purpose": "91 percent of respondents (executives and employees) who said their company had a strong sense of purpose also said their company had a history of strong financial performance." Unfortunately, however, as many as two-thirds of the respondents stated that their companies were not doing enough to instill a sense of purpose that took into account the well-being of all stakeholder groups. We still have a long way to go.

b. Profit is the result of value-creating businesses, not the goal

The aftershocks of the global financial crisis, which rattled the world economy in and after 2008, unsettled many perceived certainties – the theory of shareholder primacy among them. The idea that profit maximization would automatically be good – be best – for a company and its shareholders was brutally disproved. Bankers with profit-driven bonuses managed to drive global financial titans like Bear Stearns and Lehman Brothers to ruin – to the detriment of the very shareholders they ostensibly so prized.

The world was stunned as it saw hundreds, thousands of bankers streaming out of buildings having saved what they could – usually a cardboard box with some personal items, nothing more. The world held its breath as the collapse and near collapse of big-name financial services companies rippled through the financial markets and did untold damage to economies around the globe. The world saw proof positive that only looking out for profit in the name of shareholders could prove disastrous for all stakeholder groups – for employees and customers as much as for those hallowed investors. It was time for stakeholder primacy.

As R. E. Freeman, A. C. Wicks, and B. Parmar said in a 2004 paper:

> Managers must develop relationships, inspire their stakeholders, and create communities where everyone strives to give their best to deliver the *value* the firm promises. Certainly shareholders are an important constituent and profits are a critical feature of this activity, but concern for profits is the *result rather than the driver* in the process of value creation.

As Freeman puts it, saying that the ultimate purpose of business is to maximize profits is like saying that our ultimate purpose as human beings is to produce red blood cells. Or, as Charles Handy observed in a *Harvard Business Review Article*, we need to eat to live, food is a necessary condition of life. But if we lived to eat, making food a sufficient or sole purpose of life, we would all be obese! So, saying that the ultimate purpose of business is to maximize profits is to mistake a necessary condition for a sufficient one.

This so-called stakeholder theory brings values and ethics back into business, after shareholder theory had, in effect, separated the fields of business and economics – making money – from the rest of society – living a good life and allowing others to do the same. Note that stakeholder theory doesn't ignore the shareholders, it just makes them one of a whole number of groups who have a claim on a companies doing business responsibly.

Furthermore, US law, for example, gives corporate officers plenty of leeway – perhaps even encouragement – to factor ethics into their decisions. As Jay Lorsch has argued, a director's responsibilities are enshrined in US law as "the duty of care" and "the duty of loyalty." This calls on executives to gather all facts pertinent to a decision, and then to take decisions with due regard for all competing interests. Business scholars and people in business are discovering purpose.

As it has developed in recent years, stakeholder theory says that managers of a company have a responsibility toward all of a company's constituencies – employees, suppliers, customers as much as the people that give it money. With so many variables to consider, the task is much harder than just looking out for the interests of one sole group. Managers have to respect the ethical and financial rights of all constituencies, and they have to balance the often-competing interests of stakeholders when making decisions. The scope of this definition doesn't make the manager's task easier. But just because it's hard, doesn't mean it's wrong. The ultimate goal, as Jeff H. Smith has said, "is to balance profit maximization with the long-term ability of the corporation to remain a going concern." And that, ultimately, requires a clear sense of purpose.

Purpose clearly trumps profit when it comes to sustainability ownership. Asking managers to think about the purpose of the company they work for forces them to articulate how and where the firm adds or creates value. Looking at the world in this way, an electricity company no longer just produces electricity. Crucially, it enables its customers to heat or cool their homes, run appliances and machines, watch movies, or communicate with one another. Similarly, the purpose of an automobile company is to provide mobility to its customers, rather than simply selling cars for profit.

I recall that while teaching executives at Koc University in Istanbul, Turkey, in November 2017, a young man was having trouble with the concept of purpose in the context of his company … he said they only thought about making money. When I asked him where he worked, he said he worked for an automobile spare parts manufacturer. As we brainstormed in the class, it started becoming clear that the proper functioning of the part helped prevent cars from breaking down and causing people distress. I asked him and the class, "Wouldn't you rather think of your business in those terms rather than just making money?" There were several nods of assent and a few quizzical looks but no disagreement.

When it is meaningful and easily relatable, purpose becomes the corporate principle that employees will champion much more easily than profit maximization. One of the preconditions for ownership is that people are able to *get behind* what they want to own – the object or idea has to be personally appealing, meaningful, and identifiable to begin with. As a result, business purpose can make work much more meaningful than shareholder value ever did. Purpose that has been well contoured is typically appealing and easy to identify with and will therefore be much more effective at sowing the seeds of sustainability ownership.

People who have a moral basis for what they do will continue these actions for longer and with more commitment, according to a 2016 article, by Andrew

Luttrell and colleagues. A well-defined purpose that views the company as providing a service to society has morality embedded into it. The upside of this is clear: since morally based decisions are stronger and more resistant to change than decisions not morally based, people are more likely to stick to such purposeful decisions. In other words, a sense of purpose with a moral foundation inspires individuals to take responsibility for their decisions and to view their business through the lens of sustainability.

c. Leaders play a crucial role in contouring purpose

When I interviewed him, the boss of a big company in the European food business had spent the morning talking to colleagues from developing and emerging-market countries about sustainability. Why was viewing business through the sustainability lens so prevalent in the European operations? Why didn't the far-away markets they worked in have the same view? "They said, 'What do you need to get sustainability going?' And I said, 'Frankly, the single most important thing in my view is leadership.'"

He had become chief executive nine years before, he recalled, with a strong personal commitment to sustainability, but without a clear notion of what that meant for his day-to-day business. Getting to know his leadership team, he noticed not only its strength – the sustainability issue resonated with his top-tier colleagues. The more they talked, the more they noticed how stimulating the topic was.

> Early on, we noticed employees – like those in supply chain – were so excited about it, they were passionate about it. We thought, "We might well have something here that's a huge driver of employee engagement." Which, of course, then proved to be the case.

A leadership committed to the purpose of sustainability and a leadership driving employee ownership of sustainability – that was the difference between the food company's business in Europe and in less developed markets.

There is no doubt about it – finding purpose requires strong leadership. Purpose has to be defined and then lived from the top. As Paul Polman put it, "Every ship needs a good captain, especially when there's a storm and the sailing gets rough. So it starts with a firm commitment from the CEO." The Swiss business school IMD looked at corporate purpose in 2015 and concluded that "leaders who are perceived to be effective, capable and leading operations successfully are much more likely to be running organizations that have an authentic corporate purpose." Or, as Polman put it: "Sustainability is totally driven by purpose. The more you give, the more you receive."

Leaders that are able to infuse the work of their employees with purpose are nothing short of transformational. They make work meaningful in a new way and stimulate their employees' heads and hearts by contouring a path for them to follow. They get people to transcend themselves, and to go the extra mile by melding their work with their commitments to the environment and society. Here is a colleague of the food company boss mentioned above:

> Sustainability has always been front and center of our global operating framework and that has very much been driven by John. John's personal passion has driven his executive leadership team to provide support for the development of the sustainability plan, the signing off of our commitments.

After contouring purpose and communicating it, comes the alignment of organizational and personal values. Being convinced by purpose gives direction and inspires individuals to take ownership of their work and be part of something larger than themselves. Showing employees *how* to do something has long made good business sense. What leaders must now also do is make the employees grasp *why* they are doing it.

3.2 Communicating purpose aligns corporate and personal values

Most employees still lack the sense of purpose that's essential for seeing business through the sustainability lens. Deloitte's 2013 survey "Culture of Purpose" found that 68 percent of employees polled (and even 66 percent of executives) said that businesses were not doing enough to give meaning to work through contouring and instilling purpose. Too many people still have no idea of the purpose of the companies they work for and sometimes that lacuna is substituted by more monetary compensation. As one CEO pointed out: "Banks are complaining still that they can't attract the right people. What they're really saying is, 'We have a hard time expressing our purpose to attract the right people, so we have to throw money into it. But money doesn't motivate after a certain point of time.'"

At a higher level, if there is disconnect between a person's identity as a member of civic society and their role as an employee, there is likely an existential rift within the individual. Compartmentalizing one's roles in life results in a shattered identity. This is tantamount to an identity crisis, leading to apathy at work and the low-engagement numbers we saw before. But when you infuse work with a purpose that resonates with employee's personal values, it helps them build a consistent identity between the various facets of their existence. "Purpose" could almost be taken for a magical ingredient, something rare and elusive that motivates people to value their work and their careers.

The polling company Gallup in 2015 found that "only about one third of the US workforce" strongly agreed with the idea that their company had given them sufficient sense of purpose or mission to make them feel their job was important. Nate Dvorak and Bryant Ott concluded: "These findings suggest that organizations are struggling to develop strong connections between their stated purpose and the brand aspirations and workplace culture they create for their employees." On the other hand, companies that had been able to better align each employee's identity with their corporate identity were performing much better across a whole series of performance metrics.

One reason for employees lacking a sense of purpose is that executives talk the talk, but don't walk the walk. Surveys show that leaders see the importance of purpose, but by no means do all of them say the company they help run actually has it. In 2015, the Harvard Business Review published a report called *The Business Case for Purpose*, which included a survey by the EY Beacon Institute. The poll of 474 executives from around the world found near-unanimity about the value of purpose in driving performance. But less than half of the executives questioned thought the company they worked for had a strong sense of purpose. "Only a few companies appear to have embedded their purpose to a point where they have reaped its full potential," the report concluded.

The study highlighted the huge gap between the intellectual argument for purpose and its implementation on the ground. While 89 percent of the executives polled agreed "shared purpose" was linked to "employee satisfaction," only 37 percent said their company's business was "well-aligned" with the company's purpose. In its survey *How Authentic is your Corporate Purpose?*", the business school IMD concluded: "About a third of the executives we surveyed had considerable difficulty identifying a single company that they perceived as having an authentic corporate purpose." Indeed, while these executives generally said their own company had "an authentic corporate purpose," most also conceded that they did not always rely on this purpose to inform the decisions they had to take on a daily basis.

Data like this show that purpose is hard to implement. In another survey, the accountancy firm PwC found that more than 50 percent of the CEOs it polled were critical of their colleagues' lack of understanding when it came to translating purpose and values into clear words and concrete actions. The bigger a company, the harder this job can be. Similarly, "legacy cultures," like those formed by outdated regulation, can also be a hurdle – as can short-term investors, or outdated systems and infrastructure. The statistics suggest the company you work for is more than likely to be in the same position. Managers can do only one thing to close the paralyzing divide between leaders contouring purpose and employees embracing it.

Communicate! As the 2015 Harvard Business Review Analytic Services Report (HBR) report about purpose put it, "One key difference between the prioritizers and laggards stood out in the survey: communication. The laggards reported poor communication from top leadership as the most significant challenge in activating purpose in their organization." But before you can do that, you have to create a solid foundation for the things you want to say and do.

You need to be clear about why your business is here, as I've said before. And you need to articulate that insight. The food company boss I quoted above told me how he and his executive team come up with commitments, and then work very closely with every department in the company to make sure they are implemented. He now almost constantly addresses audiences about sustainability – both internally and externally. "Business growth has to be sustainable growth – I think we're very, very clear on that as a business," he said, noting that this demanded attention for detail and thinking things through. "If we are using more packaging, we have to be using sustainable packaging," he said. "But we really have to use less packaging, we have to 'lightweight' our bottles, we have to use recycled content. We're very conscious that the two go hand in hand." Here was a boss able to articulate a high-minded goal and some of the concrete steps that reaching it would entail.

This shows that sustainability often requires having a deeper insight and awareness of the connections that exist between the natural world and one's life and work. This insight should come naturally at the beginning of contouring purpose, because you are beginning to understand the connections. While discussing further his company's leadership development program, the food executive hammered home the point by advising: "Get to know yourself, lead others, and then lead for impact." According to him, the first step was the precondition for the other two – there is no effective leadership without insight into oneself.

Once you have clarified for yourself who you are and why your company is doing what it's doing, spread the word. This can – and should – be done by taking steps as simple as changing the language in the company's annual report. Take out any old-school references to "creating shareholder value," think about the various stakeholder groups, including the community of which your company is a part. A company might be there to "maximize value for its various stakeholder groups" or "maximize its contribution to society." Simple but clear changes to wording can have pronounced and many-sided effects.

But a company can perhaps most effectively demonstrate purpose through deeds rather than words. I still vividly remember a presentation from a manager at health insurance company AXA at my Business Roundtable in Berlin. In May 2016, the company had ended a long history of investment in tobacco companies to demonstrate its commitment to being a solver – rather than a source – of problems. "Insurers should always be part of the solution rather than the problem when it comes to health-risk prevention," then deputy CEO Thomas Buberl said in the meeting. A bold move on the investment policy front helped drive home how serious the company was about its aspiration.

Positioning your company to reflect long-term purpose sometimes requires cutting loose products incompatible with them – and in consequence putting up with short-term revenue hits. The US drug store CVS knowingly gave up on billions of dollars in revenue when it decided to stop selling tobacco products. "Put simply, the sale of tobacco products is inconsistent with our purpose," the then-CEO said of a positioning that paid off over the longer term.

A poll of consumers by Gallup may have found that many people were not stirred by the move – 51 percent of consumers were neither more nor less likely to shop at CVS. But the polling company also discovered that five times as many consumers said they were now more likely to shop there than not, 25 percent vs. 5 percent. "CVS reinforced its purpose by choosing not to continue selling cigarettes, which in turn gave it an opportunity to win new business," Gallup's Dvorak and Ott said. "And the company remains committed to the decision, recently resigning its membership in the US Chamber of Commerce to avoid a conflict with its purpose to 'help people on their path to better health.'" This followed reports that the business organization was lobbying in the US and overseas against tougher anti-smoking laws.

As effective as clear verbal communication can be, it is essential to understand that purpose is really best communicated by action. As Dominic Houlder and Nandu Nandkishore put it in a 2016 *London Business School Review* article: "Purpose isn't words. A worthwhile purpose leads to action." Purpose has to be articulated verbally, but not only that. Only if it is also communicated by actions can a sense of purpose take root.

And, like a flower, purpose won't appear overnight. Finding and contouring purpose is a process that takes time. As a sustainability officer at a big retailer told me: "One thing to remember about sustainability is that you're on your own journey." He walked me through the "five stages" his company expected to go through – employee engagement being the third, both in temporal order and in terms of difficulty. Only when employees were firmly aware of the purpose of their work could the company hope to succeed in stage four – "business model innovation" – or stage five – "to participate in wider systemic change."

This example shows that the journey and its goals are never static things: Paths lengthen or shorten, goals change. For this reason, it can easily happen that a company has to rediscover or "re-contour" its purpose more than once, either sharpening its existing definition or finding an entirely new one. Companies need to check regularly whether employees still understand the original purpose. If they don't, the corporate leadership must find out whether communication – in word and deed – is faulty. Or whether the company does indeed have to recontour its purpose. Corporate purpose is not just an announcement. It has to be a goal, an aspiration that employees believe in and work toward every day. Only if each employee takes ownership of sustainability in this way can the workforce as a whole extend its understanding of purpose in the day-to-day and beyond it.

A company with a clear and authentic purpose that incorporates sustainability goals is also attractive to potential employees. As I emphasized before, ever more people want to have purpose, not just compensation, in their jobs. In consequence, purpose can be a powerful lever to help future-proof a company for any number of challenges – starting with that essential problem of continually renewing the corporate talent pool.

An organization without purpose manages people and resources, while an organization with purpose mobilizes them. Purpose is a key ingredient for a strong, sustainable, scalable organizational culture. It's an unseen yet ever present element that drives an organization. It can be a strategic starting point, a product differentiator, and a feature that attracts users and customers. Seventh Generation, for example, a household goods company, is a top employer of millennials. It manufactures seemingly unexciting products – dish soap, fabric softener, and toilet paper – but the company's products are imbued with a higher purpose: to inspire a consumer revolution that looks out for the health of the next seven generations. Seventh Generation walks the talk of its purpose – and its employees and customers notice.

3.3 Purpose can lead employees to epiphanies

Larry Fink, the chief executive officer of Blackrock, the largest asset manager in the world, likes to kick off the year by writing a letter to the chief executives of the companies Blackrock is invested in. At the beginning of 2018, the "world's biggest investor," as the *New York Times* called him, had sent ripples through the business world when he told business leaders that profit was not everything. He said he wanted their businesses to make "a positive contribution to society" and that he would hold corporate leaders to account. His New Year's greetings stirred a huge debate about corporate purpose.

At the beginning of 2019, Fink doubled down on his message of the year before and took up some of the conversational inputs from corporate leaders. Purpose was necessary, but not enough, Fink wrote. In a divided world, companies also had to be leaders. "Stakeholders are pushing companies to wade into sensitive social and political issues – especially as they see governments failing to do so effectively," he wrote. He stressed that he had no intention of foisting purpose on companies. But he was adamant about the centrality of purpose to business: "Purpose is not the sole pursuit of profits but the animating force for achieving them."

Fink is right. Companies need purpose because people crave it – employees, customers, other stakeholder groups. The subject has attracted ever more scholarship in recent years – and ever more interesting claims. In their 2014 study of purpose and mortality rates, Patrick L. Hill and Nicholas A. Turiano concluded that "purposeful individuals" live longer than less purposeful counterparts. "Across the board, a greater purpose in life consistently predicted a lower risk of dying, showing the same benefit for younger, middle-aged and older participants," they said. "However, the sooner you discover a sense of direction and purpose, the better."

The fact that individuals crave purpose, whether it's in their business life or in their home life, is an opportunity that needs to be seized. "The full power of corporate purpose is rendered when it is aligned with the essential nature of man's being," Richard R. Ellsworth said in his 2002 study *Leading with Purpose*. Purpose can bring an uplifting quality to every employee's work. Purpose appeals to higher instincts and can unify disparate people as they strive to attain the same goal. Purpose can align every employee's private aspirations and career goals and forge a new sense of responsibility and motivation in the workplace.

Gail Klintworth, a former Unilever executive, once told me the following story. Unilever made antibacterial soap and had launched a global handwashing program to teach children about the benefits of simple hygiene – eventually the United Nations Children's Fund (UNICEF) and governments joined in to institutionalize the program as the public policy initiative it really was. The company was making a promotional film in one of its soap factories, in South Africa. "I've got the most wonderful clip of a factory worker," she told me. "We took a clip of him – his job was watching the soap go down the line to make sure that it was straight." When asked about what seems like an extremely mundane job, she said, this man spontaneously answered: "My job is about saving millions of lives around the world." Ms. Klintworth hammered her point home: "Give your employees a higher purpose, more meaning. People don't want to die having sold soap all their lives." To pass away having saved millions of lives is an altogether different proposition.

Unilever had managed to convince this employee of his higher purpose by aligning his values with the company's higher values – saving lives, not selling soap. This alignment took place as the employee came to trust that the company's espoused purpose was real and sincere – it was lived, not just preached; it was authentic. In their 2017 report "The Value of Corporate Purpose," George Serafeim, Sakis Kotsantonis, Bronagh Ward, and Daniela Saltzman define authenticity as a genuine commitment to pursuing purpose-related objectives: "Purpose-driven companies create authenticity by establishing clear goals to be achieved and ensuring that the conditions are in place to translate values into actions."

In other words, company leaders have to prove day in, day out, that purpose is not only talk. They have to lead by example – only by doing that will they be able to win over their employees to go on a joint journey to find purpose. In doing so, everyone on this journey will discover how the company's purpose can – and does – link to their personal aspirations.

"The issues are there – it's just how you apply them, that's the question," one financial services manager told me of her company's journey. She recalls a new sustainability boss coming aboard who was able to define the company's purpose clearly – "a clear, aspirational purpose." She told me how the company's chief accountant had always intellectually understood the company's sustainability drive, but that he seemed to lack motivation to take that leap himself – until the new colleague was able to win him over. "We even videotaped him to show to people at our customer conference for our biggest customers," the manager said of the colleague who found purpose.

> To have our group chief accountant sitting there saying, "This is important and this is what we need to do in our purpose." You can see that it's not a conversational message, and not the type I would have expected to get from our accountancy team [she said. Adding with delight] He's now one of our biggest advocates.

Short of hiring people who come with your company's purpose serendipitously "built in," the employee development alluded to above is the most popular method of "embedding" purpose throughout a workforce. Deloitte's

2013 survey of corporate purpose found that three-quarters of all executives rated education, training, and mentoring as effective ways to achieve a real sense of purpose in a company. Around two-thirds thought business services and products that "make a meaningful impact for clients" or that "benefit society" were also good ways of engendering purpose. However, less than half rated the adoption of "'greening' business practices," donating to non-profit organizations, or engaging in pro bono work as tools to further purpose.

If you embed purpose in your employee development, you will find that you can help some of your employees to an epiphany a bit like the one Francesco Starace had in the desert (described at the start of the chapter). It doesn't need to be as dramatic as his – it could be a more mundane one, like the one of the chief accountant we just met. But if your employees see your company's purpose as their purpose, you're well equipped for Larry Fink's New Year's greetings. And you're ready for the next stage.

Chapter 3 in summary

- It is important to recognize the need for an authentic purpose. Who are we? Why do we do what we do?
- Having leaders with a clear sense of purpose is invaluable for inspiring employees.
- Leaders must articulate how a business adds or creates value beyond shareholders.
- A company's purpose should authentically align with social and environmental causes.
- Leaders must lead by example and live the company's purpose – words are not enough.
- Companies with purpose attract talent – people want to work for more than just a paycheck.
- Purpose can lead to life-changing epiphanies and provide a clear sense of identity.
- Aligning corporate purpose with employees' personal values encourages them to commit.

Bibliography

C.A. Bartlett and S. Ghoshal (1993). Beyond the M-form: Toward a managerial theory of the firm, *Strategic Management Journal*, 14, 23–46.

R. Henderson and E. Van den Steen (May, 2015). Why do firms have 'Purpose'? The firm's role as a carrier of identity and reputation, *American Economic Review*, 105(5), 326–330.

G. Kenny (2014). Your company's purpose is not its vision, mission, or values, *Harvard Business Review*.

Aspen Institute Business & Society Program May (2014). *Unpacking Corporate Purpose: A Report on the Beliefs of Executives, Investors and Scholars*. Keller Fay Group.

H.J. Smith (2003). The shareholders vs. stakeholders debate, *MIT Sloan Management Review*, 44(4), 85.

L. Stout (2012). *The Shareholder Value Myth: How Putting Shareholders First Harms Investors, Corporations, and the Public.* San Francisco, CA: Berrett-Koehler.

R.E. Freeman (2001). *Stakeholder Theory of the Modern Corporation.* Toronto, ON: University of Toronto Press.

M. Friedman (1970). The social responsibility of business is to increase its profits, *The New York Times Magazine.*

M. Jensen and W. Meckling (October, 1976). The theory of the firm, *Journal of Financial Economics*, 3(4), 305–360.

Deloitte (2013). *Culture of Purpose: A Business Imperative.* Deloitte Publishers.

R.E. Freeman, A.C. Wicks, and B. Parmar (2004). Stakeholder theory and "the corporate objective revisited", *Organization Science*, 15(3), 364–369.

C. Handy (2002). What's a business for? *Harvard Business Review.*

J. Lorsch (1995). Empowering the board, *Harvard Business Review.*

A. Luttrell, R.E. Petty, P. Briñol, and B.C. Wagner (2016). Making it moral: Merely labeling an attitude as moral increases its strength, *Journal of Experimental Social Psychology*, 65, 82–93.

Gallup, N. Dvorak and B. Ott (2015). *A Company's Purpose Has to Be a Lot More Than Words.* Gallup Press.

Harvard Business Review Analytic Services Report (2015). *The Business Case for Purpose.* Harvard Business School Publishing. (sponsored by the EY Beacon Institute 2015).

Gallup (2017 Survey). *State of the American Workplace.* Gallup Press.

D.N. Den Hartog and F.D. Belschak (2012). When does transformational leadership enhance employee proactive behavior? The role of autonomy and role breadth self-efficacy, *Journal of Applied Psychology*, 97(1), 194–202.

W.H. Bommer, G.A. Rich, and R.S. Rubin (2005). Changing attitudes about change: Longitudinal effects of transformational leader behavior on employee cynicism about organizational change, *Journal of Organizational Behavior*, 26(7), 733–753.

C.M. Falbe and G. Yukl (August, 1992). Consequences for managers of using single influence tactics and combinations of tactics, *The Academy of Management Journal*, 35(3), 638–652.

D. Mazutis and A. Ionescu-Somers (2015). *How Authentic Is Your Corporate Purpose?* Lausanne: IMD Global Center for Sustainability Leadership.

PwC. (2017). *Connecting the Dots: How Purpose Can Join Up Your Business.* PwC.

D. Houlder and N. Nandkishore (2016). *Corporate Purpose Isn't This: Purpose Isn't Words.* London Business School.

S. Hakimi (2015). *Hit the Ground Running: Why Purpose-Driven Companies Are Often More Successful.* Fast Company.

A.R. Sorkin (2018). BlackRock's message: Contribute to society, or risk losing our support, *The New York Times.*

P.L. Hill and N.A. Turiano (2014). Purpose in life as a predictor of mortality across adulthood, *Psychological Science*, 25(7), 1482–1486.

R.R. Ellsworth (2002). *Leading with Purpose: The New Corporate Realities.* Stanford, CA: Stanford University Press.

George Serafeim, S. Kotsantonis, B. Ward, and D. Saltzman (2017). *The Value of Corporate Purpose: A Guide for CEOs and Entrepreneurs.* KKS Advisors & The Generation Foundation.

4 Concretize

4.1 Corporate leaders need to set concrete goals

I visited the sprawling world headquarters of the chemical giant BASF in Ludwigshafen, Germany, in June 2015. My hosts were kind enough to organize a tour of the facilities, a city-sized area dotted with production facilities and linked by mile upon mile of overhead pipes. It was my first encounter with BASF's world famous Verbund system, in which the by-products from one facility flow to another as a valuable input material.

This mass of metal and concrete creates efficient value chains in Ludwigshafen, producing anything from basic chemicals to highly refined products such as paints and pesticides. The system helps BASF save raw materials and energy, minimize emissions, reduce logistics costs, and exploit synergies. I also learned to my astonishment that BASF's 112,000 employees around the world make 60,000 products at a total of six Verbund integrated chemical sites, including Freeport, Texas, and Nanjing, China. On average, every German spends 60 cents per day on BASF products.

BASF's reach is huge, and the sheer scale of its Ludwigshafen site is a fitting reminder – both in a good and in a bad way. The Verbund is a wonder of efficiency, but its scale also makes it a fount of superlatives: BASF in Ludwigshafen uses about 1 percent of Germany's annual electricity consumption. It is no surprise that stakeholders have historically been critical of BASF and other chemical companies, perceiving them as environmentally unfriendly polluters. BASF had its task cut out to make itself a company that acted sustainably – and was seen by consumers to do so.

BASF had realized it had to combat negative perceptions to prepare itself for the future. That required an aggressive sustainability strategy. So, in 2013, BASF set out to identify and prioritize the tasks it needed to accomplish on the path to sustainability. Compiling a list of about 100 potentially relevant topics, executives tested them in a series of workshops and interviews with internal and external specialists. This process yielded 38 high-priority issues, such as energy and climate, water, resources and ecosystems, responsible production, and employment. Executives then solicited feedback about these issues from employees and other stakeholders around the world.

The executives finally ended up with an even smaller list of "material" issues on which to focus the company's sustainability efforts, and around which to develop sustainability goals. Not surprisingly, "products and solutions" emerged as a material issue. One key outcome of this exercise was a product segmentation approach called "Sustainable Solution Steering," which categorized products by their sustainability performance across the value chain in terms of people (e.g. safety), planet (e.g. resource use) and profit (e.g. cost saving). This process flagged products in four bands, from "accelerators," which made a substantial contribution in the value chain to sustainability, to "challenged" products, which posed "a significant sustainability concern." Between 2013 and 2018, BASF was able to consistently keep challenged products to under 1 percent of total sales, while raising the proportion of accelerators from 22 to 27.7 percent of revenues.

As I learned during my day in Ludwigshafen, another novel use for this analysis was to build bridges with customers: "We have training sessions to help us speak this [Sustainable Solutions Steering] language," one executive said. "The process is not only about the product, but services too." BASF employees were given communications brochures and learned to help customers make calculations and analyze the market. "Our main aim here was to start a dialogue with the customers." BASF set a great example of how a company can use sustainability initiatives to create new touch points with customers and opportunities for additional sales. The company was moving from defining its purpose to concretizing its goals.

Since 2013, BASF has taken big strides in sustainability in several areas of its operation to make itself future ready. In an updated strategy document it published in November 2018, the company even announced bold future steps such as achieving carbon neutrality by 2030. But, as in most other companies that have pioneered sustainability, frustrations linger: "We could do better in reaching lower emissions levels, to be more sustainable as a group – CO_2 reduction, water efficiency, etc. As individual employees, we do not think about these issues." Imagine the impact any company would have if all its employees and value-chain partners assumed ownership of its sustainability.

Once a company's leadership has committed to a broader purpose, how does it build sustainability ownership among employees and other stakeholders? The first step is to adopt a set of high-priority areas on which a company should focus.

BASF had defined its purpose through the slogan "We create chemistry for a sustainable future." In a second, concretizing step, it went on to set a priority task for itself – segmenting its 60,000 products by their sustainability performance. Prioritizing key areas of focus tied into the company's purpose was crucial for employees and other stakeholders. They suddenly had concrete goals to invest themselves in, concrete issues to get to understand. Spurring employee investment and their drive to understand in turn spurred their sense of sustainability ownership.

As a first step, any company that wants to become more sustainable by building a similar sense of ownership amongst employees and other stakeholders must be prepared to take stock of the world beyond the firm. BASF took stock of the world beyond the gates of its Verbund sites by asking how its products performed in terms of sustainability. It let the world into the company like never before – and this is something all companies on a similar path must do.

CEOs should, in a similar manner, convene their leadership team to review corporate strategy and long-term goals, business-unit heads should do the same with their senior staff. Everyone on the team must make an effort to think about trends "out there," and thus shift their gaze away from purely internal concerns. Also, everyone should accept that the formulation and implementation of a sustainable business model is an iterative process. The world is changing rapidly, with new projections about global warming or new discoveries about environmental dangers published practically every month. Sustainability priorities must change, too.

Drawing on examples from companies such as ING and Coca-Cola European Partners, this chapter argues that leaders must ask a series of questions to establish concrete priorities for sustainability. Where is the company's growth likely to come from in the future? What trends will affect demand for our products and supply of our raw materials? What do customers, employees, suppliers, and investors want from the business?

Companies should also look at hard issues like water use, waste generation, carbon dioxide emissions, and labor conditions. They need to conduct a "footprinting exercise" across the company's entire value chain, including suppliers and customers. This exercise should reveal a list of key issues a company believes it must address to ensure future success on a fast-changing planet. Juxtapose that list with what stakeholders believe the top priorities ought to be, and the company suddenly has a two-dimensional "materiality matrix" that defines its priorities. Crucially, drawing on examples from Whirlpool and Enel, I reveal that, because of cultural differences, regulatory requirements, and economic conditions, an analysis of priorities must also be done locally. As I saw firsthand, conditions in India and Chile are very different from those in the US and the UK, rendering parts of the corporate materiality analysis compiled at headquarters irrelevant in some far-flung plants.

Focusing on a few concrete areas takes time and effort, but the business results are worth it. As the chief operating officer of a large financial services company told me,

> If you don't focus on anything, in a way you do nothing, right? So we said, "Yes, we have to be concerned about everything, but let us have three areas of focus." And we wanted to connect those to our business.

The concretizing process gives leaders the chance to bring stakeholder views into the organization, and it allows the company to become more forward-looking. After setting clear priorities, companies can allocate scarce resources more effectively, allowing them to go further. Employees and other relevant stakeholders also know what areas to invest time and effort in, paving the way to their sustainability ownership. Needless to say, companies can also build considerable "market buzz" around the specific issues they choose to tackle. The environment and society win when companies set clear priorities, but so too do the companies themselves.

But where do we start? Sustainability is about a myriad of initiatives and projects, across every site a company has, in the back and front offices, and in any number of places beyond the office and factory walls. The number of potential points of focus – and the exponential number of combinations – makes this task very difficult. It takes leadership and the courage to focus and prioritize in the face of the different demands from employees, consumers, investors, and regulators. It's easier to do nothing. But that's also unsustainable.

Global warming is such a tough issue, one chief executive once confessed to me, it's one many corporate leaders like to "postpone." In fact, many issues in the sustainability space are so big that an individual can quickly feel cowed, the idea of taking action seemingly futile. Take for example the United Nations' Sustainable Development Goals (popularly known as SDGs; www.undp.org/content/undp/en/home/sustainable-development-goals.html) that are supposed to be reached by 2030, with businesses expected to be a key part of the solution. Goals such as no poverty, zero hunger, and clean water and sanitation are all so lofty and grandiose that it's easy to be paralyzed. But I want to help you not to be awed by big problems and risks. I want to guide you through a process of thinking about how you can break down big problems into workable parts, and how you're going to adapt the business models of your companies – deliberately, and step by concrete step.

4.2 Companies need to let in the outside world

Taking ownership of sustainability involves opening a company to the outside world. This can be daunting and uncomfortable on many levels, which is directly proportional to the degree of "splendid isolation" with which a company has gone about its business so far. Unlike company hierarchies or corporate silos, the outside world can be a confusing place, teeming with examples of other ways of doing things, and abuzz with a myriad of voices and opinions – some just noise, some crucial. But which ones are which?

Opening up a company to the outside world involves exposing it to the full force of others' expectations. Companies have always listened to their customers' comments about the products or services they buy. But companies today have to do much more: customers worry as much about the sourcing of a product, or its recyclability, as they do about its quality or design. As do shareholders, employees, interest groups, and politicians. And their expectations are changing all the time, as I already touched on in Chapter 3.

"We've seen over the past decade a whole range of expectations from the external world," one food company executive told me. "And perhaps the biggest challenge we face is the sheer speed at which these expectations evolve." Ten years ago, he recalled, sustainable sourcing was not an issue widely discussed. Today it is unthinkable for a company in the food business to ignore the issue – and this is only one of many. "There are expectations about calories, about what's in our product, about how we market our product. There are expectations about our factories and how we run them."

There is a good deal of research that shows this manager's impression to be true. Raphael Kaplinsky, for one, has shown that stakeholders have become more organized over the years and are now regularly forcing sustainability resolutions onto the agendas of companies' annual shareholder meetings. One of their specific targets has been sourcing – or supply chain management – to force companies to improve environmental, social, and economic performance by conserving resources, saving costs, and raising productivity.

While it has become ever more difficult to evade the expectations of the outside world, a tendency has also developed for companies to talk the talk without walking the walk, as I described in Chapter 1. As Kaplinsky notes, even the United Nations' 2013 Global Corporate Sustainability report found that companies were telling their suppliers about their expectations for sustainable sourcing. But they weren't flanking this with real steps to embed sustainability across the supply chain. There will be more detail about this in the section about materiality analysis below. First, we need to look at how to conduct strategic reviews, the first step in letting in the outside world. It is the start of a conversation, and a process of discovery.

The quality and success of your company's conversation with the outside world will depend on what you can bring to the table. A sincere willingness to engage in dialogue is a given – if you don't believe in the process, it will soon founder on your insincerity. And a deep knowledge of the course of the world and your company's place within it is a must.

a. The strategic review

An executive at a financial services company told me of her skepticism about the sector, in part thanks to encounters with lavish financial services firms' corporate hospitality. In her opinion, many of the sector's problems were rooted in an overt focus on making money for shareholders – and, by extension, for executives. She used this as a springboard for a thorough re-evaluation of her company's place in the world – a process very similar to defining purpose, as discussed in the previous chapter.

"Let's take a step back and have a look at banks and insurance companies – why do they exist at all?" she asked. They exist, she went on, because with the invention of financial services, society needed instruments for people to save or insure collectively, in order to increase the return and lower the risk compared to doing it on their own. "Really, all we are is a service that helps people become more secure. I think business in general – or certainly many sectors and definitely financial services – have forgotten why they exist."

Once the executive had convinced her colleagues to think about why their company existed, a lot of other things fell into place. The idea that the bank was there to help its customers feel more financially secure quickly led to a discussion about financial education. How literate were clients when it came to their finances? How much more literate did they want to become? The executive discovered that the need for financial education among customers was "enormous." That spurred the company to launch an education program that today reaches 15 million clients.

This is a great example of a company gaining focus through strategic review. The company asked the right question and came up with a convincing answer about its role. This, in turn, suggested a concrete path for all employees to follow – helping their customers with their financial literacy. The process is demanding not only because it requires honest self-interrogation. It's also demanding because it doesn't give hard-and-fast answers, rarely shows two companies the same path, and requires an ongoing evolution of ideas and initiatives once they're hatched. The financial services company mentioned above, for example, widened out its financial education program to help students with their financial planning, and to include responsible investment.

At Unilever, when the company's chief executive and top management started the process that would bring forth the Unilever Sustainable Living plan, they first sat down to assess the state of the world – and the company's place within it. Their review revealed that future sales growth would mainly come from emerging markets, countries in which health and hygiene needs were expected to be the greatest. The executives recognized Unilever would, as a result, have to deal with affordability issues and logistical challenges much more than in the past.

The company's top team also identified a whole range of environmental issues – such as deforestation and water scarcity – that would have implications on product development, manufacturing, and supply chain security. Lastly, the executives saw that modern communications would give stakeholders more power than ever before, and that Unilever had to forge a constructive relationship with them as a result.

These results provided a crucial foundation for the next steps. The strategic review entailed going from what I call an "inside-out" view – in which management focuses on existing products and how to sell more of them – to an "outside in" view – in which management takes stock of the outside world, where their company is heading, and their company's place within that picture. Executives who have been through this process stress the increasing importance of outside reference points. Many have told me that new issues are now appearing at an unprecedented rate, making it difficult for even the most experienced and best organized company to react well all the time.

The strategic review is but the first iteration of what should become a continuous process of self-questioning. What is the company's business purpose? Where is growth likely to come from in the future? What are stakeholders asking of the company? As the world changes, these questions have to be asked anew, and strategy adjusted or changed accordingly.

"Your company's capability must allow you to define two or three or four possible futures, and the job of the leader is to choose one of them and bring the company together to get there," one Nestlé executive told me. "And all that can be revisited. You can, three years, five years down the road, say, 'Well, there's something wrong here, a better or a preferable future has just come up." Executives have to assess the state of the world and their company's place within it. And they have to keep reassessing the world and the company's position at regular intervals to make sure their answers remain relevant

b. Footprinting

Once a company's leadership has established what the company should do, it needs to look at how the company actually goes about doing what it does. This is done by tracing its footprint in the world – what the company sources where, what it sells in which country, where its products go when discarded, how many raw materials, how much water and energy it uses. Management has to look along the company's value chain. Crucially, executives have to look at the whole chain in the real world that they are responsible for – much more than just the parts within their corporate walls. Such a holistic approach often produces vital and startling insights.

The three main things executives have to footprint are carbon emissions, water, and waste. A detailed discussion of footprinting techniques is beyond the scope of this book. But it helps to note that there is no one-size-fits-all approach. When it comes to carbon footprinting, for example, there are techniques such as Life Cycle Analysis that estimate the environmental impact of products "from cradle to grave." Or Environmentally Extended Input-Output Analysis that models interdependencies and final consumption between sectors in a national economy, or between national economies. Water footprinting uses the Global Water Footprint Standard developed by WFN in 2009. In four stages, companies have to set goals and scope, account for water use, assess water-use sustainability, and come up with responses. The method can be applied to products, companies, consumers, even entire nations. Crucially, this method bars offset activities from being counted toward water-use reductions.

If consumer goods and food companies looked only at their own footprints, they would miss huge issues of resource use that are crucial to people and planet. Unilever, a manufacturer of soap and detergents, studied its resource use and found it had a water-use issue at the very end of its value chain – its customers' water consumption. Coca-Cola European Partners was also worried about the company's overall use of resources, so it widened the analysis of its footprint to include stakeholders beyond the factory gates.

In doing so, executives found that Coca-Cola European Partners' biggest resource issue was also water, but not in the same way as for Unilever. Coca-Cola's most worrying footprint was not the water used by its customers or in its bottling plants. It was the water used by its sugar beet suppliers in producing sugar for the beverages. In a 2010 water-use assessment, the company estimated that producing a half-liter bottle of Coca-Cola in the Netherlands demanded about 23 liters of water input and dirtied another 12 liters. This result helped the company to quickly come up with new water-stewardship rules.

Coca-Cola European Partners reacted to the findings of its footprinting exercise. It looked at its entire production process from ingredient supplies via production and packaging to consumption and recycling. From those metrics, it distilled six vital issues and set specific targets – including, for example, the pledge to "reduce the carbon footprint of the drink in your hand" by a third by 2020. Since 2007, Coca-Cola European Partners has reduced the carbon footprint of every drink in a consumer's hand by 24 percent, and the carbon footprint of its core operations by 40 percent.

A company's value chain is the full range of activities it takes to conceive, make, distribute, and dispose of a product or service. David Closs and his colleagues at Michigan State University in 2011 showed how this value chain has become ever more central to sustainability efforts. Where companies initially saw sustainability as relating primarily to non-corporate issues like ethics and the environment, the shift toward looking at the value chain forced them to take a broader view – they have to see their company as part of the broader world.

In parallel to this, as Closs and his colleagues show, corporate thinking about sustainability became more integrated. Where once sustainability initiatives were anything from "greenwashing" product marketing activities to making real changes in business practice, the latter view has come to dominate – though this has not necessarily made implementation any better, as this book argues. Nonetheless, most companies have come to accept that sustainability must include both marketing and operational supply chain facets.

Jonathan Linton and his colleagues at the University of Ottawa showed how this integrated thinking developed to include by-products of the supply chain. Companies started to look at the entire life cycle of a product. They moved from looking at its current cost to the company to its total cost to company, people, and planet by including the cost of resource depletion, waste removal, recycling, and other issues beyond the factory gates. Companies, in other words, started to internalize in their accounting hitherto externalized costs. Linton and his colleagues advised companies to become early adopters as social and political trends suggested such approaches would eventually be legally mandated.

Walkers Crisps, a UK-based potato chip maker owned by PepsiCo, is a great example of how thinking about value chains has evolved. It started working with the non-governmental group Carbon Trust as far back as 2002 to reduce energy use of its operations. It now uses 30 percent less energy than it did in 2000. Just as importantly, the company got a much better understanding of the sources of its carbon emissions. It realized that its supply chain beyond its factory gates offered great opportunities to cut emissions.

In 2006, Walkers became the first company to ask the Carbon Trust to analyze the carbon footprint of its potato crisp production across the whole value chain, from the farmers growing potatoes to its plastic packaging operation.

The analysis showed that the largest contributors to each crisp packet's carbon footprint lay outside Walker's factory gates – specifically with its suppliers of potatoes, sunflowers, and seasonings. The company used the data to work out emission-reduction plans with those partners. And it became the first company to use the Carbon Trust's Carbon Reduction Label on consumer packaging, measurably raising consumer awareness, consumer education, and consumer loyalty.

Creating value-chain footprints or "heat maps" that highlight raw material use, energy consumption, or waste produced is an essential step to ready your company for its conversation with the outside world. As the above examples show, it can help a company focus on essential steps. However, as convincing as it is, executives must remember that different sectors face different challenges – every company is in some way unique. You have to commission your own analysis and you must use your own judgment.

The retailer Marks & Spencer, for example, found that the obvious targets for sustainability action were in its supply chain – "improving the water, the fish, and the cotton," as one executive put it. "We have a heat map that says it should be all about the food factories and the farming." But as a retailer with a large customer-oriented workforce, the company shied away from an all-too-drastic focus for fear that this would leave the vast majority of its employees out of touch with its strategic sustainability thinking. Quite deliberately, Marks & Spencer kept the focus wide to include shop-floor measures. Turning some lights off during shop stocking, or recycling coat-hangers and cardboard, were "low-efficiency" measures. But they were daily encouragement for shopworkers to think about acting sustainably, and eventually for Marks & Spencer's customers, too.

When approached correctly, the footprints of a company's value chain are wonderfully informative and provide solid foundations for corporate action. I will discuss them at greater length below. What is important to note here is that when heat maps are interpreted correctly, they are not deterministic in any simple sense. Sure, executives could go after the three biggest issues their heat map throws up. As one executive from another food company said: "We now have three activities, these are the KPIs [key performance indicators] we'll measure them with. And all of a sudden, we have a goal." Also scour your company's heat map for initiatives that might render poorer results numerically but galvanize your employees like no other – like Marks & Spencer did. If you can meld your business acumen with the science of footprinting, you not only equip your company with self-knowledge for that conversation with the outside world, you also strengthen the conversation by drawing more and more stakeholders into it.

c. Materiality analysis

Materiality reviews are a crucial next step after footprinting. They allow corporate executives and their various stakeholder groups to agree on areas on which to focus sustainability issues. The term materiality was borrowed from accounting and simply refers to any information from the realm of sustainability that a "reasonable investor" would want to know – how much water scarcity, say, could affect the company's business plan, all the more pressing if footprinting has highlighted a big water-use issue.

While materiality in accounting underlies strict legal definitions, materiality in sustainability does not. For this reason, there are many approaches and terms bandied about. But in essence, every exercise has the same goal: to construct a matrix in which a company lists its priority issues when it comes to sustainability, and stakeholders theirs. The points of overlap represent agreement and tend to be the best issues to pursue.

Unlike footprinting, materiality analyses can be as much art as science, qualitative rather than quantitative, and dependent on the quality of the conversation between company and stakeholders. For example, many companies like to engage with stakeholders using company-designed questionnaires. A cynic would argue this gives companies an unfair advantage in manipulating their sustainability agendas. Kinder hearts might argue it simply gives companies the chance to miss an opportunity – by asking the wrong questions.

To conduct a materiality review, a company needs to identify its various stakeholder groups and their engagement mechanism, define and describe issues to them in understandable ways, and score every input to create a priority list from the stakeholders' perspective. Having said all that, companies need to remember that these reviews are still relatively new and imperfect tools, and that most companies will have to adapt the process for themselves according to their needs. (For a good discussion on materiality analysis, see Yumasheva 2018.) But the work is worth it as materiality reviews are invaluable in engaging a company and its stakeholders in a conversation over long-term value creation and how the company can contribute to the sustainability of planet and society. In a way, these reviews are best thought of as mapping what stakeholders care about most when looking at the company, and what the company cares about most when looking at society.

In a very interesting simulated example, Robert Eccles and his colleagues at Harvard University played through the construction of a materiality matrix for a pharmaceutical company. Plotting "Society's Issue Significance" on the Y-axis against "Firm's Issue Materiality" on the X-axis, they discovered, for example, that neither constituency rates the issue of water use as significant for a drug maker, that society sees "customer satisfaction" as more of an issue than the company does, and that the company is more worried about the material impact of global warming on its operations than the non-expert public. Overlap is strongest when it comes to "customer health and safety" – an obvious point in many ways, but also an important confirmation for management to remain focused on it.

This dialogue between company and stakeholders can take the form of questionnaires, but it can also involve qualitative interviews, or roundtable discussions. In a third step, after publishing a sustainability report and consulting experts, Heineken, the Dutch beer brewer, used roundtable events to bring together different stakeholder groups. It was the penultimate stage of constructing its materiality matrix and agreeing on joint projects and initiatives. Energy use and concomitant carbon emissions emerged as one of the key areas of focus, which led to the construction of four large windmills to generate electricity in the Netherlands.

As I mentioned above, in 2013 BASF set out to identify and prioritize sustainability tasks in the same way. It put together a list of around a hundred potentially relevant topics and tested them in a series of workshops and interviews with internal and external specialists. This process identified 38 issues that were of particular importance, issues BASF then put to 350 external stakeholders and 90 key BASF employees all over the world. Out came a matrix showing the issues outside stakeholders thought most pressing, and how BASF itself saw those same topics.

Issues deemed "material" – that is, seen as crucial by both groups – related to energy and climate, water, resources and ecosystems, responsible production, products and solutions, and employment. "Energy consumption and efficiency" was the top issue for all sides. See Figure 4.1 for BASF's materiality matrix. BASF focused on these issues in its sustainability reporting and incorporated them in its steering processes – recall the Sustainability Solution Steering exercise. It then used them as a foundation for conceiving new sustainability goals. Crucially, the company showed its flexibility and open-mindedness toward the results by initiating an ongoing review, so that its sustainability priorities would be able to change as the world changed.

As a bank rather than a manufacturing behemoth, Dutch banking group ING reached very different conclusions in a materiality survey it conducted in 2015. But, like BASF, it put together a list of potential issues before circulating it to a 1,500-strong group of internal and external stakeholders worldwide. Issues that both stakeholders and the company deemed material included customer privacy and data security, stability of the bank's computer systems, and enhancing customer financial capabilities. ING stresses that it reviews the process every year, allowing it to both hone its gaze on issues stakeholders deem important and to change as the world changes.

The results of its materiality review help guide strategic decision making, stakeholder engagement, and what ING tells the world about its business practices. In this case, ING decided to focus its communication on helping its customers become "financially empowered" in order to take better decisions. And it vowed to concentrate on "accelerating sustainable transitions" to help both it and its customers become more sustainable.

Importantly, companies need to apply such insights at the right place, both in terms of corporate organization and geographic location. Issues in Chile, for example, may be very different than for business units in India. Power company Enel, for example, quickly mapped its materiality findings onto operations in individual countries. While building a power plant in Chile, the company focused on building up an ecosystem of local small- and medium-sized companies. And, while building a power plant in a water-stressed part of Brazil, Enel concentrated on technical training of local producers to enable

Materiality matrix

Relevance rating of sustainability topics for BASF

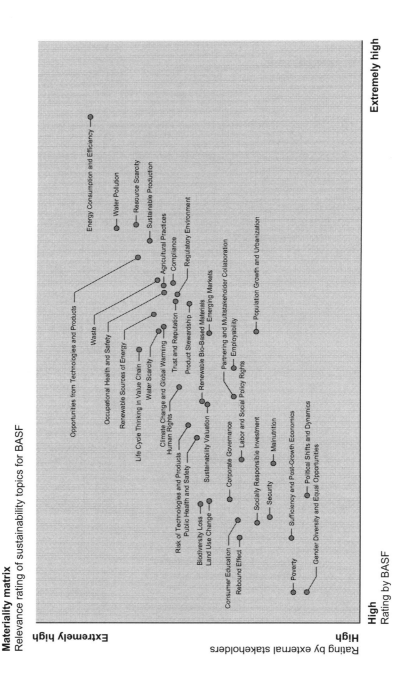

Figure 4.1 BASF's materiality matrix

them to improve their water supply. In other parts of Brazil, it tried to combat fuel theft by encouraging poor locals to collect paper and glass waste and sell it back to the company for fuel credits.

Different cultures and legal regimes can have just as big an effect on localizing company priorities as economic disparities. When a large pan-European food producer decided to focus on its carbon footprint, it did not roll out the plan in all factories at once.

> The culture in different parts of the business is of course linked to the countries they're in [an executive told me]. In our Nordic operations, it's very much second nature to be green, while in Great Britain people might need more encouragement. Or when it comes to recycling, Belgians are much happier to recycle bottles than the Brits.

You too may need different approaches depending on the countries and cultures where you operate.

Next to custom, national laws also make for big differences companies will have to take into account. An executive from Whirlpool, a manufacturer of refrigerators, air-conditioners and the like, told me how the company's waste management initiatives are influenced by local rules. In northern Europe, the retailer won't consider sending its waste to landfills because regional tax laws make it prohibitively expensive. The challenge is not the same in India, however. Waste recycling is a very different thing in India compared to Europe. In India, there is a large secondary and tertiary market for things like refrigerators and air-conditioners making it nearly impossible to track where a particular item is when it is ready to be recycled. "And that's where the challenge lies," the executive told me.

A company's sustainability efforts should be tied to its capabilities – only then will it be able to successfully implement them. This can be seen as limiting. But it should be taken as being empowering: A company should focus on areas in which it is most expert and competent. Companies are limited in their ability to influence outcomes in certain areas, but all the more powerful in others. Coupling footprinting with materiality reviews can bring real focus to a company's sustainability efforts. Indeed, Eccles and his colleagues have argued that companies that focus strongly on "material sustainability topics" – issues, as I have said, that are important to both company and stakeholders – financially outperform companies with less focus on material issues. This suggests that even in a worst-case scenario, investments in sustainability that are in line with materiality do not destroy company value.

4.3 Focus on key initiatives – but change as things change

Once you have reviewed your company's strategy, established its resources' footprint, and discovered key "material issues" on the sustainability front, you can proceed to the next stage: Choosing key initiatives. At this stage, there will be a temptation to do too much in the face of multiple issues.

After completing its strategic review, footprinting, and materiality analysis, Unilever, for example, found that its first to-do list was too long and complicated. Executives worried about confusing the workforce, but worried even more about the company's non-executive directors. Indeed, this latter group of stakeholders asked top management to simplify their message. To give their bosses a sense of the bigger picture, senior leaders agreed on the simple goal of doubling revenue growth, halving Unilever's environmental footprint and having "a positive social impact by 2020." No company had ever decoupled growth and resource use like that before. All concrete initiatives were clearly focused on contributing to this clear and ambitious goal. The disinfectant brand Domestos, for example, was given the task of building toilets to tackle the issue of defecating in public.

Every company must identify the goals and initiatives that best match its capabilities. All this book can do is provide the right method to get to those answers. A computer hardware manufacturer will end up sketching a completely different path to a sustainable business model than a bank or an insurance company. A computer manufacturer needs precious metals and rare earths, and in consequence might have all sorts of issues with environmentally and socially sound sourcing. A retailer might look at supply chain and also at educating its customers at the same time. Or it might choose to have an altogether different initiative ready in anticipation of the evolution of customer demands.

Sometimes, the goal may be clear but the path to achieving it obscure – and executives will have to decide whether to announce the goal anyway. In an effort to continue to minimize its use of materials and reduce its reliance on mining, in April 2017 Apple announced a shift to closed-loop production, even though the company at the time did not quite know how it would reach that goal. As Lisa Jackson, the vice president of Environment, Policy and Social Initiatives at Apple, told me in June 2017:

> It is an incredibly ambitious goal, but I want to be really clear it is also unusual for Apple to outline such an ambitious goal without having a complete roadmap to know how to get there. But we thought it was important at this moment in our sector to outline intentionality around that.

Defining the goal can help clear the path to get there.

If you find yourself in a similar spot, you will have to decide in consultation with your colleagues whether the moment is right for you to announce your goals and initiatives to internal and external stakeholders. Sometimes, signaling an intention is important per se. Apple, for example, was reacting to criticism from non-governmental organizations (NGOs) that the electronics industry was wasteful. It seized the opportunity to showcase its leadership.

Some initiatives, regardless of whether the company's analysis has declared them material or not, should be endorsed by any responsible enterprise as simply the "right thing to do." For example, educating the public on issues of health and safety should be an imperative for any company that regards itself as socially responsible. Thomas Jefferson once famously said that democracy can only work with an adequately informed public. We accept that dictum for voters, so why not for consumers? All too often, consumers are left in the dark. Corporate lobbyists for the food industry, for example, are currently campaigning for "dark labeling" which would exempt food producers from listing a product's potentially harmful ingredients or its genetically modified organism (GMO) content. This is wrong as it is not going to help forge a more sustainable world. Instead, companies have to help employees and consumers gain a deeper understanding of aspects of their business, of its mechanics from production to disposal.

Change is a constant on the path to sustainable business. As goals are met, new goals have to be set – and these could well be ever harder to achieve as "low-hanging fruits" are picked off. As initiatives age, they can evolve to become more inclusive. As the world changes, your company must react – thanks to global warming, perhaps more and faster than ever before. "This is not a linear journey," as one executive told me. Even well prepared companies are now regularly grappling with issues not on their radar just two or three years ago. The world is getting warmer – and the warming seems to be speeding up.

Indeed, my interviews with business leaders suggest that anyone in business today is riding a maelstrom of disruptions that only compound each other. Alongside our still unchecked slide into environmental catastrophe, business has to deal with burning social issues like inequality, and radical changes in consumer behavior, thanks to technological advances. It's hard to say where the world or your business will stand in 20 years' time.

> I can't exactly say how the world's going to unfold over the next 10–20 years, with climate change, with inequality, with issues to do with business behavior. But I do know that what's expected of business will be dramatically different than today. We're trying to create in the organization the ability to respond and adapt to whatever the world throws at us.

In this manager's view, companies need to build the skills and mindset to deal time and again with all forms of disruption: social, environmental, technological. I think there is no other way of riding out the storm.

I have talked to several senior managers who are already thinking beyond ongoing initiatives to embed sustainable business models. They want their companies to start exploring what the businesses they're in might look like tomorrow. Car makers, for example, could become "mobility providers" as car ownership gives way to car sharing.

> Already, you're looking over the horizon, saying, "We've got to change again. We've reached a certain point and now we need to push up and beyond that" [one executive told me]. Companies are good at saying

things have to change and launching lots of initiatives. But where is that taking them? Those two things – broad goals and concrete initiatives – need to be brought together in order to ensure success.

If a company goes about change in the right way, change does not have to be a burden. It can be infectious.

4.4 Getting started

Now that you've let in the outside world, traced footprints, agreed priorities with your stakeholders, taken into account internal expediencies and regional differences, you can start to pull your plan together. Set your company clear and sometimes bold goals. Not too many, but not too few. An executive from Coca-Cola European Partners reiterated this point: "Lead from the top, make sure that you have clarity on what you want to achieve." He went on to stress focus: "You can't be famous for everything. Be very clear on what is most material for your business." For Coca-Cola European Partners the most pressing issues had proved to be water use and packaging. "Water is the key ingredient in all of our products so that is why water is embedded into the heart of our sustainability plan." Making issues concrete like this helps employees and other stakeholders develop a deep understanding of the issue and come up with innovations. This then paves the path to sustainability ownership.

Lastly, when it comes to setting a timetable for your goals, be prepared to be patient. "We'd of course like to achieve all our goals tomorrow," one drinks company executive said. "But if you look at the sustainable sourcing of sugar, you realize it will take time even just to understand the challenges involved – it's a huge topic, just this one thing." But even one thing can be a huge thing, making it worthy of your attention – and your patience.

Patience is of the essence. While you wait, you must also be prepared to continually revisit your plans. Letting the world into your company is an iterative process – and so is the formulation of sustainability goals and initiatives arising from it. I think an example best serves to underline this most crucial point. When Unilever decided to "let in the world" and trace a path to a sustainable business model, top executives concluded its biggest issues were deforestation, poor sanitation, and water scarcity, while most of its future growth would come from emerging markets, many of them hard-hit by these very problems.

After footprinting and a materiality review, top management came up with a detailed plan to incrementally reduce emissions and raw material use in specific areas. Complex and extremely detailed, they found they could not sell the plan to their non-executive board members, as I said above. In the iterative spirit of implementing sustainable business models, they reappraised their findings and condensed them into a bigger picture. What I haven't said yet is that the board finally bought in. The next chapter shows how even well-made plans still need to be sold to many audiences before they can become reality.

Chapter 4 in summary

- Let in the outside world – be prepared to engage with stakeholders by having a conversation about your company's purpose and direction.
- The quality and success of that conversation depends on a deep knowledge of the course of the world and your company's place within it.
- So, conduct a strategic review that shifts your understanding from "inside-out" to "outside-in" – from existing products (and how to sell more of them) to the outside world, where it's heading, and your company's place within that larger picture
- Footprint your value chain, and then conduct materiality reviews by engaging various stakeholder groups to agree areas upon which to focus sustainability initiatives.
- Choose key initiatives with care and be prepared to continually revisit your plans.

Bibliography

B. Thier (2014). *BASF's Product Portfolio Evaluated For Sustainability*. Available at: https://www.basf.com/global/en/media/news-releases/2014/09/p-14-322.html.

S. Wettberg and T. Ballensiefer (2018). *We Drive Sustainable Solutions*. HSBC ESG DAY, BASF Report.

BASF Factbook (2017). *Information for Investors and Analysts*. Available at: https://www.basf.com/.../180614_BASF_HSBC_ESG_Day_Frankfurt.pdf.

United Nations Development Programme (2019). *What Are the Sustainable Development Goals?* Available at: http://www.undp.org/content/undp/en/home/sustainable-development-goals.html.

R. Kaplinsky (2004). Spreading the gains from globalization: What can be learned from value-chain analysis? *Problems of Economic Transition*, 47(2), 74–115.

United Nations Global Compact (2013). *Global Corporate Sustainability Report 2013*.

T. Wiedmann (2009). Editorial: Carbon footprint and input–output analysis – An introduction, *Economic Systems Research*, 21(3), 175–186. doi: 10.1080/09535310903541256.

Water Footprint Network, Global Water Footprint Standard (2009). *Water Footprinting: Identifying & Addressing Water Risks in the Value Chain*. SABMiller House.

D.J. Closs, C. Speier, and N. Meacham (2011). Sustainability to support end-to-end value chains: The role of supply chain management, *Journal of the Academy of Marketing Science*, 39(1), 101–116.

J.D. Linton, R. Klassen and V. Jayaraman (2007). *Sustainable supply chains: An introduction*, *Journal of Operations Management*, 25(6), 1075–1082.

Carbon Trust (2006). *Carbon Footprints in the Supply Chain: The Next Step for Business*. London, UK: Carbon Trust.

E. Yumasheva (2018). *Seven Tips to the Perfect Materiality Analysis*. Datamaran.

ING Group (2015). *A Step Ahead*. ING Group Annual Report.

R.G. Eccles, M.P. Krzus, J. Rogers, and G. Serafeim (2012). The need for sector-specific materiality and sustainability reporting standards, *Journal of Applied Corporate Finance*, 24(2), 65–71.

Part III

Launch
Entice and enable ownership

In Part III, I define the second phase of my model, in which companies launch their plan by enticing and enabling stakeholders to take ownership of sustainability. To entice stakeholders to take ownership of sustainability, you need to know what will make it appealing to different groups of people; people will only develop feelings of ownership toward objects and ideas they find attractive. Enabling ownership requires putting in the systems and training that allow people to understand sustainability and giving them the opportunity to control and invest themselves in it.

5 Entice

5.1 Getting employees to take ownership

I was in London on a cold but sunny day in February 2015. I hopped on the Tube, excited to visit the world headquarters of Marks & Spencer (M&S), the venerable UK retailer. The executive I was meeting was Mike Barry, the chief sustainability officer, a committed sustainability champion. He told me he had joined M&S in 2000, having been recruited by the finance director. Barry's new boss had come straight to the point: "Mike, sort this green thing out." Ever since then, Barry had relentlessly pushed his organization to move toward a sustainable business model. M&S launched its signature sustainability plan in 2007 to address all the sustainability issues affecting its business and supply chains. "Plan A," so-called because there is no Plan B, is a business plan designed to equip the company for a demanding tomorrow. It is a future in which success depends on Marks & Spencer's ability to deliver exceptional products and services in a world that is increasingly feeling the pinch of resource constraints and experiencing social change.

Barry and I were discussing my favorite question. How do you get your stakeholders to buy into sustainability? Barry was surprisingly upbeat, noting that there were actually "a very small and rapidly diminishing number" of people in the company, – and thus probably in any company – for whom any shift in attitude was impossible. Then he said something even more striking.

> The biggest group in the company is now saying, "I accept we need to change. We need a different form of business. But how do I do it? I'm paid to do a job in a competitive marketplace. I'm paid to sell more products more profitably than my rivals. You say I have to change? How? What do I do?

Barry's experience suggested that the conceptual struggle for sustainability is having an effect. Employees now need practical advice to act sustainably from day to day. People want to buy in, but don't know how to.

Crucially, Barry's experiences had convinced him that sustainability buy-in required as much emotional as technical expertise – and that companies, to their detriment, often forgot about the former. Companies, he worried, were prone to "mechanistically" pursuing targets, privileging extrinsic over intrinsic motivation. In his view, there was nothing wrong with setting targets and tying them to incentives. But he was adamant this was only one tool on a longer path. "The other side of the equation needs to be an emotional component that says, 'We cannot become a sustainable business if people only follow the word of the law – only comply with systems and processes – without understanding why.'"

After many years of pushing his company to see business through the sustainability lens, he was sure: "People have to get viscerally connected with the need for a new business model." Getting stakeholders to own sustainability is more likely to succeed if it can be embodied experientially.

Employees can experience sustainability and integrate it into their daily work through co-creation or visiting the front lines – or even by listening to the CEO speak to the company about the importance of sustainability. Mike Barry had even come up with a simulation that he believed was powerful enough to stir participants in a similar way.

> We just launched a new leadership development course that has Plan A at the heart of it [he said]. It will test our people with new scenarios, new places that take them out of their comfort zone here. I put them into communities and supply chains and say, "It might actually be a different future. This is what it's really like going into this new world. It's not a theory in a book. There's a reality here."

If the exercise is good enough, it too can stir to action.

Personal experience often has more impact on a person's behavior than a rational argument, or an abstract concept. Moving from the latter realm, detached from real-world material existence, Barry wanted his colleagues to buy in on an emotional level. It was, he knew, a big thing to ask: He wanted them to cross an emotional barrier to identify with the company's purpose in a new and very personal way. He knew they would only contemplate such a step if they had confidence they wouldn't be disappointed.

Mike Barry was making a critical point. To drive sustainable business models through organizations, companies large and small need everyone's engaged participation, the kind stakeholders have when they know why and how they should embrace sustainability. As I learned from the spectrum of companies I studied, the clearest priorities and best-laid plans are nothing without buy-in from key stakeholders, including employees, board members, supply chain partners, community members, and clients or customers. In most companies, unfortunately, leaders don't do what it takes to entice stakeholders to assume ownership of sustainability. As I touched upon in Chapter 1, this leads to sustainability seeming like a distant issue that is always "someone else's problem." As a result, rank-and-file employees don't do much to ensure the company's future – or that of our planet and society. At best, they are keeping "their heads down" in the hope that this might be a burdensome fad that will pass.

Drawing on stories from a number of companies including, Apple, IBM, Old Mutual, and Sony, this chapter runs through the various constituencies that must buy in to sustainability initiatives and describes effective practices for gaining their support. To convince hard-nosed managers, you can show them the dollar signs and bonuses, as I learned from IBM and others. But when it comes to rank-and-file employees, it's best to adopt a gradualist approach. As one sustainability officer I interviewed explained: "Keep things under the radar, keep things quiet, don't scare people. If you immediately come out with a grand idea, you run the risk that people won't think it's such a great idea — 'Goodness, we're doing that?'" Ownership is a feeling that gradually envelops employees, it cannot be thrust upon them.

You should, within reason, allow stakeholders to come up with their own projects and messaging as a way of edging toward ownership. You should, in consequence, not rely exclusively on top-down communications. The sustainability officer mentioned above described how she had fought unsuccessfully to convince a team inside her company to adopt key performance indicators (KPIs) related to sustainable sourcing. Years later, members of the team came up with a plan of their own that was strikingly similar. Sometimes, people deep inside an organization can't be convinced by their own senior leadership. They have to be allowed to convince themselves.

This chapter covers many different enticement strategies and tactics. It provides readers with arguments they can make, "ammunition" they can use to buttress those arguments, and proven rhetorical techniques. When it comes to convincing your board to act, for instance, you can point to the many direct and indirect ways through which attention to socio-environmental issues can create value — your board understands risk and reputation. To entice the vitally important cadres of middle managers, be sure to appeal to their self-interest, conveying how they and their businesses can benefit from sustainability. Try bringing them to the front lines, the point of sale, or the supplier's plantation or production facility. They can then see for themselves how they bring life to the company's purpose.

All constituencies should be made aware of the "victories" that confirm the business value of sustainability. In 2014, four years into its "Road to Zero" sustainability program, Sony Electronics wanted to see whether it could motivate employees to come up with ideas to make their workplaces greener — anything from getting rid of trash bins to using energy-saving computer settings. Sony "gamified" sustainability, offering points and prizes for the best ideas. Sony later said that during the pilot phase of the program with 500 participants, it invested about $20 per employee and yielded an average annual saving of $85 per participant, or around $25,000 in total. Sony was later able to show all its employees that 33,400 incremental steps toward sustainability had saved over 102 tons of CO_2 emissions, 36,000 gallons of water, and 2,000 gallons of fuel. In fiscal 2017, Sony's increasing use of renewable energy (5 percent of its international electricity use) has significantly lowered its environmental impact, with a reduction in CO_2 emissions of 154,000 tons, the equivalent of

CO_2 generated by over 16,000 Japanese single-family households. Greenhouse gas emissions at Sony sites are also down by 12 percent, and the annual energy consumption of products is down 50 percent.

When sustainability is "everybody's job," the results can be tremendous – and self-reinforcing. There are a number of studies that show that companies with successful sustainability strategies have a far more knowledgeable workforce than less progressive rivals. In 2011, the consultancy McKinsey surveyed executives and found that companies seen as sustainability champions had more employees at all corporate levels engaged with the issue than sustainability laggards. Among sustainability champions, 23 percent of respondents said the issue was vital to attract and retain employees. Among sustainability laggards, this awareness was shared by only 5 percent of respondents.

In 2013, the consultancy Globescan reported that 83 percent of employees it surveyed wanted more than engagement with their employer's sustainability vision. They wanted the companies they worked for to help them become more sustainable in their own lives. Put differently, eight out of ten employees wanted to achieve more consistency between their professional and private actions and values. They wanted a clear vision from their employer that they could also apply to their own lives. They wanted consistency.

One executive I talked to called it "joining the dots" between the corporate and the private world. The companies better able to align their corporate and their employees' personal priorities would obviously have an easier time transforming their business models to become sustainable, this executive said. The interests of a middle manager saving the planet in order to safeguard his children's future can align with those of a CEO who sees his task as saving the planet in order to safeguard his company.

In essence, companies can realize big gains for themselves, the environment, and society if they can engage stakeholders like this. Conversely, such gains will never materialize if companies fail to get buy-in for their purpose and sustainability goals. That's because corporate boards would then never make decisions with significant implications for sustainability, and employees would continue to believe that sustainability is "someone else's problem." A strong, profitable transformation to a sustainable business requires everyone's participation and focus. Engaged and focused stakeholders pave the path to ownership. This chapter will show you how to get your stakeholders to jump aboard the sustainability ship.

5.2 The challenge of getting companies to change

Getting companies to change is difficult. There is a wealth of academic literature that shows less than 30 percent of organizational change initiatives are successful – less than one in three. An illuminating 2004 study by Julia Balogun and Veronica Hope Hailey says the large majority of strategic changes are thought to fail because they lack an integrated approach to drive systemic change. It is hard for the process to clear the many hurdles in its path and to deal with its many knock-on effects.

In a corporate world dominated by the idea of profit maximization, most employees have for generations used a rational cost-benefit calculation to decide how to act and please their superiors. What's in it for me? This meant employees became used to making decisions that were deemed right by their employers but ran counter to an employee's personal values. Karl Marx famously talked about the alienation of the worker from the products he or she makes. By signing a work contract, this view has it, the worker agrees to these self-alienating working conditions in return for a wage: I'll do what you say, if you pay me.

In an influential 1996 paper, Paul Strebel called these old-style reciprocal contracts between employee and employer "personal compacts" that were in urgent need of change. The huge transition involved in shifting a company to a sustainable business model meant that these compacts had to become much more durable. They could only achieve this by transcending Marx's alienation. These new compacts, Strebel said, had to reconcile personal and corporate values. Without this alignment, he wrote, it was "unrealistic for managers to expect employees to fully buy into changes."

If that sounds challenging enough, remember what I said in Chapter 1 – conceiving and implementing a sustainable business model is by no means a standard change initiative, it is much more than that. Traditional change initiatives focus on the company and its strategy. But the transformation to sustainable business models along the sustainability ownership route is much more demanding. Because, as William H. Bommer and two colleagues wrote in an influential 2005 study, "What is being transformed is not the organization, but the values of the employees." Let's illustrate through an example.

In 2004, Shell, the giant oil company, was beset by doubts about its oil reserves that saw its share price suffer. The company's then-CEO concluded Shell needed to radically overhaul its structure and simplify its processes in order to survive. Global, standardized processes were introduced that affected 80 operating units. The measures were unpopular from the moment they were announced. The "change team" responsible for implementing them needed unflinching resolve and left business units in no doubt: these changes were mandatory, not optional, and the only way to achieve the goal of transformational growth. Managers got the message and gave up their resistance. CEO Jeroen van der Veer was lucky that he won this test of strength with his skeptical management.

Six years later, consumer goods group Unilever published its Sustainable Living Plan. Its blueprint for sustainable growth recognized that the company's fortunes were inextricably linked to the well-being of society and planet. Its three main goals were aspirational, and placed values over organizational detail – by 2020, as we saw in Chapter 4, Unilever wanted to improve the health and well-being of more than 1 billion people, halve the company's environmental impact, and improve the livelihoods of women and farmers in its supply chain. Then-CEO Paul Polman was successful in getting his large organization to move with him because Unilever had a clearly defined purpose and concrete goals to work toward it. The company's actions and communications managed to convince stakeholders that the values of Unilever's plan aligned with their personal values.

The two examples show the difference between going to the gym because you're forced to and going because you understand it's good for you. Sustainability champions need to approach sustainability change as they would the task of convincing a friend to exercise regularly. A sociological look at gym-going suggests that people exercise for three, usually connected, reasons: they have the right attitude – that is, they see that going to the gym will benefit them physically; they feel some social pressure – from a partner, or a doctor; and they feel they're capable of going to the gym – physically, mentally, and financially.

The process should be exactly the same when fostering sustainability in a company. Employees have to be convinced that the change will benefit them, see that other people realize that too, and also feel capable of changing. Indeed, Vernon Miller, John Johnson, and Jennifer Grau observed in 1994 that employees had "better change reactions" if they believed in positive implications for themselves and the company. Larry Greiner and Virginia Schein in 1989 noted that change-supportive social influences – for example, through official "change agents" – helped win over other people. Lastly, Deborah Terry and Nerina Jimmieson said in 2004 that individuals were more likely to support change if they were confident they themselves could act in a supportive way.

A vital underpinning to convincing employees that change will benefit them is a supportive corporate culture – one that, in the extreme, is tolerant of employees trying out new things – and failing from time to time. Also, instead of being micro-managed, employees need to be given autonomy in their work. These steps provide opportunities for employees to develop feelings of self-efficacy, self-determination, and confidence. This, in turn, increases the chance for a sense of ownership to take root.

Sustainability champions who are perceived as genuine and legitimate can close the gap between employees who agree with their company's goals because their bonuses depend on it and those that truly believe in these goals. They can help skeptics in the workforce take a vital step from technical to emotional understanding, from using one's head to also embracing heart.

The size of that gap should not be underestimated. In 2013, the consultancy Globescan found that almost 75 percent of employees of large companies felt properly informed about their employers' social and environmental commitments. But 58 percent still said there was "a gap between what my company says […] and how we actually behave." Leadership by example, from the smallest to the largest things, is key to closing that gap. I will never forget the day I was teaching executives of a large reinsurance company. They complained that their senior leadership set a bad and demotivating example for sustainability by coming to office in chauffeur-driven luxury cars.

As a sustainability champion, you need to be able to answer the colleague who accepts the business model has to change, worries about his competitors, his bottom line, and asks: "How do I do it?" You have to have concrete suggestions – and send the right signals. Don't behave like the executive who questioned the value of his company's planned local transportation initiative with the words: "All this stuff, why do we do it?" And remember that you can only establish norms and spread a culture by living both. As one executive told me: "When people see other business leaders in their peer group trying things, doing things, and being supportive through the process [of corporate change] – that inspires them."

5.3 Making the sale to employees

A financial services executive called it "having the conversation." In a company used to looking at the world in terms of hard data and cold numbers, she meant talking about the real lives of its customers. She knew colleagues who were having trouble accepting this new view of the business, who were adopting the new corporate way only mechanistically. "They'd say, 'It's the policy, it's the framework, we're doing it for compliance reasons.'"

She recalled a sustainability workshop for over 40 future leaders, many of them at the very competitive, numbers-driven "front end" of the business. They were exactly the kind of positions that might have bred mechanistic thinking, she implied. But at the end of the meeting, one of the young managers told her, "We're actually having the conversation. We're seeing how, through what we do in our day jobs, we can change lives."

The executive reckoned this insight had given them a new lease of life: "They felt like they came into work to do more than crunch numbers and spreadsheets," she said. This new alignment of corporate purpose and personal values had a marked impact on the company's operations. Managers who took part in the workshop "have been going back in as champions in the business," she said. It's a great example of the powerful role of training in corporate journeys of this sort. And it's a reminder that the best training only realizes its full potential when it's brought to bear on the experiences of employees on the front lines of the business. Only in this way can lofty goals translate into concrete actions.

Interestingly, economic rationale is by no means taboo in enticing stakeholders. Depending on the corporate culture that surrounds you, or the people you're trying to convince, numbers might be a much better bet than appealing to the heart or enlisting morals. As one executive at a large retailer put it, when talking about trying to get his colleagues to adopt the sustainability lens: "We'd go in and say, 'The world's about to end, we need to do this and that' to someone who, quite frankly, didn't care." In desperation, he recalled, his team would then take a different tack. "Someone would say, 'There's a 435 million pound opportunity that we can exploit.' And suddenly the person says, 'Ah, tell me more!'" In the same vein, Lisa Jackson of Apple told me, "The easiest and most fun part of sustainability is when you can go to the business – as we have done now several times – and say, 'This will save you money. It will save you money to reduce the amount of scrap metal that is produced. It will save you money to think about packaging in a different way.'" Head as well as heart.

These examples show how sustainability can be argued using the language of traditional, profit-maximizing capitalism. It's a way of speaking – and thinking – that is still extremely widespread. IBM in my view stands for thousands of other companies in how they go about selling sustainability to internal and external stakeholders: "We factually present the rationale and drivers behind why the company should be doing something," as an executive told me. Cold numbers can have their uses, even in the field of sustainability.

But sustainability champions should be aware that numbers and data are not always enough. There is a growing body of evidence that shows that aspirational and experiential appeals work better than rational ones. The young managers in the training program described above would surely agree with that. In a 1992 study, Cecilia Falbe and Gary Yukl found that "rational persuasion" using factual evidence, or "legitimating decisions" through rules and policies more often engendered resistance than support. More interestingly still, they found that "inspirational appeals" – like exhortations based on common values, or consultation through participation – more often engendered support than resistance. Indeed, this support was more often than not intrinsic rather than extrinsic, as Falbe and Yukl said – a truly felt "commitment" rather than mere "compliance."

So you need to choose your mode of address with care. Engendering extrinsic motivation – compliance – has its uses, though be prepared to hear grumbles: "This is another flavor-of-the-month program," "I'm going to keep my head down," "It can't be done." We're back to the analogy about going to the gym. Working-out is great, but there's a huge difference between feeling compelled to work-out and wanting to. In the same way, sustainability should become an intrinsic drive. Or, even better, a realization that not only is it the "right thing to do," but also the "smart thing to do." I call these "hybrid" forms of address as they make use of both the business case and the appeal to normative behavior. And they work extremely well.

However, unmixed forms of address also have their uses. Sometimes rational communication to the "head" is best for one stakeholder group, other times affective appeals to the heart are better for another. The Nesta Report on "Selling Sustainability," a 2008 advertising industry study, concluded that buy-in efforts should avoid talk of impending catastrophe and focus more on how "normal" such initiatives are. It recommended emphasizing fairness by stressing that all participants – companies, governments, non-governmental organizations (NGOs) – are playing their part; that campaigns be made personally relevant – it's *our* environment, not *the* environment; and that they identify areas in which individuals could take action – by reducing consumption, say, to declutter lives and save the planet.

These points have a close bearing on the advice I've extrapolated from my research: focus on the positive – companies need to sell new business models as opportunities, not struggles to avoid doom; focus on "doing your bit" – the company and everyone who works for it has a purpose; focus on the personal – both to align corporate and personal motivation, and to empower each individual stakeholder to come up with ideas and implement them. These are surefire ways to spark ownership of sustainability.

However, a food company executive cautioned that enticing stakeholders to engage in sustainability should be done gradually. He explained that, for many, sustainability is very conceptual and that they "just need to get started" getting to grips with it. He provided an interesting analogy about people who are resistant to running. How do you get someone who has no ambition to run a marathon to actually take part in one?

> You don't start off by saying, "You're going to run a marathon." That will not make them get off the sofa. Instead, just get them to take a lot of walks and get them to realize it's okay. And then ultimately, in five years, they will be running a marathon.

In a way, the same kind of trick gets stakeholders on board with your sustainability journey. Hearing about sustainability initiatives will make some skeptical and resistant. Others might be more open-minded, but complacently stick to established routines. But by defining concrete and realizable steps, you can get the ball rolling. The satisfaction of quickly reaching realistic goals will give stakeholders an experience of efficacy that can develop a momentum of its own. Once you get your stakeholders up and walking, they'll be on the path to sustainability ownership before they know it. Recognizing this point, the food company executive said: "They'll never realize how they got to that point." Again, he cautioned against sharing too much too soon about your sustainability goals, as you run the risk of scaring off employees. As we've seen before, patience is a prerequisite of sustainability.

5.4 How to sell to the board and company leadership

In 1996, the US sportswear company Nike was under pressure from NGOs that accused the company of ignoring poor working conditions at contract factories in Asia. Spurred by these allegations, Nike CEO Phil Knight asked one of his board members to take a look at the factories herself. It was the beginning of a drive that turned Nike from a seeming pariah – one associated, in Knight's own words, with "slave wages, forced overtime, and arbitrary abuse" – into a paragon of board-led efforts to bolster a company's social responsibility.

As Lynn S. Paine pointed out in an article in 2014, Nike's efforts are all the more remarkable for being so rare. Despite increasing pressure on corporate boards to improve governance, the article noted that corporate responsibility for society and environment had not yet become a mainstream issue for corporate boards. In fact, Paine pointed out, recent surveys suggested not more than one in ten US stock market listed companies had a board with a committee dedicated to corporate responsibility or sustainability.

This is very strange. After all, most of the world's corporate governance systems say the first and foremost duty of a company's board is to ensure the long-term viability of the company. What better description could there be for sustainability? In its 2015 annual report, the sustainability advocacy group Ceres called upon companies to act: "Directors have a duty and a mandate to promote sustainability priorities." Despite a recent uptick, it glumly noted only 32 percent of the 600 largest publicly traded US companies had any kind of sustainability oversight at board level in 2014. This marks a huge disconnect between boards and executives in terms of seeing value in sustainability initiatives.

This surprising lack of board-level commitment has led to a growing disparity between company directors and the executives they oversee. In 2014, MIT Sloan Management Review, Boston Consulting Group, and UN Global Compact surveyed 3,800 senior managers and executives: 65 percent of them said sustainability was a top management priority, while only 22 percent believed their boards had the same commitment to these efforts.

In an ideal world, a CEO would make sure the right people with the right mindsets get appointed to the board. More realistically, a CEO should put a lot of effort into educating the company's top body. Put simply, the CEO has to sell sustainability to his or her board. Crucially, he or she must do it in such a way that board members do not feel a conflict with their financial responsibilities toward shareholders. A CEO should quickly make the opposite case: strong sustainability initiatives can cut corporate costs and raise stakeholder loyalty – and therewith overall profit.

This is what I like to call a transactional approach. It's an appeal to the business logic, not the heart. Educating the board in this manner is nothing more than reminding it that looking out for the company's long-term health is more important than any short-term profit maximization. Profitability has to be sustainable.

In an article for Greenbiz.com in 2014, Emily Wilson from the consultancy CBRE quoted a Starbucks executive who recommended changing the conversation between management and board "from 'how to make the business case for sustainability' to 'how sustainability supports the business.'" Company executives showed their board how a rise in average global temperatures of just 2 degrees Celsius could dramatically reduce the land available for coffee cultivation. Combating climate change became a key part of Starbucks' core business. Sustainability champions need to figure out how sustainability supports core company goals. And then senior leadership need to tell their board members about those goals.

Here's a great example of how to get sustainability buy-in at a senior level. It doesn't involve a corporate board per se. But it involves the chief procurement officer, a supply chain sustainability champion at a large computer services company, whose bosses wanted to cut staff. The company was under pressure and slashing jobs was the easiest way to meet bottom-line targets. The procurement officer ran 11 programs, including one for sustainable sourcing, that the cost-cutters were eyeing because it didn't generate revenue.

"I said, 'You can unhook from any of these 11 programs, but you can't unhook from conflict minerals, because of SEC reporting requirements.'" He warned his bosses that failure to comply with SEC rules would mean products could not get shipped. "And we'll have revenue issues and customer site issues,'" he recalled warning the cost-cutters. "But I pointed out that every one of our customers has a shareholder, a stakeholder, an NGO, an investor. So these things are woven into the fabric of our new society." He recalled telling his bosses that reducing head count in any of these areas would in consequence be counterproductive. "The backlash would hit our brand image," he said. Here, a transactional approach clearly outlines the risk of reputational damage as a result of going soft on a sustainability initiative.

In other cases, a more direct link to the bottom line may offer an even more convincing narrative. At IBM, for example, the case was made to reduce the use of rare earth metals. If the company could use less and produce less waste, it could produce more efficiently and reduce the reputational risk of using raw materials from contentious regions.

Sustainability champions must continually engage with their boards. Unilever executives spent a lot of time with their board and board committees, discussing the Unilever Sustainable Living Plan and its sustainable business model. Unilever now has an external advisory committee that meets with the board three or four times a year to help explain what the company is doing. For one thing, the sessions allow board members to ask the executives they oversee better questions. At Coca-Cola European Partners (CCEP), a sustainability committee was founded over a decade ago. It initially met with the board alongside two of the five annual board meetings. But the company soon realized that sustainability needed to be a part of every board meeting. The resulting continuous involvement of the board with sustainability issues was absolutely key to CCEP'S success in the sustainability field. Institutionalizing this process also helped make thinking about and acting in the spirit of sustainability initiatives normal. These initiatives had previously been considered optional or idealistic add-ons.

Some pushback from directors is natural, but executives shouldn't be deterred. While the Unilever board eventually backed the company's sustainability moves, executives worried about several board members who had little idea about sustainability. Management had to educate them about what seemed like a radical plan to some of these board members. Thanks to this intervention by executives, directors have become more relaxed and understand that the Sustainable Living Plan is a living document, necessarily flexible in a fast-changing society.

They also realize that transparency is not a risk to the company, as some of the older board members had thought. They now understand that transparency actually strengthens the core of the company by building trust. In a similar way, the board first resisted but then supported the end of quarterly financial reporting. Increasingly, the Unilever board sees the Unilever Sustainable Living Plan as a very good way not only to ensure the long-term viability of the company, but also to build shareholder value. The company's most senior committee has come to recognize that sustainability and profit are intimately linked.

5.5 How to convince middle management

Persuading board members can be hard. But getting middle managers to buy in can be even harder. These are the people who keep the company running on a day-to-day basis, the people most immediately under pressure to deliver on time and on target. When faced with new demands from sustainability champions, it is these people who are the most torn between the traditional bottom line and the new triple bottom line.

These are the people with the least time to think about aligning their goals with your goals. "They don the corporate mask and have a hundred and one other priorities and pressures on them," one executive told me. "Sometimes they don't bring those personal [ideals] into the workplace, which means it becomes very difficult [for them] to join the dots." With that kind of traditional thinking, it remains difficult for middle managers to see what's in it for them.

Angst in the belly of any organization is a hindrance in many ways. Angst privileges the status quo. "I think one of the big barriers you've got to leap across in the organization is fear," one seasoned sustainability veteran told me.

> It's conservatism with the small c. It's the sense of, "Am I making a mistake on something that's new? I have short-term problems of trying to access this brave new world of the future. I'll just be a little cautious and keep my head down."

Angst, fear, caution – call it what you will. Executives have to fight it.

You need to give your middle managers a reason to raise their heads, survey the landscape, think about corporate goals – and about their personal ideals. You can only do that by leading by example, while at the same time showing empathy for the difficult situation middle-rank managers are in. If your sustainability plans put them in a difficult situation, you have to show them that you can and will help.

> The people in the middle have actually got to deliver the results [one executive told me]. They have actually got to deliver this week's sales. And they have actually got to build factories and make them work – and if that does not happen there are of course serious consequences for the business and for them personally.

The danger as he saw it was of overburdening middle managers, asking them to run a perfect day-to-day operation and expecting sustainability to be embedded within it without a hitch. "They will say, 'Right, okay I get that. So I need to know from you how this is going to help me.'" Executives need to be able to answer that question in a persuasive way.

Sustainability champions can do this by giving their middle management a reason to care about the new way of doing things. "Sustainability programs only thrive when each member of an organization stands to gain from participating," according to CBRE consultant Emily Wilson. Sustainability programs that require leadership at all levels allow those with conviction and initiative to take leading roles. Many people on many rungs of the corporate ladder can act as role models – just make sure you reward these people later on. "Those mentees become the mentors for the next round," according to Wilson. "Whether it's through awards, promotions, performance reviews or simply announcements, staff members need to know that their leadership on sustainability is appreciated." Recognition highlights personal and corporate gains.

It can also be of great help to have your employees help draft the rules for the new way of doing things. Sustainability consultant Gareth Kane wrote a fascinating piece for CSR Wire about machine operators being told to completely switch off their equipment under new sustainability rules. But a big problem was the fact that this approach was explicitly ruled out in the machines' training manuals. A blunt approach to cultural change was foundering on the ingrained way of doing things – for good reason.

> Over and over again we get the same old hackneyed ideas wheeled out: "switch it off" stickers, awareness posters featuring hands cradling the planet, worthy presentations showing graphs of rising global temperatures and so on [according to Kane]. None of this is in any way relevant to the day-to-day duties of employees, so it simply gets ignored.

Rules have to chime with reason.

Instead, Kane suggests executives try the "green jujitsu" approach to employee engagement, which throws the idea of changing a corporate culture on its head. A master in the martial art of jujitsu uses their opponent's strength, height, and momentum against them, he notes. It is the epitome of playing to your opponent's strengths.

To entice middle managers, you have to play to their strengths. An executive from an electronics company told me a story about energizing stakeholders by doing exactly that. His procurement staff, responsible for things early in the manufacturing process, were worried about securing supplies to get products onto the market in time. At the other end of the production chain, his customers and some of his R&D experts were trying to find ways to recycle materials people never thought about recycling before. Both groups came together as the procurement staff saw they could profit from recycling efforts beyond the end of the manufacturing process.

> Both [stakeholder groups] have different time lines, but we're really optimistic about both and we found [the whole thing] to be an incredibly energizing goal. Engineers love it because this company runs on innovation and innovating deeply, even on the things you can't see.

These stakeholders were wooed by innovation.

Another effective tactic is to develop ideas in smaller teams and get team members to spread the word.

> We had some people who were very keen on the packaging ideas and recycling [one manager told me]. They were keen on energy conservation and on water conservation, and making our plants the most water efficient plants in the system. And it really was kind of smaller groups of teams who were excited about it.

Not all employees have to be bound in at once.

Indeed, naming fully fledged sustainability ambassadors is another great way to get the message out. They are vital conduits that convey information from leader to base, but also, crucially, from the "grass roots" up to the top. This latter function is vital for enticing stakeholders. Everyone has their own worries and needs, and everyone likes these to be heard. Good ambassadors also make important multipliers:

> Our chief accountant has got it [one executive told me about the "conversion" of a colleague]. He was on a workshop specifically around financial education at the leadership program. And he's now coming back and helping us form the business case – so putting the numbers behind it. He's now really using his expertise and reach to help drive the agenda forward.

Managers buying in can really accelerate the momentum of your sustainability push.

Finally, companies have to be aware of an ongoing need to get employees to engage with the company's sustainability goals. Sometimes the conversation between company and employee has to be outside the company premises.

> It really helps getting these people to look at it on a personal basis, say over a drink after work [one sustainability officer told me]. When you contextualize [what the company is doing] using their family, their children, the world they'll come to inherit, and the things they will and won't have – then they get it. Personalizing really helps.

Getting personal helps middle managers locate their individual values in the broader context of the company's sustainability goals.

5.6 Remember that some people will get it, and some won't

Even the most adept sustainability champion will discover that he or she can't get everyone to buy in. They shouldn't worry about that. I remember a retail executive telling me about his customers' views about sustainability, and it struck me that workforces are structured in a very similar way: "Some 10 percent of them are passionately green, just like us. They're interested. They want the best product and might pay a little more for it for a greener option," he told me. On the other extreme, there were some 20 percent of consumers not interested whatsoever. And there were two groups in the middle, claiming a third of consumers each, one group interested in the issue but wary of having to change too much, the other group "slightly more defeated" and asking: "What difference can I make?"

This executive knew from experience that it was possible to galvanize some 80 percent of his customer base with appeals to the fact that "together we're stronger." Seeing the power of collective action can spur collective action. If executives can engender the same joint spirit – and optimism – in their companies, the journey to introducing a sustainable business model will suddenly become much easier. As the retail executive said of his colleagues: "I think the biggest group of people are now saying, 'I accept that we need to change. We need a different form of business.'" The widespread feeling is that younger people in particular understand that message. Now they only need a sustainability champion to show them the way.

Employees like aspirational messages. They find meaning when they can align personal values and corporate goals to forge a new sense of purpose. I have visited many companies that have embarked on the sustainability journey. In all of these companies, I have met employees of all ranks who had bought into the essence of what the company was trying to do. Typically, senior executives, with their greater exposure to trends beyond the factory walls, got it first. And so did young recruits, who are typically much more purpose-driven than older generations.

That leaves a big swathe in the middle ranks that is undecided – it needs to be shown the light. In any company up to 20 percent of employees will remain skeptical. But as other employees feel more confident and empowered, companies will find more and more of these skeptical middle rankers begin to move – they see where the success is and where people feel good. Incentives and extrinsic goals are good, as I've said above. But I hope these arguments show that alignment and intrinsic goals are better for paving the way to sustainability ownership.

The sustainability officer of a large electronics company gave me the following summary of how to harness employee enthusiasm: "Take advantage of the enthusiasm of the employees who are interested in this work and want to understand the business value that sustainability can have to the company." Sustainability programs designed correctly had the double benefit of nudging the company toward its sustainability goals and "providing a terrific opportunity for employees" though fostering their participation.

She urged executives to think about programs through which they could get employees involved, raise employee awareness, and encourage employee participation. "Start at the top, and really get the buy-in from your CEO," she advised. "I think she or he will really see the benefit of this type of work. [They] will be your greatest champion." It is executives who clearly demonstrate the business value of sustainability to subordinates. She stated emphatically that it was possible to develop programs that cascaded both business value and societal value through the ranks. "Be creative and have fun," she concluded.

While this whole process in large part depends on the initiative of the leadership and sustainability champions, it is not a one-way street. Stakeholders must be open to the appeals of their employer. But they also have to be prepared to give thought to what it is they personally want. Line workers who can honestly say, "I'm doing my part to make the world a better place" have obviously thought about their role in their company and their society. As one executive told me about his experience of corporate transformation: "You start to ask questions. What's it all about? And you have to answer those questions for yourself." This new world comes with new personal responsibility.

Chapter 5 in summary

- Engaging your employees is central to creating your sustainable business model. When sustainability is "everybody's job," the results can be tremendous – and self-reinforcing.
- Entice employee participation by aligning their personal values with your company's purpose that is oriented around sustainability initiatives.
- CEOs and senior leadership must continually engage with their boards.
- Sustainability champions can enable employee buy-in on sustainability issues by creating ambassadors as vital conduits – from leader to base.
- Learn how to harness employee enthusiasm.
- Incentives and extrinsic goals are good, but alignment and intrinsic goals are better for paving the way to sustainability ownership.

Bibliography

Sony Corporation (2018). *Sustainability Report*. Sony Corporation.

Sony Corporation (2019). *Sony Road to Zero*. Sony Corporation.

S. Bonini and S. Görner (2011). *The Business of Sustainability*. McKinsey & Company.

A.-T. Bové, D.D'Herde and S. Swartz (2017). *Sustainability's Deepening Imprint*. McKinsey & Company.

A GlobeScan SustainAbility Survey (2013). *Sustainability Leaders*. GlobeScan.

A GlobeScan SustainAbility Survey (2018). *The State of Sustainable Business 2018: Results of the 10th Annual Survey of Sustainable Business Leaders*. BSR.

J. Balogun and V. Hope Hailey (2004). *Exploring Strategic Change: Exploring Corporate Strategy Series*. Prentice Hall/Financial Times.

K. Marx (1994). Alienated labor: early philosophical writings, In: L.H. Simon ed. *Karl Marx Selected Writings*. Hackett Publishing Company.

P. Strebel (1996). Why do employees resist change? *Harvard Business Review*.

W.H. Bommer, G.A. Rich, and R.S. Rubin (2005). Changing attitudes about change: Longitudinal effects of transformational leader behaviors on employee cynicism about organizational change, *Journal of Organizational Behavior*, 26, 733–753.

V. Miller, J. Johnson and J. Grau (1994). Antecedents to willingness to participate in a planned organizational change, *Journal of Applied Communication Research*, 22(1), 59–80.

L. Greiner and V. Schein (1989). Reviewed work: Power and organization development: Mobilizing power to implement change by William Pasmore, *The Academy of Management Executive*, 3(2), 159–161.

N.L. Jimmieson, D.J. Terry, and V.J. Callan (2004). A longitudinal study of employee adaptation to organizational change: The role of change-related information and change-related self-efficacy, *Journal of Occupational Health Psychology*, 9(1), 11–27.

C.M. Falbe and G. Yukl (August, 1992). Consequences for managers of using single influence tactics and combinations of tactics, *The Academy of Management Journal*, 35(3), 638–652.

Nesta (2008). *Selling Sustainability*. London, UK: Nesta.

L.S. Paine (2014). Sustainability in the boardroom, *Harvard Business Review*.

Ceres Annual Report (2015). *The Path Taken*. Boston, MA.

D. Kiron, N. Kruschwitz, K. Haanaes, M. Reeves, S.-K. Fuisz-Kehrbach, and G. Kell (2014). Joining forces: Collaboration and leadership for sustainability. *MIT Sloan Management Review, Boston Consulting Group and UN Global Compact Survey*.

E. Wilson (2014). *How to Sell a Culture of Sustainability*. Greenbiz.com & Greenbiz Group Inc.

G. Kane (2013). *Why Most Sustainability Behavior Change Programs Fail*. CSR Wire LLC.

6 Enable

6.1 Passing on the lessons of sustainability

It was a drizzly and dreary morning in May 2015, and I was on the 8.44 a.m.
Metro North train from Grand Central Station to Croton Falls, on the edge of
New York City. I had been invited by sustainability champions Wayne Balta
and Edan Dionne to spend the day with IBM executives at their Somers campus. It was in some ways an odd place to talk about sustainability and in others
the most fitting. When IBM built the huge complex in the 1980s, Somers was
described by the *New York Times* as "a rural town of 15,000 people," debating
the social and environmental pros and cons of urban sprawl. At the end of my
commute that morning, I stood amid four broad-shouldered, pyramid-topped
office buildings and wondered whether any big corporation would tackle this
kind of project today. To me, this low-rise intrusion was a measure of how
corporate thinking had already changed – IBM moved out of Somers by 2017.

I learned a lot that day about what the company had done to embed sustainability in its folds. One striking example was how IBM persuaded the people
involved in its $40 billion global supply chain to buy into its sustainability
efforts. As one of IBM's senior executives in supply chain management told
me, the company had asked its suppliers to implement a social and environmental management system. It was meant to keep tabs on their environmental and
social footprints, and meet eight sustainability-related requirements, including
CO_2 reduction, waste recycling, and energy consumption targets. The suppliers were also required to publish results on an ongoing basis. Crucially, IBM
didn't prescribe targets for suppliers or how to meet them. It simply told its
suppliers about the company's direction and how far it wanted them to follow.
"We wanted to use our name and purchasing power to take a leadership position in the industry and advance these social and environmental initiatives,"
the executive said.

However, for all the flexibility IBM built into its new supply chain requirements, the company also let its partners know one clear expectation: suppliers
had 12 months to comply or lose the company's business. As the executive
put it, the company in effect told its suppliers: "This is the passage to being
in the twenty-first century. If you're not a strong player in this arena, being

responsive to addressing concerns such as human trafficking, conflict minerals and various environmental issues, you will be nudged out." It was a bold move designed to foster change in and well beyond the lush green campus in Somers, New York.

Some of IBM's suppliers resisted at first. The executive recalled the familiar refrain, "We don't have time for this." To help suppliers comply, he continued, IBM led by example and showed them that IBM was "doing everything" it had also asked its suppliers to do. IBM made sure that its own procurement employees could assist suppliers – for example, by helping them to implement the kind of management systems IBM was demanding, or to consider material sustainability issues to ensure supply chain security. For this latter task, IBM's internal procurement team had to learn about the company's sustainability priorities before reaching out to train suppliers. I learned that top-down messages can be extremely effective at IBM: "If the top guy says it, then everybody agrees," the executive said. In this instance, John Paterson, IBM's chief procurement officer at the time, had cascaded messages through the organization. The *New York Times* had even published an article on the company's new social and environmental requirements for its suppliers.

The story of how one part of IBM made sustainability part of every employee's job and supplier's mission is extremely illuminating. It takes educating people, re-educating them if need be, preparing an extensive list of "FAQs," and making sure that the executive message is consistent and passed down through the ranks. As the executive said,

> The fact that we've been into this for 5 years [shows] this is not going away. There's a degree of tenacity that's just part of a management ethos that we've instilled. I would say that we're winning converts. Step by step by step.

One reason for this was that suppliers constantly received applause and reinforcement for their efforts, he went on: "You're not just doing it for IBM you're doing it for yourself. You're making yourself a much more attractive supplier to clients." Creative license to find their own solutions – and recognition for finding them – had motivated IBM procurement staff and suppliers to take ownership of sustainability.

There are no hard-and-fast rules to ensure success. But at every successful company I studied, leaders implemented some mixture of new training methods, management systems, and cultural facets to pursue their sustainability goals. They knew how to balance centralized control with empowering local managers and stakeholders who know their part of the business better than anyone else. At the vast majority of unsuccessful companies, by contrast, leaders don't know how to do this. As a result, even relatively enlightened companies fail to deliver on leaders' lofty rhetoric. No wonder that a 2012 study of employees of large companies found that almost 60 percent of respondents perceived "a gap between what my company says [...] and how we actually behave." This chapter shows readers how to go beyond the rhetoric and make sustainability a part of every employee's daily experience on the job – a prerequisite for the ownership of sustainability.

Procurement is just one of several operational areas this chapter examines in relation to sustainable business models. I argue that marketing departments need to promote the environmental and social benefits of products alongside their functional strengths – no one does this better than Unilever with its "purpose" brands. Research and development departments need to follow the lead of the likes of BASF and Nestlé and use eco-efficiency tests and life-cycle analysis to determine how sustainable a new product will be. Assessing a product's environmental and social impact – alongside its quality and cost – should be mandatory steps before executives make final decisions about production. Lastly, finance departments also have vital roles in driving sustainability, especially through the dialogue they maintain with investors. SAP has started to publish financial, environmental, and social reporting data in one document, popularly called an integrated report. It's an example that shows companies need to empower and train their investor relations departments to help investors think anew.

This chapter will look at systems, structures, and training that make it relatively easy to implement sustainability for every employee of a company, be it a huge corporation or the smallest shop. I describe ways to empower and enable stakeholders by giving them the confidence and the freedom to start thinking and acting sustainably by themselves. And I look at methods and tools that lower the cost of acting sustainably and can help you make sustainability every employee's day job, regardless of whether they're in human resources, marketing, or research and development.

By making concrete changes, even in the far-flung reaches of a company, leaders can galvanize large numbers of stakeholders to take ownership of sustainability and make a difference – making real and mounting contributions – through their own daily work. If you get the implementation right, most people you work with will assume ownership of sustainability and see business through the sustainability lens, every day, in every department. At one of Unilever's tea bag factories in the UK, for example, a mere three-millimeter adjustment to the size of a seal on the bags saved fifteen huge reels of paper every shift. Over time, that one change saved thousands of trees and significantly reduced costs. What might your company save – both financially and environmentally – if everyone at all of your facilities was striving to introduce innovations like this?

6.2 Lowering the costs and increasing the benefits of acting sustainably

a. Training

The executive I was speaking to didn't say it explicitly. But it was obvious she was talking about a real period of crisis for her company's sustainability program, which at the time was already four years old. The sustainability team was trying to elicit information from middle and upper managers to help come up with new goals and concrete targets.

"We'd say, 'We don't have all the information you guys have,'" the executive remembered about her team's approach. "But then, honestly, we had senior people replying, 'Would you just write it down, tell me what you need me to do?'" The managers were obviously put off by the task. Many claimed to simply be too busy.

But the sustainability officer saw through this.

> What they would say is, "I don't have time" [she recalled about her colleagues]. But what they really meant was, "This is too hard, I'm feeling uncomfortable. There's no agreed process. None of my peers would do this sort of stuff. [...] Just tell me what to do and I'll respect your decision."

There was no buy-in.

As the executive came to recognize, the issue was not managers' time. It was their confidence – not so much in the program, but in themselves and their ability to contribute to it. "We thought, 'Well, this is great, isn't it! We've been doing this for a number of years now, but our top guys don't really know about it, and can't decide for themselves.'" It was clear, she said, that something had to change. "We couldn't just sit in the background saying, 'Here's your next goal, here's your next goal.'" That would take too much effort with too little guarantee of success. All round, the proposition seemed too costly.

The company – a big retailer – decided to launch a rigorous training program. In this instance, the training was for senior management, but other courses covered other levels of the corporate hierarchy. In each case, the executive said, the goal was to give employees "the mindset" and the technical knowledge to understand the sustainability program. The aim was to get employees to start thinking in its terms. It was, in short, a crash course in efficacy and confidence. Employees were being told: you can do it.

The example shows that systems and structures are nothing without an engaged stakeholder base. Employees, for one, not only need to feel called upon to contribute. They need to feel confident that they have something to add to the company's sustainability program. To foster a "can do" attitude, companies have to lower the costs of acting sustainably by investing in training alongside systems and structures. They need to "build" efficacy, the ability to produce a desired result. When achieved, this sense of efficacy prompts employees to take ownership of the sustainability process.

Employees perform better when they feel confident or efficacious, when they feel capable of doing the things they are expected to, according to a 2012 paper by Deanne Den Hartog and Frank Belschak. As we saw earlier when talking about physical exercise, one vital attitudinal shift when it comes to enabling stakeholders to assume sustainability ownership is to turn extrinsic into intrinsic motivation. "I have to do it" turns into "I can do it" – before morphing again into "I want to do it." Such employees cope better with change.

The Network for Business Sustainability (NBS) in 2010 published a review of business practices relating to sustainability. It underlined the central role of training and suggested that employee induction programs should include training that shows how sustainability is at the core of a company's thinking. It also stressed that the entire workforce needed ongoing ethics, environmental and sustainability courses. Sadly, such issues often still fall by the wayside because the default priority of too many businesses is still to maximize profit.

Many sustainability initiatives require employees to pick up specialized expertise, like using eco-efficiency tools when evaluating a new product. The best way this can happen is through training. Companies as diverse as BASF, IBM, Marks & Spencer, and Nestlé have invested heavily in training, and its underlying systems and processes. They can, as a result, make and implement sustainability decisions on a larger scale and in less time.

But it's important to see that technical expertise is just one facet of training. At Unilever, for example, the company's top 500 executives undergo an intensive leadership development process, which involves an assessment of their leadership skills and a program in which they have to mentor juniors. In a final stage, the executives are forced to look to the future and decide what leadership qualities might matter then – systems thinking, say, or empowerment. To bring this to life, managers are required to draw up a "Purpose into Impact" plan, which draws on personal purpose to deliver societal and business change.

Marks & Spencer has a training program for its hundred top executives that helps them discover how they and their departments can support the company's sustainability goals. As one of the program's designers told me, the course involves nine challenges with different scenarios.

> For example, they go to a town that is clearly suffering from degeneration and lack of economic development. They have to engage with the question what retailing looks like in that environment, rather than a shiny, big-city store. What does retailing mean for a town like that? They realize that there is inequality, that there are social pressures. So when, for example, we have a conversation about whether we should increase the number of disadvantaged people coming into our workforce, they're more likely to see the bigger picture and say: "Absolutely. We definitely need more of them."

Together, the hard and soft aspects of training enable stakeholders to fulfill their need for efficacy, self-identity, and belonging, making it more likely that sustainability ownership will take root. Thanks to the legitimacy and status accorded it, the cost of doing business through the sustainability lens goes down – and its benefits increase. Along with the compensation strategies I discuss a little later, integration and ownership of sustainability become that much easier.

b. Communication and hand-holding

While investment in management systems and training in various guises is necessary, it is by no means sufficient. Most of us are scared of something new and different. As a result, it is also important to communicate incessantly and to offer "hand-holding," as needed, so stakeholders can use the concrete goals of the company to inform how they act.

"We've got 7 headline commitments and 36 specific targets across our business," one executive told me when speaking of the requirements of his employer's sustainability program. He was proud of his responsibility for setting his unit's strategic targets in order to meet the corporation's overall goals. But he was equally as proud of something more humdrum: "My role is also about working with people across our business that are responsible for delivering against concrete targets." He was pleased about having been able to communicate and work across various business functions. "That's probably what I'm most proud of," he said. "We've managed to put a plan in place and then also a delivery mechanism for it." Concrete goals are one thing, communication and hand-holding another.

In the same vein, one of the sustainability officers at Enel highlighted the value of hand-holding and effective communication when it came to enabling employees to recognize and adopt sustainability goals in their daily work routines. A deep knowledge of the business was required, she argued, and employees only got this by working alongside people in every department, whether operations, business development, recruitment, or information and communication technologies (ICT). She stressed the importance of learning to "speak their language" so that sustainability leaders could "translate the concept of sustainability" into terms others understood and identified with. She concluded: "I know everybody in the company, and I know the business, I know people, I know their problems, and so this is what I try to do to help them along."

Communication is key when it comes to implementing sustainability plans, as David Lubin and Daniel Etsy argued in a 2010 paper. They showed how employees could be made to feel accountable for sustainability goals – the latter had to be embedded in business models and concrete day-to-day objectives, and their function clearly communicated. They found that employees who were acting only in the light of public information provided consistently lower assessments of their employer's plan than employees who had been consulted in the workplace and had access to full inside information.

It's no surprise to discover, then, that most of the companies that take sustainability seriously have also come to see that it's not enough to simply have one – or a few – sustainability champions at the top of the hierarchy. Sustainability ambassadors need to be placed all over the organization, at all levels. And they need the confidence and competence to hold hands and communicate clearly. Without hand-holding and communication, sustainability can just become a jumble, as this example shows.

A Marks & Spencer executive called ensuring that change spread throughout the company, "doing a hundred things by a certain deadline."

The company had supply chains in Africa, in the UK and Europe, and in Southeast Asia, he said.

> We've got thousands of different factories, tens and thousands of different raw material sources, millions of workers, and 31 million customers buying 2.9 billion items each year [he continued]. That's a huge Rubik's cube of change you've got to work on. The number one challenge for us is scale and making sure that our words are becoming reality on the ground.

Without effective communication, even a much smaller initiative, let alone something of this size, would not see the light of day.

However, there is one further factor you should bear in mind – freedom or autonomy. Employees will only communicate their expert opinions and visions if they feel confident that such bottom-up opinion is actually wanted and valued. In an influential study, published in 2012, Deanne N. Den Hartog and Frank D. Belschak of the University of Amsterdam presented some illuminating findings about proactive employee behavior.

They looked at the role of inspirational leadership, employee confidence, and job autonomy in inspiring workers to go the extra mile for their companies and bosses. They found that confident employees, those given a lot of freedom to do their jobs, were particularly open to appeals from inspirational bosses. These employees were willing to apply their professional experience and expertise to help answer the many questions the company faced. Crucially, they were willing to volunteer these inputs in a bottom-up process, confident that they would be valued rather than viewed as insignificant.

This confluence of good leadership, confidence, and institutionalized autonomy can turn every stakeholder into their own "sustainability owner," a person who believes and spreads the "sustainability creed" both by exhortation and by example. One manager with whom I spoke described his role as that of an owner and influencer, someone willing to speak up, and able, in turn, "to bring the right people together" to spread this sense of ownership. He described a meeting he'd had that morning with colleagues from other departments, and how he got them to buy into sustainability targets even though the term hadn't been "in their job titles." He said he'd tagged along to the meeting "to make sure we could get their support" for the sustainability targets. But he knew that this proactive stance was one that would have to continue: "We're only one third of the way there." Communication and hand-holding can take time to have an effect.

c. Compensation tied to sustainability

As explained in the next chapter, measuring your company's progress on environmental and social dimensions is essential. In the words of one food company executive, sustainability is best expressed through diverse key performance indicators used as targets in different parts of the business.

So if you go to talk to one of our site directors, they would tell you that sustainability is embedded in the objectives of his team: driving down water or energy use, for example. These are targets embedded at site level.

Goals are necessary, but they have to make sense to the people who are meant to reach them.

The trick, of course, is to translate a company's broad goals into that "huge Rubik's cube" of individual initiatives, whose effectiveness is then measured and turned into a myriad of key performance indicators (KPIs). If done well, one site manager's focus on water use will complement another manager's focus on sustainable sourcing, or on another colleague's quest for waste reduction. A whole mosaic of concrete – and often local – targets will make up a much finer and yet larger picture than composite KPIs can render. There'll be more about this in Chapter 7. The point I'm making here is KPIs matter a lot, especially granular ones.

No sustainability program can stay on track without careful monitoring of a myriad of metrics. And because this is so, every executive in charge of some or all parts of a sustainability program will ask him or herself: should the company link sustainability KPIs to employee compensation? One line of reasoning contends this approach is conceptually wrong. If a company is trying to make sustainability part of everyday business, it should not separate sustainability goals from metrics for output or financial returns.

As upright as that argument may be, most sustainability champions accept that we have not yet attained an ideal state in which sustainability and business goals are in perfect alignment. As a result, there is widespread consensus that at least some compensation should be linked to a set of sustainability objectives to give employees a tried-and-tested incentive. As a retail executive emphasized, "If 10 percent of my variable compensation is tied to sustainability, then it must be important." At mining giant Alcoa, up to 20 percent of employee compensation, from the production manager to the CEO, is linked to achieving the company's sustainability goals. Remember, though, that other incentive types can flank bonuses: awards ceremonies and promotions, for example, are great ways to create sustainability heroes and to spur internal competition.

The Network for Business Sustainability (NBS) emphatically calls on companies to come up with appraisal and bonus calculation systems that rely on sustainability metrics. It even calls for a "redesign" of promotions around sustainable business performance. The NBS notes that companies that have such schemes hope to incorporate sustainability thinking more quickly into traditional business models. Sustainability targets once deemed impossible can, it notes, suddenly look within reach – thanks to financial incentives.

There are two things to remember: first, when you measure things, you've got a lot better chance of achieving what it is you're trying to do [an executive told me of his company's experiences]. And secondly, if you tie the things you're measuring to someone's compensation, you have an even better chance. People are amazing in terms of those incentives. When you pay them to do something often, they'll go do it.

Rewarding individuals for their sustainability achievements creates tangible connections between the two. Companies that ground social and environmental ideals in the real world of work and material compensation also help spur employees' sense of individual ownership.

When linking KPIs to compensation, it's vital to remain open to changes. One executive I talked to recalled how easy it was "to deliver quite substantial" KPI jumps as managers naturally went for "low-hanging fruits" in the first years of the sustainability program. "The challenge gets a little bit harder as things get harder to achieve. Does one metric remain the right metric, as things get harder? I don't know." KPI-based targets have to be adjusted at regular intervals – both in degree and in nature.

Lastly, here's an example of a great tailor-made KPI, used at Marks & Spencer. Some years ago, the retailer decided employee engagement would make a great measure of managerial commitment to sustainability. Every quarter, the company polls the workers in its stores to find out how they feel about the company, their store, their manager, all components of overall employee engagement. "So if he hits his sales plan for the year, that's brilliant. But if he hits his sales plan but doesn't have a high engagement score, he won't get a [sustainability] bonus." In a "quite round about" but highly effective way, M&S linked acting sustainably to compensation – even while, the executive noted, the sustainability plan itself was not formally linked to pay.

6.3 Making sustainability part of everybody's day job

To make sustainability part of everybody's day job, every employee of a company has to adjust to the "green approach" so that sustainability is not just an add-on but is embedded in everything they do. The key difficulty is finding ways – there is always more than one – of raising sustainability awareness and making people understand sustainability by communicating clearly. We encountered several techniques for this in Chapter 5. As you likely noted, there is no hard-and-fast way to do any of this – people are different, companies are different, as are circumstances. While that suggests a multitude of different approaches, it's useful to know that many functionally similar departments throw up similar problems. This is how each department can best contribute to the sustainability journey.

a. Human resources

Sustainability as a term invokes conservatism and status quo, when in fact, as a business philosophy, it demands change and constant flexibility from employees, as one chemical company executive pointed out. To get any sustainability program up and running, human resources must work to prepare employees for change and make them ready to change, too. To do this, HR departments can invest in the different kinds of sustainability training we discussed above, or co-creation activities, idea contests, volunteering, and several other activities that prepare employees for such change.

In light of these issues, I explored the question with several executives whether it helps employees to have a common definition of sustainability. They easily agreed that this helped point staff in the right direction. But some also noted it might be necessary to interpret every company's core message differently in different regions – specifically, to take into account of concrete but local sustainability goals, as discussed in Chapter 4.

Employee volunteering also emerged as an important factor in my research. Both an executive from an industrial company and a consultant spoke about the positive effects of projects designed to get employees to volunteer help and time. By being asked for a contribution, they said, employees felt empowered and in a position to "give back" rather than just taking orders. One path was co-creation, asking employees to come up with ideas and initiatives, and to feed them into the corporate machine from the bottom up. The other path was volunteering, a route seen as very helpful in shaping corporate culture and enabling employees to assume sustainability ownership.

Finally, sustainability is a key site in the "war for talent" – and human resources can give corporations a real edge in the battle here. A case in point is Unilever, the third most looked-up company on LinkedIn, behind Apple and Google. This is in part because of its sustainability performance and because its HR department does a great job of hiring individuals with similar green values. Back in the days when executives still just talked about corporate responsibility (CR), I used to warn them that CR without well-managed HR was nothing but words – or CR – HR = PR, as I once read in Elaine Cohen's book, *CSR for HR*. Like product quality and innovation, good human resources management is a vital component of any company's sustainability plan. Do not subtract HR from Sustainability.

b. Marketing

Companies must understand that their brands are the main conduits of communication with their stakeholders. They must view their brands as ways to declare what the company does and stands for when it comes to sustainability. Promoting the environmental and social benefits of a product, encouraging its responsible consumption and proper disposal, working closely with innovation and R&D to develop sustainable successors – all these tasks are best viewed as important aspects of marketing.

Unilever, for example, uses its marketing prowess to imbue each of its brands – for example, Dove, Domestos, Lifebuoy, Knorr, and Vaseline – with a social purpose. Brand managers look at the environmental and social impact of brands and develop "brand purpose statements." The antibacterial soap Lifebuoy, for example, fights infant mortality and sickness by getting children, in particular, to wash their hands regularly; it has the stated social purpose to "help a child reach the age of 5." Seeing as much of Lifebuoy is sold in water-stressed areas, Unilever came up with an innovation: the soap's lather turns to green as soon as the user's hands are clean – a great way to garner a child's attention and save water. The company's entire workforce also participates on "World Handwashing Day," visiting schools and community centers to teach the value of regular handwashing. Helping customers reduce water use also helped to underline Unilever's sustainability credentials and to better align the company's role in addressing the UN's Sustainable Development Goals (SDGs). Only products that hit the triple bottom line – profit, people, and planet – have a chance in this company.

Next to consumer education, clear product certification also helps get the message across. That message should be the reflection of a global strategy but allow for local or country-specific implementation. But there are no hard-and-fast rules about this. The Sustainability Roundtable in Berlin saw many examples of tough decisions about whether and how to go for a local or for a global signature, and how to smooth the transition from one to another. Whereas local initiatives tend to be close to the heart of employees, global ones have greater visibility; while local initiatives are great for stimulating engagement of smaller employee groups, global ones can provide a better platform for company-wide engagement. What works in one instance, might not work in another. It can be a tough choice.

The key is to focus on initiatives that really matter to the company. A whole host of executives pointed out that it is important to focus on initiatives that are close to a company's own value chain. They must really matter to its workforce, especially at the local level. Real bottom-up approaches – local ones that can go global – are crucial. Sustainability means different things to different people in different places. So not only programs need to be localized, some of the messaging does, too.

Transparency and credibility in communication are key. A clear, consistent focus, with all departments in alignment, is crucial for the successful communication of sustainability goals and initiatives. A company "living" its sustainability program is one that sends subtle, repeated signals in the hope of informing – and being seen to inform. It does not merely go through the motions of now and again selling a message. Also, the internal communication of failures is vital for establishing credibility and for enabling learning by doing.

Sustainability can absolutely drive brand value. Remember that this deserves high consideration as brand value is crucial to long-term sustainability. No brand, no revenues, no company – it's that simple. Remember that customers and other stakeholder groups reward sustainability. For example, they prize relevance and engagement: if sustainability initiatives meet emotional demands relevant to stakeholders, a company will profit.

c. Research and development

Companies need to make the case for sustainable innovation to help sustainability be appreciated as an integral part of business strategy and not just a cost-cutting exercise. Today, companies have the ability to access proper tools to evaluate environmental sustainability and are developing tools to monitor nutritional and social aspects. Sustainability assessments using eco-efficiency and life-cycle analysis are mandatory at some leading companies – for every project before it goes to development.

Sustainable businesses need to take a broad view of research and development. R&D is not just about coming up with innovative products – it's about coming up with innovative processes, services, and markets. And there are some already established best practices that no company should do without. The just-mentioned sustainability assessments that look at eco-efficiency and product life-cycles should be mandatory for every project before development begins. Managers should take a deep look at consumers' environmental and social needs during this development phase. Lastly, companies should encourage their employees to adopt a clear vision and take a broader perspective of what the company does – a carmaker no longer just makes cars, it helps the world stay mobile.

At Unilever, managers are charged with looking at consumers' environmental and social needs during product development. For example, when developing products for markets that tend to be water-stressed, managers not only worry about reducing the water footprint of their own manufacturing, but also think about ways to reduce water usage in the consumer's home. This led to Unilever managers developing soaps that don't use any water at all. As already described, they turn green in the hand-washing process to signal users – for example, children in disease-prone areas – that they have washed their hands long enough. Such joined-up thinking is crucial to better integrate sustainability into the innovation process. Sustainable innovation is about doing palpable good.

"Innovating through doing good" is how an insurance executive described sustainable innovation at his company to the Berlin Sustainable Business Roundtable. He talked about the company's interest in micro-insurance and how it delivered a double bottom-line return – for the company and society. But to make micro-insurance successful, challenges had to be overcome through innovation – in areas as diverse as definition, products, processes, distribution, and education. The company made sure to provide a clear definition that guided values and transparency. The executive pointed out that the latter in particular pushed stakeholders to improve performance and drive internal innovation. To reach various target groups, they came up with simple and customized products, such as weekly payable education insurance, monthly payable funeral insurance, or index-based rainfall cover for farmers. The key aim of helping these customers drove innovation.

Process innovation, on the other hand, needed to focus on low transaction costs but high efficiency, he continued. Alternative distribution channels with a large customer base could be created, for instance, by selling insurance by mobile phone or, more sustainably, by cooperating with consumer goods companies that could provide free insurance to small-shop owners, for example. Finally, promoting financial literacy using games, comics, even Bollywood-style films, contributed to overcoming consumer challenges.

Another example of sustainability-driven innovation came from a food company executive. She noted that customers wanted to know more and more about where their products come from, how they were made, and what they contained. In response, the company integrated sustainability into each stage of the food value chain. Expert networks, mandatory sustainability assessments before and during development, and market-introduction processes quickly became crucial tools. Most importantly, the company integrated a life-cycle analysis process across the entire value chain. It focused on a few relevant indicators and made data available quickly for non-expert users via an easily understandable databank. Everybody involved knew and understood what was going on.

The executive acknowledged that sustainable innovations sometimes have to come in stages along the value chain. While they might at first not appear useful, they can eventually render huge contributions. Her key message was that sustainability could never be regarded as an afterthought, it had to be built into the DNA of every product from the very beginning. This was hard to communicate on small product labeling, but pointers to web-links could show interested consumers the way to get more of the information they required. She asked Roundtable participants to remember that groundbreaking innovation often came from the business side, not from the input or explicit demands of customers.

d. Supply chain

Companies are going to find it increasingly difficult to reach sustainability goals in this area. Many of the supply chain lapses in recent years – I'm thinking of examples such as the horsemeat-in-food scandals or the fires in garment factories in Southeast Asia – are in no small part the result of increased single bottom-line pressures. In 2010, a survey by the consultancy McKinsey found that improving customer service was only one of three supply chain priorities over the next five years. Reducing operating costs and getting products or services to market faster were the other two.

On the other hand, companies do seem to recognize that they need to be not only profitable, but also a sustainable supply chain. The 2012 Accenture Outlook found that 90 percent of companies saw sustainable procurement as a top-five priority.

Companies need to make all management levels aware of the importance of good supplier relationships and performance. Supply chain issues need to be part of corporate strategy. Companies that take this ambition seriously will have to increase supply chain security, improve sustainable sourcing through training and developing better relationships with suppliers, and cut waste. A key factor will be to train procurement teams on material sustainability issues, so that they can have informed conversations with suppliers. Procurement teams need to be encouraged to think beyond mere compliance issues in order to develop real partnerships with suppliers. Cross-industry perspectives, relationship management as well as supply chain transparency will prove vital for this.

An executive from a consumer electronics company told me about the transformative power of good supply chain partnerships. Companies, he said, were keen to end "the cat-and-mouse game" with suppliers. They wanted to go beyond policing them and explain the benefits of a broader, deeper relationship. He emphasized that companies needed to start sharing information. To manage materials successfully and to relieve suppliers of outsourcing burdens, his company was using a global database to manage supplier declarations regarding substances and materials. By cooperating with its home government and non-governmental organizations (NGOs), the company had created a closed supply pipeline. Recall the IBM story at the beginning of this chapter – the company had led by example and offered expertise where needed, but the suppliers had had to come up with their own ways to meet environmental and social targets. And IBM's confidence in its suppliers paid off.

e. Investor relations and finance

When it comes to sustainability, there is a big gap – real or perceived – between companies and the investment community. The latter complains that companies don't volunteer any or enough sustainability information, while many companies say they never get asked for it. Both sides need to shift the conversation to close the information gap.

We have, for one, seen real progress in environmental-impact measurement and sustainability standards. The group controller of a food company noted growing investor interest in sustainability issues. But he lamented that investors were still unable to distinguish between material and immaterial factors in sustainability reports. He called for more progress when it came to impact assessment and standards, especially when it came to looking at the whole value chain and taking a holistic approach.

I said earlier in this chapter that interdepartmental, internal communication is key. But here we can also see the importance of external communication, between companies and investors. It needs to be improved in the area of sustainability, for example, by using the targets and metrics now coming into play. When it comes to explaining sustainability, sustainability officers need to be able to "speak the language" of finance. They have to be able to explain why their projects should be chosen over other investment opportunities by linking them to strategy and to metrics. As finance is and always will be at the center of the business, sustainability needs to learn to translate its results into this language.

Sustainability must be able to justify why resources should be allocated, say, to an environmental project and not to another department's project. The greatest intersection of sustainability and finance is in the appreciation of risk, which is inherent to both functions. These risks need to be evaluated and weighed against one another in an overarching evaluation system encompassing both finance and sustainability. For this to succeed, sustainability needs to speak more of the language of finance – and finance needs to be willing to look 10 or 20 years ahead, just like sustainability has always done. Using resources sustainably and realizing environmental risks has always required taking a long view.

6.4 Making use of any tail winds

Knowing your purpose, cultivating good leadership, enabling your employees to take ownership of their work – these three moves pave the way for success in an increasingly social and environmentally conscious world. This chapter has focused on the last of those steps. One CEO I talked with left me with an important thought. He stressed the critical need for any company to gauge where the world is, in terms of sustainability challenges, and where its business is heading. He stressed the importance of recognizing what key sustainability issues are, and acting on them.

For his industry, it was palm oil, for example. He recalled how that problem had come into view – and how that could help other companies.

> We better do something about that. All companies I am sure will have a few of those things [he said]. Choose those things and come up with a plan. A plan about what you could start to do to adapt your business model to that future.

Especially if customers wanted companies to do this, he added.

> If Walmart decides it is going to really push sustainability, it is easier because then you have got a customer driving for it. You have an actual bottom-line reason for doing it. Because, if you can do it better than your peers, you can grow your business faster than the market.

The foresight to implement sustainability initiatives into your business model is based on being able to see where consumer trends are heading. The executive argued that progress is not antithetical to profit. In general, he suggested, "Look for the tail winds, look for the places where you could make some progress because there is a benefit for doing it." He argued that getting employees to support and creatively embed sustainability into their everyday work routines can actually lift employee performance because they are working for something they believe in.

As I have said all along, it is not a waste of time or resources to do things in an environmentally friendly and socially responsible way. Rather, it is making an investment in the future. The stakes may be high, but the dividends include having a healthy world to pass along to future generations and make money in the process. Remember that courses can be adjusted, past decisions revoked. Remember IBM once moved to Somers, New York. And eventually moved away again.

Chapter 6 in summary

- Enabling employees is key to implementing a sustainable business model from the ground up, fostering employees' confidence and competence.
- Good leadership makes sustainability part of every employee's job, it encourages autonomy that can turn every worker into their own "change agent."
- Employees can be further motivated by linking sustainability goals to their compensation –KPIs can be very useful for this.
- Good marketing recognizes the importance of communicating company purpose through its brands – and it and new KPIs can help you better deal with investors.
- Recognize the importance of local innovation for solving problems sustainably and recognize the need for every company to know its supply chain.
- Ensure your company has a future by recognizing where its sector is heading and what the company's role in it should be – and use the tail winds to get it there.

Bibliography

B. Brown (1983). With mixed feelings, Somers awaits I.B.M. and Pepsico, *The New York Times.*

D.N. Den Hartog and F.D. Belschak (2012). When does transformational leadership enhance employee proactive behavior? The role of autonomy and role breadth self-efficacy, *Journal of Applied Psychology*, 97(1), 194–202.

SAP Integrated Report (2017). *Intelligent Enterprise, SAP.* Available at: https://www.sap.com/integrated-reports/2017/en.html.

S. Bertels, L. Papania, and D. Papania, Simon Fraser University (2010). Embedding sustainability in organizational culture: A systematic review of the body of knowledge, *Network for Business Sustainability.*

D.A. Lubin and D.C. Esty (2010). The sustainability imperative, *Harvard Business Review.*

E. Cohen (2010). *CSR for HR: A Necessary Partnership for Advancing Responsible Business Practices.* Greenleaf Publishing.

Y. Malik, A. Niemeyer, and B. Ruwadi (2011). Building the supply chain of the future, *McKinsey Quarterly.* Available at: https://www.mckinsey.com/business-functions/operations/our-insights/building-the-supply-chain-of-the-future.

T. Gyorey, M. Jochim, and S. Norton (2010). *The Challenges Ahead for Supply Chains: McKinsey Global Survey Results*. Available at: https://www.mckinsey.com/business-functions/operations/our-insights/the-challenges-ahead-for-supply-chains-mckinsey-global-survey-results.

T. D'Emidio, D. Malfara, and K. Neher (2017). *Improving the Customer Experience to Achieve Government-Agency Goals*. McKinsey & Company.

Accenture (2012). *Sustainable Organizations? Start with Sustainable Procurement*. Accenture.

Part IV

Entrench
Demystify, enliven, and expand ownership

In Part IV, I explain the third and final step of my model – entrench. When ownership is entrenched, it is firmly integrated into the company's culture and ethos. To entrench feelings of ownership, *demystify* or make evident stakeholders' contributions to achieving sustainability targets, which allows them to feel accomplished and competent. *Enliven* ownership through communication, co-creation, and celebration, which maintains the momentum of sustainability. Finally, *expand* feelings of ownership by building the broader industry collaborations required to solve complex, systemic problems, which demonstrate an authentic commitment to sustainability above and beyond business imperatives.

7 Demystify

7.1 Show stakeholders their role in achieving sustainability

In June 2015, I was in the bustling city of Mumbai, the commercial and financial capital of India and, according to the World Health Organization, the fourth most polluted megacity in the world. One of the companies I was visiting that day was Ambuja Cement, a subsidiary of the global cement manufacturer LafargeHolcim. The Swiss-based company was a giant in what has traditionally been seen as an energy-intensive and dirty industry. But over the past few years, it had become one of the pioneers of social impact measurement – it used hard data to see where, how, and how much its business affected society. Subsidiaries like Ambuja Cement in India had themselves become pioneers of sustainability, actively measuring and addressing the strains their business is putting on communities – even and especially on hot, sprawling, teeming municipalities like Mumbai.

I was on my way to meet Ashwin Raykundalia, a senior vice president at Ambuja Cement, who is one of the pioneers of quantifying social and environmental impact and expressing it in monetary terms. He welcomed me into his modest office. It was a Friday and he was dressed in polo shirt and blue jeans. Soon into our conversation in English, he asked, "Do you understand Hindi?" I knew that as the official language of India, Hindi was still dominant for the operational parts of most businesses and realized that it was perhaps easier for him to explain a few things to me in Hindi. "Yes I do speak Hindi," I replied with a smile. "Sometimes it will come out," he said with a wise nod. Having established that our conversation would be linguistically sustainable, we settled into our discussion.

In 2012, three years before merging with French rival Lafarge, Holcim executives decided to redefine the company's sustainability goals for 2020. One of the goals of "Sustainability Ambitions 2020" was to create environmental- and social-impact accounting to get a sense of the "true value" of the company. New hard data, it was hoped, would generate new ideas for Holcim's strategy. Ambuja was chosen to conduct a pilot program, whose learnings were to be rolled out across the whole group if they proved successful.

At the time, thanks in part to a British organization called Trucost, methodologies were just being invented that allowed companies to calculate and monetize environmental impact, or to account for "natural capital" in terms of emissions, water, and waste. But there weren't any obvious approaches to measuring social impact. Holcim and Ambuja decided to use employment, health, and well-being of workers as direct measures of its social footprint. Measuring the most significant number, jobs impact, would entail looking at direct employment, indirect employment through suppliers, and induced employment as a result of Ambuja's employees or suppliers' employees spending their wages locally.

The company built an "impact pathway for employment" that measured the following: inputs, or money spent to run the company; activities or operations in specific countries; output, or jobs created and destroyed; outcomes, or changes in income along the whole employment chain; impacts, or changes in community well-being as a result of changes in income. Using a mix of in-house and government data, "guestimates," and basic calculations, and the help of the consulting company KPMG, Ambuja was able to estimate both the positive and negative impact of its environmental and social footprint. When the company placed these metrics alongside its financial performance, it came up with a single index number that gave a very good idea of Ambuja's overall societal impact. So good, in fact, that the company's methodology became the foundation of a very good Harvard Business School case study about corporate true-value calculations.

Raykundalia told me what an eye-opener the exercise had proved to be. True, he said, the overall evaluation was and remained sensitive to assumptions – Ambuja warns its "social and environmental profit and loss statement" can change "as valuation techniques and methodologies evolve." But, he continued emphatically, it did give managers a new foundation upon which to assess their business and invest in it. "It was a big shift in mindset." On top of profit, executives saw that Ambuja's social activities were a net gain – economic value-added results minus health issues. But they also saw its environmental activities were a drag on true value – the impact of emissions, water, and land use exceeded the gains from rainwater harvesting, alternative sourcing, quarry restoration, and renewable energy.

Nevertheless, managers weren't dispirited by such bad news, Raykundalia continued. This is because the new accounting made it easier to steer investments into true-value creation to counteract environmental impacts. More money flowed into water retention initiatives, for example, and into skills development for employees. While Ambuja couldn't avoid all negative effects – cement making requires a lot of energy – the metrics did allow management to identify important points of leverage. As a result, executives could run the company so it would have a net positive effect on environment and society. "You [discover it's easier to] invest more on the social, environmental side to offset your negativity and create more true value," he said. True-value accounting had shown the company that it was easier to create more positive externalities than reduce all existing negative ones.

Ambuja also found true-value analysis to be an effective internal communications tool. It raised sustainability understanding within the company and helped shift the conversation toward materiality and business performance. When I visited, Ambuja was preparing to break down its true-value key performance indicators (KPIs) to show the performance of each of its 16 plants. The company hoped spurring constructive internal competition would improve site-specific true value every year. Plant managers would be sharing the numbers with their employees, providing positive reinforcement for their engagement in sustainability, and demystifying the progress they had made. This strengthened sustainability ownership.

At some point, Ambuja planned to link these new KPIs to management compensation. And Raykundalia even thought the true-value approach could one day prove useful when considering acquisitions, allowing LafargeHolcim to consider total value and not just single bottom-line returns when sizing up companies to buy. By now, Ambuja's pilot attempts have been extended to many LafargeHolcim subsidiaries worldwide. As a result, many, and ever more, employees are beginning to get a sense of sustainability ownership in an industry both vilified as a polluter and essential to the way we live. Its efforts saw Ambuja land fifth place in the construction material category in the coveted Dow Jones Sustainability Index in 2017. A year later, the company managed to hold on to its top-five spot, scoring full marks in, among others, materiality, sustainable construction, environmental reporting, environmental policy, and water-related risks.

"We treasure what we measure," as Unilever's Paul Polman likes to say. Best-in-class companies apply this dictum in many areas, including sustainability. I have seen factory workers visualizing CO_2 emissions on whiteboards, office employees receiving pop-ups on water usage when they turn on their laptops, and dashboards and tickers galore posting progress on various sustainability KPIs. Such information-sharing leads to conversations and becomes the basis of motivation, pride, and a stronger sense of sustainability ownership.

Many companies, by contrast, don't have this discipline when it comes to comprehensively measuring and communicating sustainability KPIs. They only measure the traditional, revenue-generating parts of their business – and some ad hoc metrics they want to put in their sustainability reports. As a result, these companies and their key stakeholders don't know how much water they use, for instance, how big their carbon footprint is, or which business units contribute the most – and the least – to waste reduction. In consequence, employees don't understand the impact they, their teams, and their organization are having. Ownership fails to take root, sustainability remains unsustainable.

Measuring things is a great way to end such torpor. Compiling key performance indicators can make companies extremely transparent, allowing management and stakeholders to see how they are performing, both in financial and socio-environmental terms. Measuring can tell you what you and your stakeholders are doing right – and what's going wrong, what needs to be tweaked or abandoned. These are all essential steps in investing in the subject – enabling management and stakeholders to acquire a deep understanding of it and thereby strengthen their sense of ownership. Measurement is an excellent basis for communicating with stakeholders. It can motivate them to keep up the good work or challenge them to do more. When goals are clear and progress demystified, stakeholders are better able to pursue their work, while also taking ownership of people and planet issues.

What precisely should be measured? As ratings agencies and industry regulators seem to demand ever more KPIs, executives might already feel overwhelmed. As one executive told me, his industry was suffering from "death by KPI's," with measurement even becoming counterproductive. Drawing on my research, this chapter argues that we should adopt two basic types of measurement for sustainability initiatives: direct and indirect. Companies should measure direct progress on sustainability goals – amounts of CO_2 emitted, volumes of water used, tons of waste created, numbers of suppliers trained. But companies should also measure the indirect impact of the goals they are working toward – how stakeholders react to such initiatives; how employee engagement, customer satisfaction, and productivity develop; how investors react to sustainability communication.

7.2 How to measure sustainability value directly and indirectly

"We're constantly walking a tightrope," a sustainability champion at a big retailer told me. While the company wanted to embed sustainability in its strategy and daily operations, it also saw the need to highlight these efforts in the form of stand-alone sustainability KPIs. The problem, he said, was that the company was striving to integrate sustainability into every corporate thought and deed, while at the same time separating out sustainability efforts by targeting specific data saying, "Look, here are the big metrics, the big numbers that show we're shifting toward a sustainable business."

I touched upon this paradox in Chapter 6, when I noted that efforts to embed sustainability within a company also needed landmark projects around which employees could rally. Sustainability is meant to be second nature and fit in seamlessly with bottom-line thinking and action. But landmark projects requiring bespoke sustainability KPIs seem to contradict that. This paradox is one with which management and stakeholders have to live as their company – or shop or department – converts to living and breathing a sustainable business model. Sustainability ownership is fostered by visibility and momentum, and the right KPIs, carefully chosen and communicated, can engender that crucial sense of ownership.

Given the complexities of an embedded system and its diverse effects, sustainability KPIs make every step on the path toward a sustainable business model satisfyingly transparent and tangible. Measuring makes things concrete and comparable and provides ongoing feedback on sustainability targets. That demystifies stakeholders' contributions and gradually propels them to own sustainability, making it indivisible from their jobs.

a. Direct measures of progress on the path to sustainability

John Brock, then CEO of Coca-Cola European Partners, told me in 2015: "If you go back 10 years the question is, 'What the hell's a carbon footprint?' I mean, 10 years ago, it was not even on the radar, except in limited circles." Today, calculating carbon footprints is not only popular for companies, but starting to gain traction among individuals, too.

I make my students calculate their carbon footprints using one of the many online calculators available. The World Wildlife Fund (WWF), for example, provides an individual footprint calculator (www.footprint.wwf.org.uk). In a five-minute questionnaire, users are asked about their diet and food waste, household energy consumption, personal and public transport use, and shopping habits. Using these inputs and an underlying model that quantitatively relates lifestyle to footprint, the calculator spits out the quantity of resources users are consuming. Try it yourself – my students are often astounded that many of us consume resources that would collectively take something more than three planets to support. Sadly, we so far have only one planet to live on and pass on to future generations.

To keep global warming within the 1.5- to 2-degree Celsius band by 2050, the WWF says each person should by then be producing no more than 1.05 tons in annual carbon emissions. As many of my students are constantly surprised to discover, people living in developed countries currently have footprints way larger than that. "But this should not discourage you," the WWF notes. "Do all to reduce your own footprint, and with your help we'll continue to fight for action from businesses and government." The WWF's website shows that measuring helps engage people in planet-saving conversations. The footprint calculator allows people to participate in the process and it helps demystify climate change. Measuring the impact of your own actions is a critical step toward sustainability.

Measuring carbon emissions is by no means the only way of monitoring environmental impact – land-use figures, for example, have long been used to show the amount of land needed to grow the things we eat, or to swallow up the things we throw away. But as Sarah West and colleagues argued in a 2015 study, carbon footprints are particularly useful in an age of globalized supply chains as they can be used to link local consumption to global greenhouse gas emissions. Such tools allow people and companies to assess their footprints and compare them with those of peers in their community – and to take remedial action, if necessary. Recently, this practice has been taken a step further by assigning a dollar price to each ton of carbon produced, allowing citizens, executives, and policymakers to more easily undertake cost-benefit analyses of anti-emissions initiatives. I will talk more about carbon pricing in a later section of this chapter.

You might recall I said in Chapter 4 that footprinting is but one way to measure your company's (un)sustainability and its movement along the path of more people- and planet-friendly operations. Life-cycle assessments, eco-efficiency analyses, social impact studies, and environmental cost measurement are another ways. They can directly determine the sustainability of business outcomes, and the shifts taking place therein.

A good example of the benefits of measuring environmental impact comes from Greif, a US-based industrial packaging and services company with operations in over 50 countries. Between 2007 and 2008, an increasing number of Greif's key European customers, such as chemical giant AkzoNobel, were asking for more environmentally responsible products. As a result, Greif conducted a life-cycle assessment (LCA) to determine the full scope of environmental risks arising from its product catalog, which included steel and plastic drums and containers, and so-called big bags.

Greif made a bold decision to expand its business model. That's because the LCA results contained valuable information that allowed the company to better understand the environmental impact of its products – and the options it had to reduce those impacts. Customers had worked on the assumption that Greif's various bulk containers were best filled to the brim to improve emissions in transit and environmental profiles. Greif itself had assumed that "thin-gauging" – making these bulk containers lighter by using fewer materials – would be the best option to reduce each product's environmental impact.

The LCA data showed that transportation emissions were a factor in the environmental profile of bulk containers, but that the bigger impact did indeed come from the raw materials used to make the containers. Engineering the containers to extend their useful life, and reducing raw material inputs would prove to be a substantially more effective option for improving the environmental performance of Greif's bulk containers.

As a result, the company determined that its core business would in future include the recycling and reconditioning of these containers. The life-cycle assessments helped Greif identify environmental risks in its value chain – and employees took ownership of addressing them. This, in turn, enabled the company to develop stronger relationships with its customers. Many of Greif's customers now contract with the company across all packaging types, and Greif is now able to offer a bigger selection of industrial packaging to help customers reduce their environmental footprint and meet other sustainability goals.

Greif is an excellent case study that shows how sustainability measurement helps inform strategy, leads to the development of new and more sustainable products, and fosters stronger stakeholder relationships. There are other examples of companies benefiting from such analyses, but now might be the time for you to think about how similar steps might help you and your company start the journey.

b. Indirect measures also plot how a company should move forward

To get a clear picture of the indirect impacts of corporate sustainability, companies need to measure various stakeholder reactions to sustainability initiatives. Critical KPIs like employee retention and customer loyalty rates, the reputation of a company's brands, levels of in-house volunteering, corporate rankings, and even financial performance are all in some way affected by the sustainability policies defined and pursued by management.

Measuring the indirect effects of sustainability initiatives does have its challenges, however. Direct effects like emissions footprints are relatively easy to quantify, comparing carbon dioxide emissions in year one with those in year two will give you a clear measure. They are also usually easy to interpret – if emissions are rising, the company is backsliding. Tracking employee engagement does not allow the same certain causal connections. Yes, your company's sustainability initiatives might be raising employee engagement. But what about the possible effects of pay levels or recent pay rises? What about charismatic line managers? Or a generally vibrant culture in the company or in a certain department?

Energy use creates carbon dioxide. But many things contribute to employee engagement, making it an unreliable measure of the effects of sustainability programs if used unfiltered. To get an accurate representation of the impact of sustainability on employee engagement, for example, we need to control for all other factors and isolate the impact of sustainability. Students in my executive education seminars often jokingly complain that I take them back to math class at school. I explain that we need to use regression-type methodologies to isolate the impact of sustainability on any of the stakeholder-reaction KPIs they might want to use. Mathematics allows for such analysis to be done – and in fact demands it be done to avoid drawing erroneous conclusions.

Recently, Daniel Korschun from Drexel University in Philadelphia, Scott Swain from Clemson University in South Carolina, and I looked at sentiment among hundreds of employees at a large financial services company. Using regression-type statistical methods, we developed a model that allowed us to determine how far sustainability initiatives boosted the motivation of front-line workers and the customers they dealt with.

We found that factors other than sustainability – though most often pay – have a major role in motivating employees and determining employees' customer orientation and overall job performance. But we were also able to demonstrate tangible effects on employee motivation by engagement in sustainability. Initiatives like charitable giving, environmental programs, and ethical practices schemes demonstrably boosted motivation. We found that sustainability is an effective inducement for frontline employees, all the more when managers and customers are supportive of such initiatives.

Interestingly, we were able to unpack the effect of higher employee engagement on customer orientation. Our analysis showed that employees used themes relating to sustainability as "icebreakers" in conversation with customers. If employees discovered a customer shared their interest in the topic, they bonded more with their interlocutors, became more motivated to serve them, and more confident that they knew what their customers needed. Sharing their enthusiasm for sustainability created the conditions for an emotional identification to develop between them, and a kind of intimacy that provided the space for a constructive bonding experience. With a few statistical calculations, we were able to trace the positive impact of sustainability on frontline job performance. "Programs for social good create more satisfaction at every level," the *Guardian* newspaper headlined our findings. Integrate sustainability initiatives that reflect an employee's moral position into their work, and you have a win–win situation.

The indirect measures of sustainability performance can often be as revealing as the direct ones. You just need to consider other possible influences on the phenomena you're trying to measure and then find statistical means to hone in only on the effect you're interested in. One of my favorite stories is about research I did with my colleagues Sankar Sen and Shuili Du about the yogurt industry. We were trying to isolate the impact that sustainability initiatives had on consumer purchases for the three major US brands, Danone, Yoplait, and Stonyfield Farm, the US organic-yogurt producer.

The statistical analysis showed that, as expected, product attributes such as quality, taste, and nutrition played the biggest role in driving customer loyalty. But the analysis also showed that customers valued sustainability initiatives sufficiently to influence buying behavior – being seen to be sustainable could drive sales. Sustainability was by no means the only driver of customer loyalty. But it did have a significant impact on customer behavior after controlling for the impact of product attributes and price. I still remember the smile on the face of Chris Shea, then executive vice president at General Mills, when I presented these results to her and her marketing and strategy colleagues in Minneapolis in 2006.

c. Relating sustainability KPIs to financial performance

Relating the impact of sustainability to financial performance makes sustainability skeptics and non-believers sit up and take notice; that helps shift the discussion from whether to what and how. The software giant SAP is a classic case study for this development. A senior human resources executive in charge of sustainability initiatives at the software maker recalled he was having trouble making his voice heard at regular senior management meetings. His boss constantly asked him to cede his slot – which was already low on the agenda – to other participants who were more oriented toward the bottom line.

Frustrated, this executive told his boss that he was ignoring critically important HR issues. As the executive recounted, "The only question he then asked me was, 'Can you show that to me? If it really has an impact, you should show me a figure. If it really has an impact, we will keep your points on the agenda.'" The executive went to work with his team and, using in-house data and statistical models, developed a range of indicators that measured the influence of non-financial KPIs on SAP's profit. The executive could now confidently tell his colleagues at the senior management meeting that a 1 percent rise in employee engagement added 35–45 million Euros to the company's annual operating results, while a 1 percent reduction in carbon emissions added Euros 4 million.

Later, the executive and his team expanded the scope of their work and developed a "Business Health Culture Index" (BHCI), a measure of the facets of corporate culture that enabled employees to stay healthy and balanced. For every 1 percent increase in BHCI, they discovered, SAP increased operating profit by 85–95 million Euros. According to SAP, the internal models used for this quantification took due care to account for indirect effects and interdependencies. For example, sustainability is only one of the factors that impact employee engagement; issues such as salary and work environment matter a great deal as well. In other words, as with the frontline employees and yogurt examples above, the various measures had to be filtered or weighted, or both. In SAP's case, BHCI increases and carbon dioxide reduction were both credited with having positive effects on employee engagement. Math again helped shine a light on the value of sustainability.

The SAP manager's bosses probed his methodology and, finding no holes, were quickly won over. They decided to cascade the insights to all management levels. Operating managers were now obliged to ask their finance staff not only about production forecasts, product pipeline, and product costs, but also about trends in employee engagement, energy consumption, and CO_2 emissions. These KPIs are now on every SAP employee's radar. "That is what I call shifting the discussion," the HR executive told me. Today, SAP uses this and other models internally to encourage decisions about resource allocation that are more sustainable and aligned toward the triple bottom line. The company also developed a business model to sell this service to other companies to help them explore similar linkages.

d. Using proxies to save the planet

But it is not always easy to measure the impact of sustainability on outcomes such as sales and profitability. As a result, companies should use proxies to get an idea of trends. In Chapter 6 I described the retailer Marks & Spencer that polls shop-floor employee engagement. The company uses these measures to gauge line managers' commitment to the corporate sustainability program. In other words, where direct measurement is difficult, the solution can be measures that are easier to generate combined with managerial judgment.

A financial services group I visited measured the effects of sustainability on its corporate culture by asking whether employees were proud to work for the company. At the same time, an executive told me, the company measured its progress in the "community space" by its advance toward a straightforward spending target, of then 1 percent of pretax profit. Proxy measures are good because they can be collected with little effort. But each one needs to be analyzed carefully by management to ascertain whether the measure of choice is "vaguely right" and worth a try, or "precisely wrong" and to be avoided. Nowhere is the dictum "garbage in, garbage out" more true than in the realm of measurement.

7.3 Environmental rankings can spur management

Luckily, a company doesn't have to rely solely on homemade KPIs. In parallel to company-specific measurements, a number of organizations over the years have developed voluntary reporting standards and initiatives to help companies adopt them. The Global Reporting Initiative (GRI), for example, issued its first sustainability reporting guidelines for companies as far back as 1999. Soon after, it became a permanent institution within the United Nations Environment Program (UNEP) and the United Nations Global Compact. The GRI's aim to standardize reporting was to enhance the comparability and the credibility of reports published by individual companies.

Its guidelines set out to quantify and standardize the environmental, social, and political costs (and benefits) of any company's activities. Over the years, it honed thirty so-called performance indicators that allow companies — and third parties — to assess the impact from corporate activity and the supply chain. Indicators range from recording materials used by weight to tallying environmental expenditures by type of investment. Over the years, the GRI also worked with the International Labour Organization (ILO) to develop a host of social reporting standards.

Over time, the GRI guidelines have become increasingly more complicated and have come to cover an ever broader range of issues. A common complaint is that the framework focuses on reporting and not on producing "actionable" numbers, that is, data that could spur management to act and allow executives to measure progress in a clear way. Also, because of the level of detail in GRI reports, readers often find it difficult to trace causality — which set of data are driven by which strategic decision or operational action.

This has helped spur other organizations to develop sustainability measuring systems of their own. Perhaps the two most well-known alongside the GRI are the Sustainability Accounting Standards Board (SASB) and the Dow Jones Sustainability Indices (DJSI). In response to increasing pressure from financial markets, SASB was launched in 2011 to allow businesses and investors to talk about the financial impacts of sustainability in a more focused way. The DJSI is also the result of investor demand. It began tracking corporate sustainability performance as far back as 1999 and is now a family of indexes that benchmarks the largest 2,500 stock listed companies worldwide.

The businessman and former mayor of New York City, Michael Bloomberg, is one of the driving forces behind SASB. His data and news company Bloomberg LP was the first company to disclose sustainability data using provisional SASB standards. SASB subdivides corporate performance into five categories — environment, human capital, social capital, business model and innovation, leadership and governance — and calculates a number of specific KPIs for each category. SASB standards were developed using extensive feedback from companies, investors, and other market participants as part of a transparent, publicly documented process. These standards differ by industry but are the same within sectors, enabling investors and companies to compare the performance of competing peers. While GRI was designed both for sustainability practitioners and a broader community of stakeholders from customers to investors, SASB's mission is narrower in that it aims specifically to inform people seeking to make investment decisions.

DJSI publishes industry-specific rankings of companies based on their sustainability performance and is currently more visible as a result. Owned by S&P Dow Jones Corporate Indices and Robeco Sustainable Asset Management, the DJSI tracks each company's answers to regular sustainability questionnaires, as well as company data, stakeholder and media analyses, and interviews with corporate executives. DJSI's best-in-class approach means that its measures are much more readable than reports compiled under GRI guidelines. Little wonder that the DJSI has become an important part of many big companies' thinking.

In an advertising feature in the *Guardian* in 2014, André Veneman, sustainability director at Dutch chemical company AkzoNobel, described how his company's performance was measured every year against that of 86 competitors. While AkzoNobel often came out on top, he stressed that DJSI's usefulness wasn't restricted to marketing aimed at outsiders – it was a tool to spur continual improvement within the company.

"Being ranked first means you are doing a lot of things right," he said. "But, more importantly, the assessment also highlights areas for improvement. And you need to take action … [otherwise] you'll drop down the list or fall off it altogether." He noted how the company's 2013 ratings had highlighted operational eco-efficiency, and the winning and retaining of new recruits as areas in which AkzoNobel could do better. This spurred management into action. At the time, the company had linked its DJSI-performance – "a barometer […] of our success" – to the pay package of its top 600 executives.

7.4 Putting environmental and social impacts in monetary terms

Making sustainability measures more readable and comparable has in recent years led companies to try to measure their sustainability impact in monetary terms. Even ratings agencies like DJSI have begun to place more emphasis on "monetizing" corporate impact on the environment and society. In 2016, it asked DJSI companies to include an "impact valuation" in its measurement. While many companies were developing products and services "to address social needs," RobecoSAM executives said, fewer companies were "actually measuring the benefits derived from the programs." But companies are starting to respond to this call, as Ambuja Cement demonstrated at the beginning of this chapter.

Stating environmental and social impact in monetary terms perhaps started with attempts to price carbon, which goes back over 20 years. In 1997, more than 2,500 economists signed "The Economists' Statement on Climate Change," which called for pricing – and taxation – of carbon dioxide to reduce emissions and raise money to deal with their consequences. In Europe, this led to the founding of the Emissions Trading Scheme (ETS), under which companies are given emissions quotas and have to buy extra permits if they exceed their limits. Priced at 20 Euros per ton at inception in 2005, permit prices tumbled to around 5 Euros for many years, with experts blaming an over-allocation of permits. But in 2018, the European Union finally agreed to measures to lower allowances and support ETS prices, causing the market to soar by over 200 percent. An EU certificate allowing a company to emit one metric ton of carbon dioxide currently costs a little over 23 Euros.

Sadly, President Barack Obama shied away from introducing a similar "cap-and-trade" system in the US. But his administration did provide an important contribution to cost-benefit analyses by estimating the social costs of dealing with every ton of carbon dioxide released into the atmosphere. In 2009, it began to consider what monetary burden to assign to greenhouse gases. Such a comprehensive measure was meant to reflect, among other things, the cost of property damage from storms and floods, declining productivity, and rising mortality rates. The Environmental Protection Agency eventually published an estimate that said releasing a ton of carbon dioxide into the atmosphere in 2015 would lead to about $36 in social costs over the coming decades. However, it also conceded that the time span and variability of underlying assumptions of its forecasting models meant this cost could turn out to be as low as $11 or as high as $105 per ton.

This broad estimate for the current social cost of carbon has emboldened climate-change skeptics to reject the exercise. But the project's honesty in dealing with the perils of forecasting should not undermine its central point: emitting carbon comes with real costs that society will have to cover; and the cost of dealing with the emission's effects will rise significantly as the planet gets warmer. While it could cost "only" $36 to deal with the effects of one ton of carbon dioxide released in 2015, the clean-up expense is expected to have almost doubled by 2050 to $69 for every ton of carbon dioxide released.

The Obama administration policymakers Michael Greenstone, now an economist at the University of Chicago, and Cass Sunstein, a professor at Harvard Law School, said in a 2016 op-ed for the *New York Times* that these numbers were "necessary guideposts" to help the world balance today's cost of investing in sustainability against tomorrow's costs of looming climate change – they even acknowledged plenty of experts thought their forecast too low. "Wishing we did not have this trade-off will not make it go away," they concluded. A number of companies already embed a carbon price within their strategies, allowing them to better allocate resources to sustainability initiatives or research and development, and to reveal hidden costs in production and supply chains.

Natura, for example, is a Brazilian company and brand leader in cosmetics, fragrances, and personal care. Like IBM in Chapter 6, Natura wanted to find a way to drive environmental performance through its supply chain. It wanted to engage its suppliers in a program aimed at improving their social and environmental contribution. The program, called "Strategic Sourcing Triple Bottom Line," encouraged Natura to work with its suppliers to put a price on externalities like carbon dioxide emissions, water use, and waste generation. This "shadow price" for each environmental impact helped Natura to select suppliers based on both pricing and environmental impact. This approach improved the economic, social, and environmental performance of its supply chain, while also saving the company money. The company estimates that the net benefit of this program would total R$1.9 million (more than US $960,000) over a four-year period.

Advances in environmental impact measurement have also spurred executives and academics to look at the much trickier task of measuring and then monetizing social impact. This is much harder to quantify because different people see social impacts differently – they're subjective and more qualitative. Also, social impacts can be the vicarious result of a company's direct environmental and economic actions. Thirdly, the effects of corporate conduct unfold over the short and long term, making continued measurement advisable.

As a result, there is a wide array of methods for a company to choose from. Social impact measurement tools abound, but you shouldn't let their number confuse you. What tool fits best depends on what type of company you work for, what its sustainability goals are, and what it wants to measure. An important player is the World Business Council for Sustainable Development (WBCSD), which in 2016 teamed up with accountancy firm KPMG to provide some guidelines for what they called "social capital in decision-making."

By trying to measure social capital, the WBCSD has tried to hone a whole set of more diffuse goals that can be used by any company – whether an HR executive wanting to grow their talent pool, or supply chain managers trying to make suppliers more socially responsible. Ideally, social capital should be a measure of how a company profits from its employees' skills, from social values and institutions, and from relationships with stakeholders and peers. "Together, these resources need to be maintained and enhanced to make society more cohesive and resilient, and to make business more successful," the WBCSD said.

Driven by the insight that quantification and even cold-seeming monetization are the best way to incentivize managers to assume sustainability ownership, the WBCSD suggests companies come up with consistent scoring or rating systems. Whether at corporate or portfolio level, for example, or focused on a product's life cycle, they should enable social impacts to be represented in numerical form. Systems that consistently attribute monetary value to the performance of social capital can lead to new quantitative insights about phenomena like Social Return on Investment (SROI), or social profit-and-loss accounts.

The most tangible outcome of the WBCSD's thinking is the impact pathway – we saw one in the Ambuja example. Also known as the results chain, executives can use it to translate corporate actions into numbers about social – and economic – impact. The impact pathway is a flow diagram that schematically represents: a company's inputs, such as resources and their cost; ensuing activity, such as manufacturing and, say, compliance with standards; and its output of products or services, expressed in units sold and customers reached. Crucially, the pathway also looks at how these three steps affect outcomes – for example, by measuring how many people in the target population now have access to new opportunities – and impacts – expressed by quantified, longer-term social changes in health or education.

The schematic diagram of a social impact pathway in Figure 7.1 is from the WBCSD website and shows the impact of investing resources on suppliers and

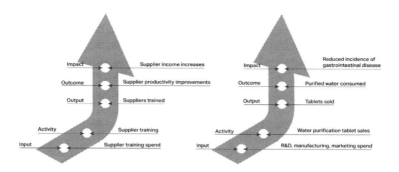

Figure 7.1 Example impact pathways from WBCSD's "Measuring socio-economic impact: a guide for business"

R&D. Stakeholders all around the world find it more meaningful to look at the ultimate impact of their actions and investments rather than at simple inputs or outputs. I encourage you to trace the impact of your social and environmental initiatives, monetize them as far as possible, and then disseminate your findings to relevant internal and external stakeholders.

7.5 Companies should communicate what they measure

Ambuja Cement is a reminder of something I've said repeatedly: companies need to communicate what they know. Once Ambuja had come up with readable and meaningful KPIs, it not only used them to measure operations and to define strategy. It saw their company-wide communication could incite sustainability ownership and spur healthy internal competition. And the company realized it could usefully engage external shareholders when it came to dealing with negative externalities like emissions, and to reminding locals of the positive ones like wealth and water in the community.

It bears repeating that communicating evidence-based progress internally serves as a vivid reminder of the company's purpose in practice. It enables employees to see themselves as part of the solution, or at least as part of the journey, solidifying sustainability ownership. Thanks to a variety of media – from whiteboards to hallway signs to computer pop-ups – employees in the best companies can acquire a remarkable awareness and understanding of their company's sustainability progress and of its future goals.

When it comes to communicating with external stakeholders, some companies can boast of a history of disclosing environmental and social data stretching back into the 1980s. At first, companies mostly included these new types of data in the reports they published already, mainly financial ones. But, over time, data became more detailed and technical, triggering a trend to publish social and environmental information in separate reports – although that did raise questions of whether they were of any use to non-specialists.

These reservations and investors' increasing interest in sustainability KPIs have in recent years seen a welcome return to publishing financial and sustainability figures in joint publications. In what is today called "integrated reporting," an ever larger group of companies is tacitly assigning its social and environmental KPIs the same status as its financial ones. The International Integrated Reporting Committee (IIRC) is perhaps the most prominent of a handful of associations now promoting common standards.

Integrated reporting brings together information for investors from strategy, governance, finance, and sustainability departments. The best reports give a clear and concise view of how a company both makes a profit and creates social and environmental value. They show how these strands are linked, and how they affect the company's ability to create value over the long term. SAP, as we saw, publishes the monetary value of carbon emission reductions, and increases in employee engagement in its integrated report.

But, sadly, there is still no global standard for the information that integrated reports should contain. In part, this is because it is not easy to agree on what issues and areas are material to investors – or immaterial to investors, but still crucial for other external stakeholders. Also, as we have seen, the lack of standards leaves much room for creativity within a company but throws up the problem of non-comparability.

Nonetheless, these problems should be seen as teething troubles that the corporate world is addressing. Even you can still add your voice to the conversation. Measuring and communicating KPIs – and progress toward them – remains one of the best ways of focusing people's attention, inside and outside your company. People want to succeed in measurable ways – they respond to measuring. This virtuous cycle of action and feedback becomes the basis of motivation, pride, and a stronger sense of sustainability ownership.

Chapter 7 in summary

- Measuring key performance indicators tells a company what it's doing right and wrong; measuring makes things concrete, comparable, and motivates employees.
- Where poor communication can hinder the efforts of sustainability initiatives, measuring is a clear way of explaining corporate decisions and implementation.
- Measuring demystifies stakeholders' contributions and lets them own sustainability as part of their jobs; measuring engages them in planet-saving dialogue and decisions.
- Demystifying sustainability means converting it into terms that resonate; for example – CO_2 emissions are a tangible link between a company's activities and global warming.
- Measuring can represent social impacts in numerical form; associating with organizations like GRI and DJSI helps skeptics see the importance of sustainability.
- Assigning a monetary value to social capital can lead to new quantitative insights about phenomena like Social Return on Investment or social profit-and-loss accounts.

- People are more likely to claim ownership of things to which they feel connected – measuring fosters this connection, so be sure to publish what you measure.

Bibliography

United Nations (2012). *Sustainability Ambitions 2020*. LafargeHolcim. Available at: https://www.lafargeholcim.com/sustainability-ambitions-2020.

S & P Dow Jones Indices and RobecoSAM (2017). *Results Announced for 2017 Dow Jones Sustainability Indices Review*. S & P Dow Jones Indices, RobecoSAM.

S & P Dow Jones Indices and RobecoSAM (2018). *Our Warming World: How Much Difference Will Half-a-Degree Really Make?* WWF. Available at: https://www.wwf.org.uk/updates/our-warming-world-how-much-difference-will-half-degree-really-make.

S.E. West, A. Owen, K. Axelsson and C.D. West (2015). Evaluating the use of a carbon footprint calculator: communicating impacts of consumption at household level and exploring mitigation options, *Journal of Industrial Ecology*, 20(3), 396–409.

A. Perera, S. Putt Del Pino and B. Oliveira (2013). *Aligning Profit and Environmental Sustainability: Stories From Industry*. Washington, DC: World Resources Institute.

D. Korschun, CB Bhattacharya, and S.D. Swain (May, 2014). Corporate social responsibility, customer orientation, and the job performance of Frontline employees, *Journal of Marketing*, 78(3), 20–37.

S. Du, CB Bhattacharya, and S. Sen (2010). Maximizing business returns to corporate social responsibility (CSR): the role of CSR communication, *International Journal of Management Reviews*, 8–19.

A. Schmitz (2015). *The Value of Health*. SAP.

SAP (2018). *SAP Integrated Report*. SAP. Available at: https://www.sap.com/integrated-reports/2018/en.html.

R. Blinch (2014). 'Not all about the bloody return': how social programs affect employees, *The Guardian*.

The Global Reporting Initiative (2013). *G4 Sustainability Reporting Guidelines*. The Global Reporting Initiative. Available at: https://www2.globalreporting.org/standards/g4/Pages/default.aspx.

United Nations Global Compact. *Global Goals in Action*. United Nations Global Compact. Available at: https://www.unglobalcompact.org/sdgs/global-goals-in-action.

Sustainability Accounting Standards Board (2016). *Case Study: Unlocking Value of the SASB Standards*. Sustainability Accounting Standards Board. Available at: https://using.sasb.org/wp-content/uploads/2016/01/Bloomberg-SASB-Case-Study.pdf.

RobecoSAM (2016). *DJSI 2016 Review Results*. S & P Dow Jones Indices.

A. Veneman (2014). Dow Jones sustainability index: why winning isn't everything, *The Guardian*.

Redefining Progress (1997). Economists' Statement on Climate Change.

United States Environmental Protection Agency (2015). *The Social Cost of Carbon: Estimating the Benefits of Reducing Greenhouse Gas Emissions*. EPA.

M. Greenstone and C. Sunstein (2016). Donald Trump should know: this is what climate change costs Us, *The New York Times*.

WBCSD and KPMG (2015). *Social Capital in Decision-Making: How Social Information Drives Value Creation*. WBCSD and KPMG. Available at: https://www.wbcsd.org/dsfup.

V. Kasturi Rangan, S. Srinivasan, and N. Arora (2017). Measuring true value at Ambuja Cement, *Harvard Business School Case 518–063, November 2017. (Revised June 2019)*.

8 Enliven

8.1 Collective reaffirmation and celebration of new thinking and new goals

I was in Rome, Italy, on a sunny June day in 2016. Traffic-choked, smoggy, and loud, the city may seem a strange destination on the sustainability trail. Ancient Rome didn't have enough drinking water to quench the thirst of its huge population, the region's aqueducts are testament to that, and the wood that it needed for ships, furniture, cooking, and heating led to the disastrous deforestation of northern Africa, once called "the granary of the world." But in other ways this venerable city had blazed a trail that should inspire every sustainability leader. There is probably no other city in the world in which old buildings have proved so sustainable, possibly outnumbering modern constructions. Not only has their ancient, solid masonry allowed old or ancient buildings to be reused time and again. It has also kept inhabitants warm in winter and cool in summer with minimal energy use.

I was visiting the headquarters of the electric utility behemoth Enel at the invitation of Ernesto Ciorra, the chief "innovability" officer, in charge of both innovation and sustainability. He had chosen the day with care, as there was an event scheduled that afternoon for which managers had come to Rome from all over the world. My day was full of interesting meetings, including one with Mr. Starace, who you met in Chapter 3. But I had no idea about the treat that was in store for me that afternoon. An auditorium packed with 500 people, a large video screen flashing a series of headshots of about a dozen employees on stage, and an announcer relating these individuals all had one unusual thing in common: they had all made significant mistakes at work. No, they weren't about to get sacked. They were being celebrated, and by no one less than the company's CEO.

The ceremony, the only one of its kind I have seen, is an annual awards presentation called "My Best Failures." It demonstrated to employees that making mistakes in the course of trying something new wasn't only acceptable, it could bring vital insights that could make the company better. The contest was just one of the measures Enel had introduced to keep employee-engagement high and support its sustainability efforts. The company had realized making mistakes and learning from them was vital if it was to move toward a sustainable business model. It was now seeking to convince its employees of this approach.

To counteract the stigma of and break down the resistance to failure in the workplace, Enel in 2015 had launched "My Best Failure." It was an online platform that invited colleagues from all over the world to share instructive failures and came to include efforts to launch a more sustainable product, a new work technique, and even everyday calculation errors. Since going live, the platform has catalogued Enel's setbacks, expanding the overall corporate experience by demonstrating time and time again that failure can be constructive. The initiative serves as a first step toward building a culture of failure, in which people are not afraid to speak about their errors and are even open to discussing them publicly in the hope of avoiding similar errors in the future. Such creative freedom and the ability to help come up with innovative and sustainable solutions for the company are crucial. This process of so-called co-creation fosters a real, lively sense of sustainability ownership among employees and other stakeholders.

The mistakes on the "My Best Failure" platform were well meant – they were made in an attempt to do something new, something that had not been tried before. They represent a necessary risk for a company that truly believes in innovation for a sustainable future – and an opportunity for the company to multiply its chances of success. On the one hand, shining a spotlight on what did not go as planned allows stakeholders to take note of negative results. But looking at failure in an altogether different light also allows for an in-depth analysis of what to do better next time. Failure can be extremely instructive.

Enel and a handful of the other best-in-class companies I studied understand what so many companies don't – that culture plays a critical role in underpinning sustainability initiatives and instilling ownership. Many companies succeed in building initial momentum around such initiatives only to see them slowed to a dead stop by entropy and inertia at the grassroots level. As soon as sustainable business starts seeming humdrum, unworthy of the attention of top bosses, the skeptics inside the company again become emboldened. Perceiving sustainability as a passing fad, they decline to take action to work toward it. Others around them follow their example and revert to seeing sustainability as someone else's job. Soon, only pockets of the workforce are engaged, and sustainability ownership fails to take root. Only an enlivened sustainability culture can protect against entropy and inertia. An analysis of 179 company case studies spanning 15 years found that the most important driver for embedding sustainability in day-to-day business activity was culture, all of those more-or-less informal practices that bring colleagues together.

A fresh coat of paint or interesting art enlivens your home and deepens your sense of ownership. In the same way, activities and rituals that keep the topic of sustainability fresh in the organization are key to maintaining salience and enthusiasm. According to scholars Beggan and Brown, a feeling of ownership comes about through association with an object. The more a person associates with an object or ideal, the more they feel they know it; the more they know it, the greater their sense of ownership. In this chapter, I will discuss what steps you and your company can take to stir ownership in and to keep it alive among employees. What I call enlivening is all about increasing association with corporate purpose and sustainability. If you succeed, your colleagues or employees will quickly find that making business decisions through the lens of sustainability becomes routine.

Collective reaffirmation and celebration of new thinking and new goals is one way to build such association – just ask Enel. This chapter examines three guiding ideas under the rubric of what I call "The Three Cs": celebrate, communicate, co-create. Celebrating projects and initiatives that have succeeded – as well as some efforts that have failed – is key to inspiring by example, giving legitimacy to sustainability, and keeping it salient. Leaders must communicate sustainability on an ongoing basis, and in an authentic, sincere way. Consumer goods maker Unilever stays in touch with its stakeholder groups using dashboards, internal information cascades, and webcasts. Sustainability leaders can also appoint sustainability deputies – what the company calls "sustainability ambassadors" – throughout the corporate hierarchy. Their goal is to enliven the company's culture around sustainability initiatives by keeping them fresh and up-to-date.

Finally, companies should invite employees and managers to co-create initiatives together. When employees see that the potential benefits of sustainability outweigh the potential costs, they start believing that they have a real role to play. They integrate sustainability into their everyday jobs more enthusiastically and take ownership – and soon, new ideas begin to flow. Some companies put programs in place to solicit and reward ideas from the rank-and-file. Shop-floor workers at heavy machinery manufacturer JCB, for example, formed teams to propose sustainability solutions. The winning team was allowed to take its idea on the road and present to colleagues at other factories – and then also to me during my visit in 2017. Chemical company BASF's scheme "Connected to Care" enables employees to form a team, develop a volunteer project in the areas of food, smart energy, or urban living, and submit it for approval and funding. In 2015, some 35,000 employees submitted 500 ideas, with 150 projects eventually being implemented. In this chapter, I'll describe a number of smart, innovative programs like this that you can use to help employees and managers identify closely – and sustainably – with your company's sustainable business models.

8.2 The "Three Cs" that create shared understanding

A company's ultimate goal is to get every stakeholder to think along similar lines, as if by second nature. Acting and working sustainably should be routine, a habit, not a chore. It is widely accepted that "theory" has to be driven by practice. In an article in Greenbiz.com, Stephanie Bertels, a management professor at Simon Fraser University is quoted as saying "Embedding sustainability [... is] an area where practice leads theory."

Bertels looked at 179 studies of companies going back over 15 years and named three important drivers for embedding sustainability in day-to-day business activity. According to her research, informal practices like collaboration, education, and knowledge management – practices through which colleagues came together – were key. Indeed, Henry Mintzberg of McGill University said in a 2009 article: "Companies must remake themselves into places of engagement, where people are committed to one another and their enterprise." Note how "enterprise" suddenly means more than "company."

In the article "Rebuilding Companies as Communities," Mintzberg took the example of animated-film studio Pixar. Its then boss, Ed Catmull, lauded its "vibrant community where talented people are loyal to each other and their collective work" as the cornerstone of Pixar's extraordinary box office success. "Everyone feels like they are part of something extraordinary," he is quoted as saying, an expression of a collective state of mind that not only produces great results, but also attracts new talent. It is a great example of how building community can satisfy the need for esteem and lay the ground for satisfying needs involving meaning and purpose. Remember that Maslow's third-level social need involves belonging.

Community is also a vital instrument to turn chore into habit – through the example of others, through identification with them, through engagement with the collective. As one executive I interviewed said: "You've got to develop that. This isn't something you have to do, but rather something that you get to do." As I touched upon in a previous chapter, you should think about it in terms of running or going to the gym. Both activities can be onerous chores. But giving rewards, highlighting benefits, tracking progress, and demanding accountability can be transformative and turn them into willed-for habits.

The website Lifedev.net prides itself on "making creative people create." It offers an illuminating "11 steps to becoming addicted to running," or better, a way to turn the chore of running into a good habit: make running an important part of your day to help avoid excuses not to run; run with other people to keep you accountable; reward yourself for milestones passed; keep the benefits in mind, like how much weight you've lost; track and measure your progress and watch those key performance indicators (KPIs) to motivate yourself; recognize these steps as making running something that you get to do, not something you have to do.

If we transfer the analogy to the corporate world, it means turning sustainable words and deeds from the particular obligation of a sustainability officer into a natural, normal part of everybody's day job. As an executive told me: "Sustainability has got to be mainstreamed in the organization. It has got to be all countries, all brands, and all divisions." There could be no exceptions, he warned. Everybody had to see everybody else doing it as if it were a matter of course. "If you think of it as a day job, then you have a chance of doing it."

In this vein, one big drinks manufacturer I visited was trying to instill the habit of recycling into each employee's day job. To do this, the company had removed the waste-paper baskets from every office. An executive told me that the move had initially caused consternation. "Everyone moaned about what are we going to do with our rubbish." But the company stuck to its guns and every employee got a "recycler," whose contents they had to sort into separate waste streams – like food and plastic – at the end of the day. "Now, for everyone, recycling is just second nature," the executive said.

The company was able to use the initiative to instill the importance of recycling bottles at work – and then also at home. Reusing bottles and their materials is a crucial way to reduce the carbon footprint of each bottle. The company saw the need for employees to recycle bottles at work if there was any chance of persuading them – and consumers, too – to do the same at home. "I think the message we've given out ... about recycling is pretty strong," the executive said. By constantly reminding employees of the purpose and benefits of recycling, the company had been able to make it "second nature" at work – and hopefully at home as well. "You can't work for us without understanding that bottles aren't waste, they're a valuable resource that we need to get back."

Curiously, I came across a very similar initiative pioneered by the Chinese subsidiary of the engineering stalwart Bosch when I visited their premises in Suzhow, China, in March 2019. The company had started a "Zero Waste" campaign with no individual trash bins but a centralized sorting facility. The company emissary I spoke with highlighted the powerful secondary benefit of this initiative, "That way they will go home and influence their family members to make less waste," reaffirming my belief that companies are a great conduit to shift civil society toward sustainability – a theme I shall revisit in the Conclusion.

Instilling consciousness – and even a degree of self-consciousness – in colleagues and employees is a vital step toward making sustainable actions second nature. The UK retailer Marks & Spencer in past years has become a poster child for its sustainability efforts, known, as I've said, as Plan A. Beyond setting many different concrete targets in all parts of its business, the company was also happy to let employees know that they were leading the way. "All the employees are aware of Plan A, which I think they would describe as Marks & Spencer doing the right thing ... the right thing for the environment,'" one manager told me.

The manager described how this thinking had come to permeate the company, so that sustainability wasn't just about meeting targets, but about acting in a (self-)consciously sustainable way.

> When you're helping yourself to more napkins than you need in the cafeteria, someone might tap you on the shoulder and say, "That's not very Plan A." Or when you're printing excessively or doing other things that people perceive as being unsustainable, colleagues will turn to you and say, "That's not very Plan A."

He was adamant the Plan A campaign had changed the retailer's culture. "Plan A has gone from being a program to being more of a verb – 'to be or not to be Plan A.'" This is a great example of a vibrant culture in which all employees share the bond of sustainability ownership.

Marks & Spencer has also started using large solar photovoltaic arrays and introducing new eco-friendly stores. One executive told me these steps had given a huge boost to employee motivation and self-esteem: "You can't underestimate the importance of having the feeling of working for a brand that has integrity." As I mentioned in Chapter 6, having a brand with sustainability woven into its very fabric gives it a moral legitimacy that no amount of green advertising can match. Sustainability ownership is a dynamic resource.

Once a company has created a shared understanding of what it and its employees should do to make their business actions more sustainable, it needs to codify this new way of viewing the company's business. As the above examples show, this is best done through employee engagement and leadership commitment. Strong, honest leadership by example motivates employees and gives them the confidence to assume ownership and change their actions. As one chief executive told me: "When people see other business leaders in their peer group trying things, doing things, and being supportive – that inspires them, too."

Steve Zaffron, a sustainability adviser and author, told *MIT Sloan Management Review* in 2015 about the long-term benefits of supportive corporate cultures and their effects on employee behavior. He was advising a copper mining company, which had long been beset by tense relations between management and workers and their unions. The situation reminded me of my experience with Rio Tinto in Madagascar, where the mining company's management and local workers have butted heads since the company started operations there in early 2006. In Zaffron's account, business was not going well, and all sides came to agree that something had to change for the company and its jobs to survive. It was a crucial sliver of shared understanding on which to build.

Instead of investing in new equipment, Zaffron recalled, the company worked to change its culture over three years. It got all employees – management and workers – to change the way they saw their roles and, crucially, saw each other. An antagonistic culture turned into a collective one. Job satisfaction jumped, employee churn plummeted, and efficiency and profitability – and employee bonuses – rose sharply.

"A culture like this," Zaffron was quoted as saying, "Is inherently self-sustaining because it lives in the employees. They really experience this change, this new way of working together, and they don't want to lose it." Indeed, the rather sad twist to the story reinforces Zaffron's point: after the company was taken over by a competitor, the new owners didn't understand the collectivist approach and abandoned it. But the employees for their part refused to abandon what they had learned about the power, pleasure, and profits of work based on mutual trust – little by little, they all left the company.

a. The first "C": co-creation

The right company culture is vital to empower employees. The right company culture stimulates them to think and act sustainably, without fear of making mistakes and with the confidence that their ideas count too. An executive at a drinks manufacturer told me how the managers who run bottling plants had come to value – and to no small degree depend on – employee-driven, small-scale innovation in order to hit sustainability goals.

> An employee who decides that he can make changes to a valve that will save energy or save water; an employee who decides to do something differently with the way water flows through a line, or our electricity use, or turns down the temperature on a particular piece of kit; an engineer or local line engineer who chooses to tweak something – add all of those up [the executive said]. You get a very big difference.

Once ownership takes effect, it becomes a crucial driver on the path to sustainability.

You can kick-start co-creation through town hall meetings or idea contests. Small companies will find the process of opening the sluice gates of ideas easier to construct than large companies with tens of thousands of employees and complicated supply chains. But the example of BASF, the huge German chemicals manufacturer, shows that even size is not a deal breaker in getting your employees to volunteer ideas and time.

As I mentioned before, "Connected to Care" was a 2015 corporate contest that allowed employees to realize projects together with non-profit organizations. Small teams of employees pitched ideas in the areas of nutrition, energy use, and urban living – and all employees worldwide got to vote for their favorites. The top 150 projects received up to 5,000 Euros, payable to the non-profit organization, and employees each got one paid day's leave to work on their idea with the non-profit they had chosen.

BASF estimates that conceiving and choosing projects engaged around a third of that year's worldwide workforce of 112,000. The most popular initiatives were supporting a children's hospice in Germany, helping young widows and female refugees in Sri Lanka to found companies of their own, ensuring a safe water supply for an orphanage in West Africa, and placing beehives in a communal garden to increase the yield of its plants.

As I've discussed before, giving employees autonomy to develop ideas and confidence to table them is crucial to instilling sustainability ownership. As Robert G. Eccles and his colleagues pointed out in a 2012 article in the *MIT Sloan Management Review*: "Because sustainable-strategy execution requires behavioral change by individuals, the personal engagement of employees is crucial." The article goes on to note that sustainable companies are twice as likely to have a strategy for engaging employees than traditional companies – 72 percent compared to 30 percent, to be precise.

My own 2011 study of corporate sustainability initiatives showed that employees yearn to play a leadership role. They want to co-create value. I heard similar things from dozens of executives. Co-creation is the best way to instill sustainable action in your employees – and the best way to sustain that sustainability perspective. Beyond the voices I've already quoted, I came across a manager lauding sustainability as one of his colleagues' favorite areas of volunteering time and ideas; and an executive exhorting his employees: "I want you to be the entrepreneur in the organization who invents new approaches to sustainability, from a middle I cannot see." A sense of sustainability ownership will go a long way to spark that entrepreneurial spirit and fulfill that executive's wishes.

Marks & Spencer is a great example of engaging employees through co-creation. Take, for example, its hugely successful "Shwopping" initiative, through which Marks & Spencer passed on customers' old clothes to the Oxfam charity. That was an idea hatched by employees and embraced all the way up the hierarchy. Since 2008, the retailer has collected more than 20 million items of clothes, worth some £16 million to the non-profit Oxfam. Marks & Spencer even tied the initiative into some of its marketing initiatives to reward devoted Shwoppers.

However, while successfully managing centralized campaigns like this, Marks & Spencer also set about empowering local stores to come up with schemes of their own. "What is Hereford's concern? What is the town's preoccupation?" one manager asked me. "What is M&S's role in solving them? We can't solve everything. But it's about bringing our people out of the box called Marks & Spencer into the community that they serve." The idea was to go beyond intermittent initiatives like fund-raising to have shop-floor employees immerse themselves in their communities, legitimizing Marks & Spencer's wish to do business there.

As another executive explained it to me: "If we don't engage our store colleagues, they can at best ignore, or even override [what we're asking them to do], and actually do the opposite. That makes their being on this journey with us so important." It is people who make and perpetuate the sustainability culture, people talking to other people. That process might start with sustainability champions talking to colleagues. If done right, it should ultimately morph into shop assistants viewing business through the sustainability lens and advising their customers accordingly. The executive voiced the hope that this cultural change on the "supply side" would ultimately spur a reinforcing "demand side" change.

"That demand side change will only come if we dialogue with our end-customers in a way that helps them understand that they can be motivated, too," he said. This was not the job of senior executives delivering speeches about lofty goals.

> It's going to come from Jane in the food hall and her colleague in the next department. They will now tell their local customers: "Look at this new product. It's fair trade. Did you know what fair trade is? This is what fair trade is all about. Look at this organic product, look at this product for which we've reduced the packaging by 30, 40, 50 percent. Soon it will have no packaging."

Those are the kinds of conversations a company needs to encourage to bring about systemic change.

I remember an energy company executive summing up his strategy for stimulating sustainability thinking along the whole value chain. He declared:

> Deliver for today, inspire for tomorrow. It's about doing everything we can today and then inspiring not just our own people, but our suppliers and our customers. Inspiring people for tomorrow – that's been very much at the heart of our strategy.

A workforce engaged in sustainability thinking will spread the word beyond the factory gates, reinforcing the engagement effect.

Oliver Wendell Holmes Sr., a well-known poet and doctor in the nineteenth century, famously said, "A mind that is stretched by a new experience can never go back to its old dimensions." If you can galvanize your colleagues or employees to co-create solutions to challenges that sustainability demands, they will have to stretch for answers and stretch their minds. How could you ever go back to your old corporate thinking after that?

b. The second "C": celebration

Celebrating successes – or even successful failures, as I described at the start of this chapter – is a less formal complement to the metrics and bonuses I discussed in Chapter 7. Celebrating is about naming-and-faming, making people feel good through recognizing their efforts. It's about attention and association more than financial incentives or material rewards. My, what a beautiful house! Why do we complement friends or relatives when we visit a new home for the first time? Because recognition makes ownership resonate. As my experience in Rome shows, there are many different ways to signal recognition for successes and initiatives. And there are many ways to do the celebrating – the quirkier, the better, perhaps, to keep things top-of-mind. Celebration raises awareness.

Apple, for example, has found fun ways to bring people into a larger culture of belonging by linking employee success to environmental initiatives. Apple uses "Earth Day" as an opportunity to encourage its employees to unify around environmental issues. One way it does this is by celebrating employee accomplishments: "Once a year we just take a second and commemorate all the work we do and it turned into a real celebration company wise," an Apple executive told me. "We do Earth Day celebrations around the world, our retail stores all change their Apple logo to green. For months before and after, we wear green shirts instead of our normal blue or red." Apple also uses this time window to throw parties to rally its employees. The gatherings are meant to give workers the opportunity to share their thoughts and concerns about the direction in which the company is moving.

"There are lots of different levers you can pull, right from recognition," one retail executive told me. "There's a very clear sense that people willing to go the extra mile, who relate from the shop upward, can get awards. That sense has been very, very important." A sustainability executive mentioned the importance of maintaining a culture of inclusivity. For example, whenever her company wins a sustainability award, she makes sure that the achievement is shared among all the employees who contributed.

> I make sure that these [accomplishments] are promoted within the organization [she said]. Anyone who helps me, even though they might be a lesser actor – I make sure that everyone gets credit so that they can feel that they've been part of moving this ball forward.

Timothy Galpin from Colorado State University, and J. Lee Whittington and Greg Bell from the University of Dallas looked at rewards and awards in a 2015 study. They concluded that they could be essential in giving employees the right signals – not only that top executives are paying attention, but also that good work gets rewarded over merely average work. They quoted a raft of earlier research – by M.B. Metzger and colleagues from 1993, and L.K. Treviño and K.A. Nelson from 1995 – that demonstrated that a reward system "significantly influences the decision-making of organizational actors." Note that these observations also apply to bonus systems. The crucial difference with celebrating people is that it allows colleagues to learn by example – from successes, or constructive failures.

That is what makes Enel's "My Best Failure" awards so noteworthy. The initiative is a combination of celebration and cultural reinforcement. The company is showing – not just telling – its employees that it's acceptable, even good, to make mistakes. This breeds the kind of trust and confidence a corporate culture needs to manage the swing to a sustainable business model. As Ernesto Ciorra, director of innovation and sustainability, says on Enel's website: "My Best Failure reflects our Open Power spirit. Looking for new products and solutions means risking making mistakes, daring to follow new, unknown roads."

He goes on to explain that the awards are designed to share mistakes and the important lessons they provide. As quirky and tongue-in-cheek as the initiative might at first appear, it is about nothing less than instilling two crucial insights: well-run businesses rely on "continuous improvement" and sustainability is a "moving target" that demands constant refinements. It is a way of constantly keeping top-of-mind the vital idea that tomorrow's triumphs are built on today's successes and successful failures. People learn from them – so it is important to show employees what effects these lessons have. Awards can stimulate employees and make them open for change – a prerequisite for sustainability.

One retail executive summed up his company's efforts to celebrate successes and failures as follows: "We made the business more able and willing to accept risk." As a result, the company had come to make greater use of the ability to trial different ideas and initiatives in different parts of the company. For example, energy saving technologies were tested in one store and found not to be up to the job, he said.

> There are two or three energy saving technologies that didn't work for us. In that one store, we spent quite a lot of money getting it wrong [he explained]. But actually that was very powerful learning. Because it meant that we didn't repeat that mistake anywhere else.

Celebrating insights like this will have a huge effect on you and your company. It is a way to signal that, for one, lessons learned are relevant for everyone in the company. It is also a way of showing the workforce that these lessons were generated in the community, a clear signal that more inputs like this are always welcome. If done well, celebration can create real momentum, with one celebration spurring the next co-creation initiative and, in turn, the next celebration. Celebration spurs the kind of self-empowered and grassroots work that defines continuous improvement on the path to sustainability.

c. The third "C": communication

One of my MBA students once recounted how the consultancy he was work-ing for at the time introduced a sustainability program. As part of this, the com-pany reconfigured the communal kitchens in its offices. Out went one-way plastic cups and in came biodegradable dishes and implements that were col-lected for recycling after use. There was, he recalled, some skepticism among colleagues about the value of a move that seemed more symbolic than actually planet-saving. But soon the initiative became a real talking point.

Clients, in particular, were intrigued. They would ask all sorts of questions about the arrangement, the student recalled. That was usually a prelude to a more wide-ranging conversation about sustainable business plans – and how the world needed more. Far from being a vain symbol of lofty ideals at the top level of the consultancy, biodegradable knives and forks encouraged other companies to think about what they were – or, more usually, weren't – doing. It is a wonderful example of how to communicate saliently.

According to Nerina Jimmieson and colleagues, the salience of a fact is defined by the extent to which it dominates a person's "working memory." If a fact is – and deserves to be – top-of-mind, it is salient. In the above anecdote, knives, forks, and cups drove home the salient point that the consultancy was actively engaged in becoming more sustainable. And that it wanted its employ-ees and other stakeholders to know and be inspired.

At first, examples like this may strike you as being trivial efforts. After all, these small acts are merely symbolic of what needs to be done on a much larger scale to make business models sustainable. However, setting up easy goals for stakeholders gets them to act and reflect on being environmentally and socially responsible. This, in turn, helps to normalize sustainability practices and turn them into standard aspects of daily work routines. When employees eventually face more challenging issues, they are at least already thinking in sustainability terms. They are already viewing a part of the world and their business through a sustainability lens. Sustainability has become second nature in a part of their lives. These programs are invaluable steps toward entrenching sustainability ownership.

Next to co-creation, keeping sustainability salient via communication is perhaps the most important tool to sustain sustainability within an organization. Keeping sustainability salient is to constantly remind your company to view business through the sustainability lens. As one CEO put it to me: "I never give a speech without talking about sustainability." Another described company-wide scorecards that mapped energy and water use, carbon dioxide emissions, and waste production, as well as health and safety metrics. They were discussed every quarter with all managers via webcast. "We ask them to cascade these materials to the factories, to the employees." To be truly salient, sustainability communication also has to be as good as constant.

Signage, metrics, dashboards, webcasts, browser pop-ups – there are many, many ways to time and again remind your colleagues or employees of what's in play and what's at stake. Modern technology aside, one of the best communicators of salience continues to be people – in the form of sustainability ambassadors who remind everyone of their goal.

The more engaged and "co-creative" employees are, the easier and more natural they will find it to assume ownership and spread the word to others. Ideally, every employee should be a sustainability champion. Sustainability owners should be encouraged to practice advocacy and hand-holding. This helps others become owners and advocates, in turn.

You must be keenly aware that it is not enough for your company to have sustainability champions only at the top. You must cultivate such champions at all levels and in all geographies of the organization. Marks & Spencer has sustainability "champions" in every store, a volunteer position that employees fight over. And Unilever has sustainability "ambassadors" working constantly throughout the organization to instill ownership into colleagues and other stakeholders. No wonder, then, that 76 percent of Unilever's 160,000 plus employees feel their role at work enables them to contribute to the company's sustainability agenda. About half of all new employees entering the company from university cite Unilever's ethical and sustainability policies as the primary reason for signing up.

Unilever is a great example of how to encourage employees to become active proponents of sustainable actions. The sustainability website Coresponsibility. com relates how the company promoted sustainability awareness and engagement inside and outside the organization. It made use of traditional media and internal channels like a quarterly magazine, town hall meetings, and leadership forums. On top of that, the company launched a training program called "Green Ambassadors." It cultivated a generation of young ambassadors through experiential learning and training.

To continue communicating sustainability achievements, Unilever has created its own video hosting website, "Unilever Tube," which enables employees to share the sustainability stories of all the company's factories. This medium has allowed the company to create a simple yet effective way to bridge its organizational culture – it's a form of a smart connectivity that makes things happen. According to a company executive I interviewed, communicating was all about giving employees "a source of inspiration so they can feel they are making something good" and that they are making a difference. "That's part of our ethos," he said. "It's a 'number one' embedded factor: it makes us so proud about what we've done that we actually end up doing much more."

The key to such efforts is to make people aware of the impact that their actions – and the actions of the company they work for – are having on people and planet. Henkel, a German consumer goods group, published a fascinating online interview with one of its sustainability ambassadors. She was based in the company's Lebanese subsidiary – "a challenging region in terms of sustainability," as the employee herself said. But she said making people aware of the impact of their actions was very fruitful. "What's important to keep in mind is that there is no such thing as a small action," she said. "We should not underestimate the importance of our day-to-day choices on both a professional and personal level." Small actions make a big difference when adopted by many people.

Henkel not only communicates sustainability throughout its organization, it also carries word outside. The sustainability ambassador talked about her experience of making schoolchildren aware of looking after people and planet. "Every session is unique, because it involves a new interaction with a new group of students. But it's always rewarding. The students' enthusiasm and passion for the topic feeds my own commitment for sustainability." A company can galvanize outside stakeholders, who, in turn, bring fresh momentum into the company. Being a sustainability ambassador can be self-sustaining.

But sustainability ambassadors do need looking after to make sure the focus of the message they are spreading aligns with their often intense motivation. My visits to Marks & Spencer brought some interesting insights about that. A number of executives admitted that the role of sustainability champions went through cycles of greater and lesser importance, in part because of attitudes right at the top.

> You need to give them a sort of career guidance and career motivation to make sure that they are really well supported from the center [one executive said]. These people would motivate the hell out of anyone, because they're so proud of what they do. So, for us, it's more about building capability and capacity to certain degrees, not about motivation.

Isn't that refreshing? If you and your company communicate correctly, it is message and not motivation that becomes the issue.

8.3 Using the Three Cs to entrench sustainability ownership

The ultimate goal of co-creation, communication, and celebration is to firmly root sustainability ownership in your company. The Three Cs do this by evoking employee engagement and giving jobs meaning. T. J. Erickson in a 2005 study called engagement "a desirable condition" for every company as it drives organizational purpose. According to him, it is a measure of the "enthusiasm … effort, and energy" of a company's workforce. Which makes it so odd that it is so lacking in many companies today.

Unilever CEO Paul Polman told me in an interview that "only 20 percent" of employees the world over went to work "feeling happy or motivated" – even less in some countries. "Because there's no purpose, they see the [corporate] values as being different from their own values," he explained. Polman contrasted this with Unilever's attempts to win over employees to its "Sustainable Living Plan." The company sought to keep its workforce engaged by continually repeating and reinforcing key messages. You know by now that when personal and corporate values match you have a higher chance of satisfaction, which enables individuals to develop themselves to their fullest potential. "That's an incredible competitive advantage in itself," Polman said. "The fact that we have 2 million young people applying to join our company each year might have something to do with this."

By Polman's account, co-creation, communication, and celebration lead to enormous rates of what Michael Pratt and Blake Ashforth called "self-transcendence" in a 2003 study: "A connection to something greater than oneself, such as a cause or other people." I mentioned him before, so you might remember the man in the Unilever soap factory whose job it was to keep the soap bars aligned during production. He didn't make soap, or work to pay the rent. No, he simply said: "My job is about saving millions of lives around the world."

Such engagement is crucial for people and planet. And such engagement is crucial for profit. The consultancy Tower Watson looked at employee engagement levels in 50 global companies, as Anna Clark of the consultancy EarthPeople Media noted in a Greenbiz.com blog in 2011. The consultants found that so-called "high-engagement companies" were able to increase operating income by 19 percent on average over a 12-month period, while low-engagement organizations saw operating income drop almost 33 percent.

Clark also noted a 2008 study that said highly engaged employees were 26 percent more productive than their less engaged colleagues. "Happy people who want to work together to make the world better by greening their own workplace – a CEO's dream," she concluded. "The challenge is making the dream come true." The Three Cs, coupled with the other steps outlined in this book, are the surest way of ensuring that.

I want to make sure you've understood the importance of this central point. If a colleague or employee conceives of their job as something they have to do to receive a paycheck, a corrosive disconnect exists. If they see work as a place apart from their actual life, they can develop feelings of alienation akin to those that Marx identified in the nineteenth century. But if that colleague or employee feels part of something larger and feels his or her work is valued, he or she is more likely to identify with and grow in the job they do.

If you and your company can encourage colleagues and employees to take the same pride in their accomplishments at work as they do in their successes at home, they will come to feel a camaraderie for and excitement about the company. You can stimulate people to claim ownership of their work as they do of other aspects of their life. You just have to remember the Three Cs as essential instruments for making sustainability sustainable.

Chapter 8 in summary

* Create an enduring company culture of tolerance and collaboration to keep ideas flowing and to stimulate sustainability thinking among employees.
* Encourage employees to take pride in their accomplishments at work as they do in their personal lives – this will allow them to claim ownership of their jobs.
* Create opportunities for employees to celebrate both their accomplishments and constructive failures – both are essential lessons on the path to sustainability.
* Co-creation, communication, and celebration can inspire self-transcendence among employees – and a connection to something greater than themselves.
* Co-creation makes it easy for employees to participate in working toward bigger goals and is a great way to instill and maintain sustainable thinking and action.
* Celebrate employee contributions by naming-and-faming – make people feel good by recognizing their efforts and allow others to learn from their example.
* Communicate the salience of sustainability to employees by keeping ideas fresh and up-to-date – and watch as employees pass these ideas on to other stakeholders.

Bibliography

J.K. Beggan and E.M. Brown (1994). Association as a psychological justification for ownership, *The Journal of Psychology: Interdisciplinary and Applied*, 128(4), 365–380.

M. Wheeland (2010). *CEOs Can Embed a Culture of Sustainability Beyond Their Departure: Embedding sustainability in Organizational Culture.* Greenbiz.com (on Stephanie Bertels)

S. Bertels, L. Papania and D. Papania, with research assistance by Sara Graves (2010). *Embedding Sustainability in Organizational Culture: A Systematic Review of the Body of Knowledge.* Simon Fraser University, Network for Business Sustainability.

H. Mintzberg (2009). Rebuilding companies as communities, *Harvard Business Review*.

G. Unruh (2015). Sustaining sustainability: Investing in the intangibles are what keep sustainability policies alive – and evolving, *MIT Sloan Management Review*. (on Steve Zaffron).

R.G. Eccles, K. Miller Perkins, and G. Serafeim (2012). How to become a sustainable company, *MIT Sloan Management Review.*

CB Bhattacharya, S. Sen, and D. Korschun (2011). *Leveraging Corporate Responsibility: The Stakeholder Route to Maximizing Business and Social Value.* Cambridge University Press.

T. Galpin, J.L. Whittington, and G. Bell (2015). Is your sustainability strategy sustainable? Creating a culture of sustainability, *Corporate Governance: The International Journal of Business in Society,* 15(1), 1–17.

D.R. Dalton and M.B. Metzger (1993). "Integrity Testing" for personnel selection: An unsparing perspective, *Journal of Business Ethics,* 12, 147.

L. K. Treviño and K.A. Nelson (1995). *Managing Business Ethics: Straight Talk About How to Do It Right.* New York: J. Wiley & Sons.

N.L. Jimmieson, D.J. Terry, and V.J. Callan (2004). A longitudinal study of employee adaptation to organizational change: The role of change-related information and change-related self-efficacy, *Journal of Occupational Health Psychology,* 9(1), 11–27.

T.J. Erickson (2005). *Testimony Submitted Before the U.S. Senate Committee on Health, Education, Labor and Pensions,* May 26.

M. Pratt and B. Ashforth (2003). Institutionalized spirituality: An oxymoron? In: R.A. Giacalone and C.L. Jurkiewicz eds. *The Handbook of Workplace Spirituality and Organizational Performance.* M.E. Sharpe, pp. 93–107.

W.T. Watson (2011). *Viewpoints Q&A: Employee Engagement to the Power of Three.* Towers Watson.

A. Clark (2011). *Eco-Leadership: Why Employee Engagement Is Critical to Sustaining Sustainability.* Greenbiz.com.

O.W. Holmes, Jr. Available at: Quote. Available at: https://www.brainyquote.com/quotes/oliver_wendell_holmes_jr_109160.

9 Expand

9.1 Why companies need to think beyond their entire value chains

In early August 2016, the UK was baking in temperatures "hotter than the Med," the *Daily Mail* newspaper reported. Hotter than the Mediterranean – and yet, the newspaper pointed out a curious fact: UK supermarkets were wonderfully cool, some apparently "more bracing than parts of the Arctic." Even in that very hot summer, the newspaper measured temperatures of 10.5 °C at Tesco and "a chilly" 5.4 °C at Sainsbury's. The *Daily Mail* speculated that these results were the result of a cynical use of air-conditioning systems: "There's a theory that when we're colder [...] we may subconsciously think we need more food." But it also hit upon a more mundane, but no less shocking reason: to make stores more convenient for shoppers, supermarkets stocked products that needed to be cooled in open refrigerators. "Can you imagine how much your electricity bill would rise if you left your fridge or freezer wide open all day?" the newspaper asked. It went on to note refrigerator doors could cut food retailers' voracious power consumption by as much as half.

As my subsequent research revealed, the "refrigerator door issue" was one of the UK retail sector's dirty secrets. All food retailers in the UK market, including Marks & Spencer, Sainsbury, and Tesco, knew that the sector was using up to 4 percent more electricity for refrigeration than necessary. Many players had experimented with doors, and some even used them in small, urban shops. But "the big stores" still went door-less for fear of alienating their customers. "We really ought to talk to each other," one executive told me. "We ought to agree on a voluntary declaration that all refrigerators will have doors." A sector-wide agreement would resolve the problem any one player faced going it alone: "There would be no competitive disadvantage of a barrier in the way of the customer."

The refrigerator door issue points to a key limitation of many sustainability initiatives: their efforts are confined to the company itself. All too often, corporate leaders don't go further to build broader coalitions to drive systemic change – the kind of industry collaborations required to solve complex issues like supply chain and distribution challenges. That means that the really big, sweeping changes that our planet and its population need – and that businesses need too – all too often never materialize.

Until recently, most executives laughed at the idea of collaborating with competitors. In their zero-sum world, competitors were there solely to be vanquished, and knowledge represented an advantage not to be shared. Luckily, today's business world is very different. Most executives now recognize the tragedy of the commons I talked about in Chapter 1. Most recognize they are responsible for helping to protect the common good.

However, like my students playing the "Fishbanks" simulation near the beginning of this book, many executives still have difficulty making the next logical connection: to save the fish or the commons or the planet, our conception of sustainability ownership has to expand and become more inclusive, even collective. To make your company truly future-ready, you must do what the leading companies I studied do – recognize that you cannot go it alone when it comes to sustainability. After all, as one executive told me, there is no point in doing business responsibly if your competitors carry on as before and take the fish or the commons or the world – and you and your company – down with them.

Are you prepared to rethink the role of competition? Is your company ready to use its size, influence, expertise, and resources to lead systemic change beyond the factory gates and its ecosystem of direct stakeholders? Many of the companies I studied are. As Nestlé's global head of public affairs told me: "Unless you shift the whole industry, you're only going to solve pockets of the problem." Such enlightened awareness has allowed the food industry to launch a number of partnerships that would have been impossible a generation ago.

For example, retailers and consumer goods makers came together to form the Consumer Goods Forum and agreed to sustainably source raw materials whose unsustainable sourcing was driving deforestation – mainly palm oil, beef, soy, and timber. "That was a pretty special moment," one executive told me, "Because there were Unilever, P&G, Nestlé, Coca-Cola, Pepsi, and many more suddenly agreeing on this agenda." It spurred governments to go one better by bringing state, non-governmental organization (NGO),-and commercial actors together in the Tropical Forest Alliance – and to pass a UN declaration to end deforestation by 2030.

As I show in this chapter, when one company is willing to lead and inspire others to take collective ownership of the planet and its people, the effects can quickly ripple across an industry and into society as a whole. Commercial rivals can fall into line, lending the initiative real sectoral heft. This in turn spurs NGOs and governments, again raising the scale of collective ambition, resources, and potential for change. The fundamental point I want to make is this: companies have to take action and push sustainability because they have the means and the expertise to do so – as opposed to governments which don't, as they are often paralyzed by politics. If companies can get their act together, governments will, however, draw strength from them and begin to follow suit. But companies need to work together, sharing knowledge and expertise. A single company, acting alone, won't heal what ails planet earth. Every sustainable company needs others to be good alongside it.

Take refrigerator doors in supermarkets. My example might appear trivial to some, but if you want to see business through the sustainability lens, you must be able to take problems like this seriously for two main reasons. Firstly, as I've said, the "refrigerator door issue" is a classic tragedy of the commons. It might not be as striking as the problem of overfishing, but it is a prime example of extracting private gain at the expense of the common good – convenience for consumers and sales for retailers achieved by socializing the effects of higher CO_2 emissions through excessive energy consumption.

Secondly, you must be able to recognize problems of this type and be prepared to address them. As I hope my example shows, no issue is too small, obscure, or trivial-seeming to make a difference. But how can you and your company start tackling tragedies of the commons? As the fishing game with my students shows time and again, individual players do come to recognize the perils of overfishing. But they also come to see the futility of doing anything about it themselves – if Team One stops fishing in an attempt to avert disaster, Team Two will only scoop up extra fish and disaster will strike as quickly as before. It's a shocking realization – one that regularly seems to paralyze companies big and small.

Even "enlightened" players of the fishing simulation rarely have the nerve to interrupt the game to try and make their rivals see the tragedy into which they are collectively sliding. That is a mistake you must avoid, regardless of whether your company is a global behemoth or a small local player. Once you identify an area in which your company is extracting gain at the expense of the commons, you must be prepared to act. And once you're prepared to act, you must reach out to your rivals, because only collective ownership and joint action will resolve the problem. The same rules apply to big and small.

So, for example, the only way to solve overfishing is either through self-regulation or the power of law. Regardless of whether they own one boat or a huge fleet, fishermen must recognize the need for everyone to agree and abide by fishing quotas, legally or voluntarily defined. The only way to do away with the UK food retailers' dirty secret of refrigeration is to jointly agree and implement a program to retrofit doors. In both cases, the people and companies involved must recognize that if nothing gets done, everybody will ultimately lose. They must embrace the insight that a collective response lets everybody gain.

Collective psychological ownership is as an extension of the personal sense of ownership that I introduced in Chapter 2. As personal as this latter feeling of ownership can and should be, it is the foundation for the sense of shared ownership in an organizational setting. This allows a group of individuals to forge a collective mindset that allows them to claim a particular target of ownership. Criminal gangs, prostitutes working a street corner, or a group of homeowners in a neighborhood are classic examples of groups with a collectively held notion of an "us" – and, crucially, a collective sense that any target of ownership is "ours."

This chapter will show you how to build the same sense of ownership for societal and environmental problems too big for individual companies to address on their own. In earlier chapters, we discussed the need for a shift from an egocentric form of ownership to a more ecocentric one. An important step on this journey is to de-individualize ownership of very big problems and to turn them into more collective issues. Rather than any one person or corporation trying to solve all the problems facing the earth and its population, people and businesses must come together to co-manage the bigger ones.

But practicing sustainability ownership at that level demands that individuals and companies embrace a perspective beyond their own. Collaboration is the future. The question is whether you and your colleagues are in a position to see that. Are you ready to expand and extend your sense of sustainability ownership to partners and competitors?

9.2 Competing companies need to collaborate to save the planet

Doing business through the sustainability lens changes your company – and it changes you. If you have taken all the steps on the path to sustainability I've outlined in the previous chapters, this last step to collaborating with competitors should seem like second nature. On my travels along the front lines of corporate sustainability, I met people who, all by themselves, had come to the realization that this step is inevitable. But given the competitive nature of business, it is understandable why many people hold back from making that conceptual and practical leap. After all, this sizeable step demands a paradigm shift: competitors are no longer simply enemies and threats to your corporate profit; they are also allies in the greater cause of ensuring planetary and human survival.

Food giant Marks & Spencer, for example, made that leap. It recognized that its own sustainability efforts were not enough. What helped make the company's "Plan A" initiative different was that it was encouraging participation in wider change. This striving for a broader perspective on sustainability meant taking stock of a larger portion of the world and the company's place in it. As an executive told me:

> This is not just Marks & Spencer trying to put its own house in order, but humble recognition that we're part of a wider economy and society. Unless the economy and society are changing and functioning well, we'll fall with it.

The message, he added, was crystal clear: "If everything fails around us, we fail too."

As he told me this, I recalled a consumer goods executive ticking off the steps his company had taken to do business more sustainably. "We operationalized things, we innovated," he said. But these successes had also made the company more aware of the world around it – and its deficiencies. "There comes a point where you realize you have to change the society and the economy around you," he added. Executives had come to see that it wasn't enough to feel pride in their company as a green oasis in the desert. They saw they had no choice but to agitate for and participate in efforts for wider change – for example by having their company support business bodies like the Consumer Goods Forum or the World Economic Forum, and work with the World Wildlife Fund, Oxfam, or Unicef.

An executive from chocolate manufacturer Ferrero described a similar realization to me. She told me how the company she worked for had worried about child labor in one of its supply chains. Having "shone the light on what the problem was," the company soon decided it couldn't usefully address the problem on its own. So it teamed up with a trade body and an NGO that already had an eye on and expertise about child labor in the sector. "They explained to us where we were weak, where we were strong. This wasn't something we could fix alone," she said.

Seeing oneself as part of a wider collective is an essential insight during the transition to a sustainable business model. As I have said, this shift to accepting the need to collaborate with competitors and other institutions is difficult for many, perhaps most employees. As the Marks & Spencer executive elaborated: "Many businesses are naturally not happy with that level of looking outward, of being in touch with others." He said it had been his employer's signal achievement to create a culture that encouraged everyone to "look beyond the immediacy of our world, to the wide world around us."

If you defined your corporate purpose and followed the steps I outlined in Chapter 4 to build sustainability ownership in your value chain, you too should come to realize that you have no choice but to collaborate. I used the chapter to emphasize how important it is to "let the outside world" into your company. And here, again, we see why that is so important: without outside reference points, without some awareness of what people, planet, and other players are up to, you will remain precariously uninformed. You will be trying to save the oceans by foregoing fishing while your rivals scoop up the last of the fast dwindling catch. Without outside reference points, you and the world are doomed.

Openness to the world is part of your transition toward a sustainable business model. An executive at Nestlé once candidly told me about how, just after the beginning of the new millennium, his company and its customers all found themselves "beginning this journey" and "trying to figure out what it all means" by talking to each other. He described how this often haphazard, disorganized conversation had eventually drawn in suppliers, too. Consumer-driven demands for more sustainable food products had trickled all the way down the value chain. Nestlé and its partners had let the outside world in.

But the process didn't stop there. One company talking to a competitor soon turned into a sectoral and then a cross-industry conversation, and soon widened into a dialogue also involving governments and NGOs. "Ten years ago, we didn't talk to these groups," the Nestlé executive recalled. "There was a major chasm between us." But an acrimonious relationship was changed by companies "trying to figure out what it all means" – and talking to governments and NGOs, as well. "Some of them helped show us where to go, in a positive fashion, and we helped some of them understand who we were." Circumstance forced all sides to start a conversation that dramatically changed relations. "We may still not always agree on ways to reach our goals," the executive said. "But we do now tend to agree on the end result we need." This is how feelings of collective ownership can come about.

Understanding the tragedy of the commons and seeing the need for collaborative action leads to remarkable results, on many levels. I would never have expected an executive at one of the world's largest drinks manufacturers to praise an NGO: "I think they've been a highly engaging partner, one that continues to push us, while being willing to also work with us [...] We've learned a lot by the way they pushed us on certain topics."

The common thread here is the understanding that social and environmental problems are increasingly often impediments to sustainable business and corporate profits. NGOs and civil society more generally have become so aware of corporate (co-)responsibility for many of the world's problems that doing nothing about protecting and restoring the common good is an ever less tenable option for companies. As Mark R. Kramer and Marc Pfitzer said in an influential article "The Ecosystem of Shared Value": "No company exists in isolation; each exists in an ecosystem where societal conditions may curtail its markets or restrict the productivity of its suppliers and distributors."

Once a company recognizes its part in creating the problems that threaten its business, it should turn to addressing them with as many like-minded parties as possible. Kramer and Pfitzer call these "shared value efforts" that address problems too big for any one company to deal with. "Businesses must foster and participate in multi-sector coalitions – and for that they need a new framework." Borrowing from an earlier article by Kramer and John Kania, they call this "collective impact." This allows companies to improve society and reap economic opportunities they would otherwise have missed.

9.3 It's safer and more effective to address risks together – and it creates higher purpose

Tackling large problems that no one company can fix on its own is the most obvious reason to collaborate. Together, companies have more resources to deal with the problem – while each individual company expends less of its own. Together, companies share expertise and network, and they bring corporate planning and goal definition to sustainability processes – skills that NGOs and governments often can only dream of. Together, companies deal more efficiently with common threats to business, reduce reputational risks, foster new technology and standards, and communicate with consumers, regulators, and investors. Collaboration also leads to one vital side effect that can greatly help the relationship between a company and its stakeholders: showcasing corporate higher purpose.

In 2010, a host of food manufacturing companies formed the Consumer Goods Forum by putting together three separate trade bodies. The companies used this new neutral ground to hammer out a groundbreaking agreement to end deforestation. By itself, the production of palm oil, beef, soy, and timber, one executive who had been involved told me, accounted for half of all deforestation around the globe – which in turn accounted for 15 percent of total greenhouse gas emissions. The companies presented their agreement on the first day of the 2010 UN Climate Change Conference in Cancun, Mexico, in November 2010.

A Unilever executive I spoke to was adamant about the social significance of such a coalition: the world's top consumer goods companies had been able to put aside their differences and unite to tackle a huge global issue like deforestation. "Part of the theory of change that lies behind companies stepping up to be a force for change in the world is really about aligning like-minded businesses to reach critical mass in the marketplace." That, he said, was what had happened in the fight to save the forests of the world.

The business-led effort in turn "helped the governments raise their level of ambition," the executive continued. He recalled how some governments took their cues from the companies involved and proposed the Tropical Forest Alliance. Formed in 2012, it came to combine the corporate initiative of the Consumer Goods Forum with the skills and experience of governments and NGOs. This led to the UN-sponsored Declaration on Rainforests in 2014, in which all agreed to work toward ending deforestation by 2030.

"This was a huge contribution on the part of governments, NGOs, and companies," the executive said. "It was the kind of system-level alignment that would not have happened five years before." At the start of the decade, he noted, there had been a "single-digit percentage commitment" from companies to source palm oil sustainably. Thanks to the Consumer Goods Forum, the Tropical Forest Alliance, and the Declaration on Rainforests, countries such as the Netherlands, Belgium, and the UK pledged by 2015 to import only palm oil certified as sustainable. A year after this deadline, according to the European Sustainable Palm Oil (ESPO) project, some 69 percent of the palm oil imported to refineries across the whole European Union for use in food was certified sustainable palm oil.

Getting institutions to make pledges takes a lot of work and turning them into reality takes even more. But having taken collective ownership of the problem, participants are quite optimistic about the prospects of curbing deforestation. If they can realize their ambitions, they should be able to end an ecologically devastating agricultural practice that contributes significantly to global climate change. And they should be able to empower and help smallholder palm oil farmers increase their incomes and meet global demand without cutting down any more trees – a transformation from a net negative to a net positive. As one food company executive stated:

> For me, that's the power of business, it's not just one company. One company can lead, but it's only when others in the sector align around a common purpose to create a critical mass that you can get NGOs to say wow, you guys are really serious, let's raise our collective ambition and scale.

The example shows how the collaboration between companies, NGOs, and governments turned every supply chain officer's niche problem into one relevant to every citizen – saving the rainforests to help stop global warming. While making the problem appear bigger, the collaboration also showed each stakeholder involved that they can make more of a difference by collectively tackling global problems. There's no better boost to employee motivation and reinforcement of sustainability ownership than employees' realization they're helping to save the world.

Nevertheless, employees away from the front lines or not actively engaged in supply chain work can find it hard to see the forest for the trees when part of a collective action initiative. I recall a food company executive telling me how her initial professional reaction to her employer's sustainability efforts was very much numbers-driven. She told me how she'd come to see sustainability costs as investments, and then had tried to quantify returns on the sums invested. But it was her personal reaction that was more profound and hugely influenced her eventual stance, both as a private individual and a corporate employee.

Prior to her employer's sustainability efforts, the executive said, she had had a clear view on environmental and social issues: "This is not my responsibility." But her involvement with her company's efforts in both areas made her see the scale and complexity of the tasks in hand. "I used to think it was the role of the government to take care of climate change and social issues," she told me. Now that she understood more, she still thought governments had an important role. "But I now see governments can fail or cannot do everything themselves – and this is why citizens and companies need to play a role." Every company must foster employee awareness of "commons problems" such as deforestation or child labor; and then every company must win its employees' support for its role in addressing them collaboratively with outside partners, even corporate rivals.

9.4 Why companies have to collaborate, even if they find it hard

MIT Sloan Management Review, Boston Consulting Group (BCG), and the United Nations Global Compact in 2014 found that 90 percent of some 4,000 executives polled in 113 countries regarded collaboration as an essential driver of sustainability. Roughly 60 percent said they collaborated with industry associations, with other businesses in other sectors, with rivals in their own industry, or with some combination of these three variants.

The report said companies were moving from "the old model [...] of ad hoc or opportunistic efforts" that often created friction with governments and NGOs "toward strategic and transformational initiatives that engage multiple entities." This trend was driven by the growing realization within companies that sustainability issues were too complex, too global, and too important for a company to grapple with on its own.

With their report, the three institutions that had authored it provided a rare piece of evidence that the tragedy of the commons and the need to combat it are being understood in the corporate world. Sadly, for all these signs of enlightened self-interest, or selfish altruism, the survey also showed a worrying shortcoming – that of "practice lagging behind belief" at many companies. While nine in ten executives said collaboration was important for sustainability, only 47 percent said their companies were actually engaging in such partnerships. On top of that, more than two-thirds of this sample of corporate leaders suggested most corporate initiatives were anything but impressive: According to the report, less than 30 percent of executives thought their companies were collaborating usefully.

This is an initially baffling statistic. If the benefits of collaborating are so clear, why do companies find it so difficult to collaborate with other companies or organizations? If collaborations allow companies to benefit from partners' expertise, networks, political contacts, and other resources, if collaborations allow easier standard setting and a greater ability to influence public opinion – why are collaborations still so hard to achieve? At the most basic level, because companies are all very different. In an influential 2009 study about corporate interaction with NGOs, John Peloza and Loren Falkenberg pointed out companies have different cultures and sustainability goals. At a more fundamental level, companies compete with one another, which makes trusting one another difficult. Kramer and Pfitzer see this as the biggest hurdle to clear – can you trust your competitors enough to reach out to them? "Although companies are often respected, they are more likely to be feared than trusted. After all, they're in the self-interested pursuit of profit. So they may be viewed as not having the legitimacy to initiate social progress."

This lack of trust can lead to a relatively benign fear of free-riders – companies that aren't fully committed to a jointly stated goal, but still profit from the environmental, social, or financial investments of another company or group of companies. But it can also make companies worry about partners discovering commercial secrets or making off with intellectual property. Both are examples of shared value with unfairly shared costs.

Secondly, collaboration is real work and demands executives' intellectual energy and management time. Companies need to integrate the views and goals of all stakeholder groups, many of which will have very different – and often even competing – claims. The process of edging toward cooperation presents management with any number of difficult tasks. And note that if executives are having problems getting internal constituents on board, how long might it take them to get external ones to align?

Lastly, as Kramer and Pfitzer note, too many companies still separate operations and strategy from social and environmental problems. The latter pair is in consequence still seen as a cost factor, not as an investment in a license to continue doing business. But the pair's proposition of "shared value creation" demands that companies analyze their environmental and social initiatives like any capital investment. If they fail to do that, companies won't understand why an initiative is worth the allocation both of money and of management time. In other words, you must be prepared for internal roadblocks and to work continuously on fostering cultural change, as I have discussed in previous chapters.

The hard work becomes easier to manage if you keep firmly focused on the upsides. Management scholars Lori DiVito and Garima Sharma give a great summary of these in their "how to" guide to collaborations, which they wrote for the Network for Business Sustainability: "Competitors come together to: reduce reputational risks that threaten an entire industry, support new technology development by sharing uncertain returns and pooling knowledge, develop shared standards for businesses within an industry, communicate effectively with regulators on public policy." The results of successful collaborations regularly far exceed what one company can do on its own.

Even in this light, the concern of many companies that collaboration is really about losing profits and commercial secrets remains understandable. But it also shows the limitations of self-interest. To become a sustainable business, a company will at some point have to favor collective gains over selfish, individual ones. Collaborative sustainability – sharing sustainable solutions and innovations between companies and working together to address complex environmental and social issues – requires expanding definitions of ownership. Once a company has persuaded its stakeholders to switch mindsets, it needs to build trust with unfamiliar partners, investing extra resources and overcoming internal skepticism. These are necessary sacrifices to yield the collective benefits of a healthy planet.

9.5 How companies can collaborate even with their biggest rivals

I first heard about "conflict minerals" while talking to Florian Nehm, the chief sustainability officer of the media company Axel Springer. He was worried that NGOs such as Greenpeace might campaign against his company as it was serving up a lot of content on digital devices that contained these raw materials. Gold, tungsten, tantalum, and tin – collectively often referred to as 3TG – are often called conflict minerals because they are sourced from militia-controlled mines in the troubled Democratic Republic of Congo. Revenues from the mines are used to finance military conflicts, putting companies that make or rely on smartphones, say, at risk of being associated with these abuses.

Human rights abuses abound in the Democratic Republic of Congo's mining sector – teenage boys and girls work 16-hour shifts in extremely hazardous mines. The country's civil war has killed over 5 million people in the past two decades as the demand for 3TGs has soared worldwide. The minerals, which are key components in modern, everyday items like smartphones, tablets, computers, and televisions, are at the same time widely considered to be key drivers of government corruption and large-scale deforestation.

Companies started grappling with the problem in 2008 when they founded the Responsible Minerals Initiative (RMI), which today has 350 corporate members. The RMI then became part of a multi-stakeholder partnership in which the Organization for Economic Cooperation and Development (OECD), NGOs such as RESOLVE and the Enough Project, and other organizations, came together to begin sourcing minerals responsibly. Legislation like the US's 2010 Dodd-Frank Act also provided a boost by asking companies that were sourcing metals from the Congo to report where their raw materials were coming from.

The example shows that when companies large or small come together, they can address problems of a scale once reserved for the attention of governments. When companies think big and conceive initiatives with a cross-industry perspective, sustainability shifts from being a small-bore strategic and operational issue into one addressing some of the biggest problems the planet faces. Of course, proper implementation is key – I'll get to that in a minute. But the foundation is confidence and openness. Your company has to be prepared to let in the world – a stance we first encountered in Chapter 4 and one you should quite naturally have picked up over the subsequent steps described in the book. Looking at your company's entire value chain drives interdepartmental cooperation and better relations with your suppliers. This is excellent preparation for broader collaboration.

One drinks company executive told me how his employer had recognized that close collaboration with its suppliers could bring sizeable benefits when striving for more sustainability. "They have much more knowledge on the ground [...] They have a relationship all the way back to the growers of the sugarcane, the farmers that grow the sugarcane we use." The company saw the clear benefits of this way of working, which meant its readiness to cooperate with people and organizations outside the company rose.

"Companies that understand the importance of sustainable sourcing need to take that example and build on it," he said. "They come to understand that it's really important to also work in partnership with civil society organizations and NGOs." By the time we talked, the company was collaborating "across the board," this executive told me, reaping benefit through cooperation with partners beyond its immediate value chain where it could.

This man's boss, the chief executive, later told me about a whole series of initiatives the company was now part of, projects relating to a wide range of issues from sustainable sourcing to sensible nutrition. "We work with our competitors," he said. "Sometimes we work directly with our rivals. Other times more with NGOs. Other times with governments." The drivers of such changes in mindset can be external as well as internal.

The companies that got together under the RMI umbrella a decade ago had been confronted with evidence showing the connection between 3TGs and conflict. In the consumer electronics industry, in which metals are a critical component, companies decided they had to do something collectively. Collaboration, they realized, was the only way to achieve "collective good" when sharing supply chains, similar processing facilities, similar mining sites. No one company could take on the task of cleaning such a complex supply chain, with conflict five tiers removed from any one company's manufacturing sites.

With the RMI's help, the companies agreed on definitions about responsible sourcing and materials to prioritize and aligned expectations. Approaching supply chain issues collectively sent a powerful signal to suppliers that the companies were serious about finding out where their raw materials came from. The founding companies were very different and had different policies, priorities, resources, and levels of patience, but this did not prove to be a deal breaker. Jay Celorie, global program manager of conflict minerals at Hewlett-Packard recalled: "What was fun about it is that we were a bunch of different company representatives working together for one common objective and we all brought different skills and abilities." It was the RMI's job to keep the companies in check and to manage their expectations. According to Leah Butler, one of the RMI's senior executives: "Our job is to provide a path forward for companies no matter where they are in the journey."

To get your company to move down a similar path requires openness, as I've said. It requires the power to analyze problems and ask the right questions. For example, as a first step, you have to be honest enough when in-house solutions to problems are obviously failing or going to fail. You have to be honest enough to admit to yourself, your boss, and your employees that solving the problem will require others' help. Jose Lopez, who had a storied career at Nestlé and was its chief sustainability architect, told me that making a commitment across and beyond the value chain requires a degree of humility. "If you don't go out of your individual [corporate social responsibility] CSR moment, you will never have that big an impact. You can outsource responsibly but that doesn't mean outsourcing the responsibility," he added. So, as a next step, look for competitors or NGOs that are battling the same practical problems.

In a second step, your company and the organizations you have identified must build a joint vision and shared sense of purpose, both to be effective and build trust. John Peloza and Loren Falkenberg used the term "meta-problems" in their 2009 study of how companies can interact with NGOs – in many ways a template for corporate interaction with all the other players in civil society. Signaling a growing awareness of the size and complexity of issues, the business studies scholars noted that companies had been told much about building relationships with individual NGOs, but "relatively little attention" had been paid to making more complex alliances work. Their analysis of different types of collaborations showed that the bigger the problem, the bigger the consortium should be.

The problem of conflict minerals illustrates this point. As they grappled for the best way to source 3TGs reliably, the founding companies held intense technical discussions, formed working groups, and convened workshops. With the OECD acting as a facilitator, they talked to other private sector players, on-the-ground NGOs, and even the US government. Together, they hit upon the crucial idea that the smelters to which the minerals were brought from the mine was a great "choke point" that could be policed.

Thomas Osburg, who used to work at Intel, spoke at one of my Berlin Roundtable meetings about the issue: "In contrast to more than 16,000 mines, there are only about 160 smelters." Over time, the RMI used member dues to set up audit and assurance programs for supply chain partners, design supplier training programs at smelters and mines, and develop online risk-assessment tools and databases. As these resources are capital-intensive, companies would be hard pushed to build these on their own. But they all benefit from the collective facilities they build – with the help of the OECD, NGOs, and the US government.

The simplest type of collaboration that John Peloza and Loren Falkenberg identify is also the oldest – one company joining forces with one NGO. The authors show how McDonald's enlisted the Environmental Defense Fund as far back as the 1980s to help it reduce waste. This model allows a company to be identified with certain issues, which can be good for motivational and reputational issues. But it can also expose the company to accusations of not being ambitious enough. McDonald's, for example, redesigned its packaging, but was then accused of focusing only on this and ignoring issues like obesity.

A more ambitious type of collaboration is the cooperation between a number of firms and a single NGO, which can be sectoral or regional in nature. When Caterpillar opened a production facility in the Brazilian city of Piracicaba, it and several other local firms ended up supporting a new regional development NGO. But Peloza and Falkenberg warn that this construction demands that companies and NGO have a strong ethical compass to mitigate the danger of the collaboration being brought off course by corporate interests.

One way of dealing with that problem is for a company to enter a collaboration with several NGOs, not just one. The idea is that several NGOs have a better chance of keeping one company focused on maximizing the social impact of the initiative. Starbucks, for example, set up a successful multi-NGO collaboration in coffee-growing areas of Mexico. The scheme helped Starbucks and its farmers to source coffee more sustainably, benefiting the communities. But note that administering such a structure takes time and skill.

And note also that option four is even more ambitious. Tackling a big social or environmental issue that affects many different regions of the globe takes a coalition of many companies with many NGOs. As we've seen with the conflict minerals initiatives, such broad alliances can tackle questions no government can – or wants to – tackle on its own, although, as we have seen, individual governments can sometimes provide real help to such initiatives.

One example Peloza and Falkenberg cite is the Fair Labor Association, founded by Nike and 19 other apparel manufacturers to lay down labor standards – for example against child labor and harassment and abuse – across a whole number of national jurisdictions. These multicompany, multi-NGO initiatives have done much to address big issues. The Waste Electrical and Electronic Equipment Forum, for example, shares ideas and best practices for waste management among a network of companies and other collaborators.

What all of these constructs share is a non-corporate entity that acts as a facilitator or "neutralizer." Existing trade bodies or associations founded to tackle a particular issue are great ways to bring companies together. The food retail executive I introduced at the start of the chapter praised the cooperation of his employer and its rivals in areas like emissions and energy – with the obvious exception of refrigerator doors. But he noted that the intense competition of these companies meant these exchanges best took place "on middle ground" provided by NGOs, trade bodies, academia, or even government.

"Our cooperation has not yet got to the point where I can call my colleagues at [a rival food retailer] and ask them to come over for a meeting about a [collective] problem," he said. Long-established rivalries, different cultures, even anti-trust issues made it much safer to meet on the neutral ground provided by a facilitator. He told me about a meeting at a university engineering department, at which representatives from the UK's major food retailers talked about reducing emissions that are released when manufacturing the materials for shops, or when fitting out retail units. "We were on common ground, we all felt comfortable, and we were all quite open with one another." Neutral ground is a catalyst.

Sharing best practices with competitors may not be an obvious or intuitive choice for most companies. However, opening up on these issues allows the corporate world to put sustainability in a "pre-competitive space," as one chemical company executive described it at an industry conference I attended. He stated emphatically: "Sustainability is not competitive. Yes, it helps you become more efficient. But to really unlock all [its potential] opportunities, let's put it into the pre-competitive space and deal with it as such." Coming to such a bold, shared understanding is a great way to overcome hesitation.

The campaign for conflict-free minerals shows that even complex collaborative approaches can work. Much work remains to be done with regard to responsible sourcing of minerals, but a lot of progress has been made. An OECD report published after five years of the initiative notes that "at sites visited in 2009/10 the percentage of 3TG workers engaged at mines affected by interference from non-state armed groups and public security forces was 57%, compared to 26% of workers at sites visited in 2013/14." By June 2018, according to the RMI, over 81 percent of smelters and refiners worldwide for the four conflict minerals had passed or were participating in independent audits by the Responsible Minerals Assurance Process. Even with the Dodd-Frank Act in jeopardy under the Trump administration, companies like Apple,

Intel, and Tiffany say they will continue their responsible sourcing. Customers and employees now absolutely expect a metal be conflict-free, they say.

But remember that complexity is not necessarily built in. Your answer to the question of whether and how to collaborate will differ from case to case. If you have identified a problem you know your company can't solve on its own, look for other companies that may face the same problem. Only then ask yourself whether you need to involve civil society organizations like NGOs, or governments, or regulators that can monitor progress and also pinpoint collaborators who aren't pulling their weight. Lastly, take a view on whether a "neutralizer" might be the best-placed host to bring every organization and all those different goals and ideas together. Juxtaposing all options, you will find that there are any number of formations in which collaboration can take place – complicated and simple ones.

DiVito and Sharma's analysis points up this tension. They also outline different types of collaboration, distinguished by where these models sit on the competition–cooperation and the formal–informal axes. "Cooperative collaborations" are for companies that are "similarly motivated to address an issue" – putting an end to deforestation, say. Achieving collective goals and long-term engagement from partners is more likely in this case. In contrast, "competitive collaborations" pool companies "that emphasize their own interests at the expense of collective goals." For example, the Alliance and Accord agreements were formed between apparel brands, NGOs, trade unions, and governments to improve standards after the 2013 collapse of a garment factory in Bangladesh. Firms are directly competing to get the best prices from respective suppliers, so understandably are more hesitant to share information or expend resources in this collaboration type. A formalized structure with oversight by an NGO or regulatory body can be useful in this instance.

The Network for Business Sustainability report shows clearly that choosing between different ways to collaborate depends on the company and the issue it wants to tackle. Beyond the cooperation–competition dichotomy, the authors identify important subsidiary properties on the formal–informal front. Formal collaborations have higher entry and exit barriers than informal ones: they build trust with tools like scorecards rather than leaving the job up to individual firms, they can make decisions more quickly as they typically have more resources, and they make "free-riding" by any one firm harder than under more informal mechanisms. Based on all this knowledge, you will need to identify the kind of collaboration best suited for your company and its goals.

Do bear in mind that you don't always need to found a new trade body to address an issue your company might be concerned about. Increased corporate awareness of – and striving toward "higher purpose" – has seen the foundation of numerous groups. Under the umbrella of the Consumer Goods Council alone, companies can opt to join subgroups dealing with deforestation, refrigeration, waste, and environmental impact measurement. And remember the initiative I described in the latter part of this chapter, the Responsible Minerals Initiative, and that there are now many other such institutions.

There are also organizations such as the UK's Blueprint for Better Business (BBB). It was founded by Unilever and others to help companies see that they are able – and in many ways obliged – to imbue what they do with higher purpose, to connect what they and their stakeholders do to the world around them. The organization runs workshops and thought-leadership classes to engage and motivate people in business, with the goal of stimulating creativity and innovation in sustainability and beyond. The BBB says it is driven by the beliefs "that business has the ability to do tremendous good and mitigate harm to society" and "that the values of society should shape the values of business and those within business." If you are sitting on the fence waiting for inspiration to strike, this kind of organization can be very helpful for peer-to-peer learning – or even peer-to-peer inspiration.

"Blueprint for Better Business is a good example of how to bring more purpose to business," Paul Polman, Unilever's then-CEO, told me. In his view, initiatives like BBB help executives and middle management maintain an outward focus, even when criticism from investors or the media – or simply tough economic conditions – lead to an understandable urge to be "more inward-looking." Unilever's transition to an even more sustainable business model did draw some skepticism and criticism. But Polman and his team were undeterred. "Leadership for me is not just driving a company, [it's] about making it do the right thing. It's really about helping to transform entire markets and behaviors beyond those your own company is engaged in to the benefit of all."

True leadership in turbulent times is about having the vision and fortitude to establish a new normal. In the case of sustainability, this means that executives must forge collaborations with competitors, NGOs, and regulators to tackle the abundant commons tragedies. The only way to foster change on the scale required is to take collective ownership of and share responsibility for the planet and its future. Maybe an alliance of retailers, NGOs, and governments will one day put doors on in-store refrigerators.

Chapter 9 in summary

- Companies must act on sustainability because they have the means and the expertise to do so, while governments are all too often paralyzed by politics.
- If you notice your company is extracting gain at the expense of the commons, you must reach out to NGOs and rivals – only joint action will resolve the problem.
- Shift the old paradigm about competitors being the enemy – view them as allies in a greater cause that demands collective psychological ownership as a prelude to action.
- Let the outside world in: cultivating openness to the world comes at the very start and at the very end of your company's journey toward a sustainable business model.

- Companies can better deal with common threats to business collectively, although such collaboration will require them to extend current definitions of ownership.
- Sharing best practices from a trove of sustainable solutions and innovations with competitors demands that companies shift sustainability to a pre-competitive space.

Bibliography

C. Coleman (2016). The cynical reason your supermarket's colder than the Arctic: FEMAIL takes the temperature of food chains to see which is the chilliest, *Daily Mail*.

J.L. Pierce and I. Jussila (2011). *Psychological Ownership and the Organizational Context*. Cheltenham, UK: Edward Elgar.

M.R. Kramer and M. Pfitzer (2016). The ecosystem of shared value, *Harvard Business Review*.

J. Kania and M. Kramer (2011). Collective impact, *Stanford Social Innovation Review: Informing and Inspiring Leaders of Social Change*.

Press Association. (2014). UN climate summit pledges to halt the loss of natural forests by 2030, *The Guardian*.

O. Balch (2013). Sustainable palm oil: How successful is RSPO certification? *The Guardian*.

European Sustainable Palm Oil (ESPO) Project (2017). Europe on its way to achieving 100% sustainable palm oil, *The Sustainable Trade Initiative*, 5th annual European Palm Oil Conference, Brussels.

D. Kiron, N. Kruschwitz, K. Haanaes, M. Reeves, S.K. Fuisz-Kehrbach, and G. Kell (2015). Joining forces: Collaboration and leadership for sustainability, *MIT Sloan Management Review*, 56(3), 1–31. (Boston Consulting Group and UN Global Compact Survey.)

J. Peloza and L. Falkenberg (2009). The role of collaboration in achieving corporate social responsibility objectives, *California Management Review*, 51(3), 95–113.

L. DiVito and G. Sharma (2016). *Collaborating with Competitors to Advance Sustainability: A Guide for Managers*. ResearchGate.

OECD Publishing (2009). *OECD 2009 Annual Report*, The Organisation for Economic Co-operation and Development.

Secretary General of the OECD (2018). *Alignment Assessment of Industry Programmes with the OECD Minerals Guidance*. The Organisation For Economic Co-Operation and Development. Available at: mneguidelines.oecd.org.

Conclusion

1 A generation of parents needs to be inspired by its children

Much of the northern hemisphere was in the vicelike grip of subzero temperatures when I visited the Atacama Desert in Chile for three days in January 2017. I was there to see firsthand the work of Enel, the Rome-based company we have encountered a few times in this book. The energy company had been helping villages in this part of northern Chile become more resilient and had built a geothermal electricity plant in San Pabellon that was to about to go on stream. One morning, my hosts and I woke in the small hours and drove out to see some famous geothermal springs, which I was told were best seen in the fresh light of dawn.

The springs were majestic, their hot, bubbling water breathing forth long trails of steam across the low, warm rays of first light. My group and the dozens of other people who had also risen early that morning were awestruck. My group and I enjoyed the breakfast the hotel had packed in this almost surreal atmosphere. But by 7 a.m. the sun was rising high in the sky and shining brightly. The show was over, and we started driving again across the desert plateau.

We traveled long distances at high altitudes, sometimes exceeding 4,500 meters (almost 15,000 feet). No wonder I had had to get special medical clearance to make the trip. And no wonder the Internet service was patchy as we drove in the car. Reception was intermittent, which meant that whenever there was a signal, beyond very occasionally checking my emails, my favorite thing to do was to play music from my Spotify account. My hosts seemed to enjoy the change from all the Spanish-language music CDs the driver had in the car for entertainment.

At one point while we did have an Internet signal and were enjoying a popular sing-along, the music was interrupted abruptly by another voice singing, "I love you, you love me, we are a happy family." It was the unmistakable voice of that toddler sensation, Barney, and a song I had heard a thousand times before, when my son Felix had been two or three. But why and how was this song playing here and now, in the world's highest and driest desert? Then it struck me. Of course, it was the work of Felix, then 13. We shared a Spotify account and he had overwritten one of my songs with his. He was trying to send me a message of love – I had been away for some time and he was missing me. That was truly a special moment and I got a bit emotional. After all, when you cut to the chase, what is more important than love and being able to care for those you love?

Felix is now 16 years old. As I look at him, his school friends, other teenagers, I cannot help but wonder what kind of world we are going to pass on to them. Do you ever have similar thoughts? As some sustainability leaders I've met like to say: "We don't inherit the earth from our parents, we borrow it from our children." How true that is. But the mess our generation has created is prompting teenagers to take to the streets to highlight all sorts of dangers that have appeared on our watch. After the school shooting in Parkland, Florida, in February 2018, my son and his friends walked out of their own school to protest against gun violence.

More recently, in February 2019, the *Guardian* reported that thousands of schoolchildren and young people had walked out of classes to join a UK-wide climate strike amid growing anger at the failure of politicians to tackle the escalating ecological crisis. Organizers said more than 10,000 young people in at least 60 towns and cities, from the Scottish Highlands to Cornwall, joined the strike. They defied threats of school punishment to voice their frustration at the older generation's inaction in the face of the mounting environmental impact of climate change. The school-strike movement started in August 2018 when Greta Thunberg, then 15, protested outside the Swedish parliament. You can see her stirring speech on YouTube, and it seems to have galvanized many. According to the *Guardian*, 70,000 schoolchildren are currently holding weekly protests in 270 towns and cities worldwide.

Youth activism is inspiring and downright necessary. But it leaves me ashamed. We have failed our young – perhaps the very last group any adult wants to disappoint. But the good news about these protests is that they show that the young people around the world are taking ownership of the problem – and even urging the older generation to finally do the same. "Don't go breaking my earth," read one of the young people's banners, as I saw in one of the pictures of the live protest. The phrase was a memorable play on the popular Elton John song, and its identification of "my earth" testament to a vibrant sense of sustainability ownership, whose importance I have discussed in previous chapters. "Don't go breaking my earth" is a call-to-arms that must be heeded. We may still feel the urge to fly away from all this mess. But most of us now would agree with what Pink Floyd sang prophetically in *The Wall*: we have "nowhere to fly to."

So, no more excuses. Let's do this. Let's get to work. There are no guarantees that even spirited collective efforts will be enough to surmount the challenges facing us now. It could be that we are doing too little too late – the refrain I hear all the time from my students. But even with this possibility in mind, inaction is precisely wrong. Taking ownership of sustainability is the way to go, and companies and their employees are the right place to start.

Why? Because they have incentives – remember all the good outcomes that come from sustainable business. Secondly, because the consumerism that has helped cause our social and environmental problems was socially engineered. Per capita consumption has doubled in many developed countries in the past 50 years. Companies can play a vital role in un-engineering consumerism and bringing in an era of responsible consumption. And, lastly, because every corporate stakeholder grappling with sustainability is probably also a parent or a sibling, and certainly a member of civil society, with all the responsibilities that that entails. Executives and their employees are in an excellent position to spread the sustainability bug far and wide.

We saw instances of this in previous chapters – the Unilever employee who was harvesting rainwater at home in India, the European beverage manufacturer employees who were urged to recycle bottles at home, the Bosch employees in China who were expected to influence family members to sort waste. Ultimately, each one of us must take ownership of planet and people. Imagine the leverage we would have if every employee, supply chain manager, or community member caught the sustainability bug and started to spread it to others in society.

Why is sustainability a prime candidate for ownership within the corporate setting and beyond? Because, as the youth activism stories above demonstrate, most of us are yearning to do something about the dire situation facing us. Issues such as global warming, inequality, and poverty – and many, many more, as outlined in the UN's Sustainable Development Goals (SDGs) – are now becoming visible and in consequence have gained urgency. In the United States, 2.2 million workers earned only $7.25 an hour or less in 2016; the Federal minimum wage that hasn't increased in a decade, making the debate about what should constitute a living wage a frontline issue.

Taking ownership of issues like this and taking action in their name forms our identity and self-esteem. We see ourselves – and, even better, we also come to be seen – as being "part of the solution." Moreover, we can all take small actions to collectively make a big difference – imagine what would happen if we all reused shopping bags whenever we were out and about. Initiatives like this fulfill our need for efficacy, our need to make a difference. We feel less guilty as we are doing our part to make our and our children's lives better.

The model of ownership developed in Chapter 2 and beyond addresses the all-important "how." The three broad stages of incubate, launch, and entrench describe the steps to sustainability ownership in walkable chunks. No one can place a foot on this path before realizing that profit is the consequence of value creation for all stakeholders, and that the value you and your company create has to be in line with your corporate purpose.

In a recent article, journalist Charles Duhigg tells an interesting story about going to his Harvard Business School MBA reunion 15 years after graduating.

He found that many of his former classmates were miserable in their professional lives. I was intrigued to learn that one of Duhigg's friends earned $1.2 million per year but hated going to the office. Why? Because his job was all about earning an extra percentage point of return on the investments he was making. It was not about improving the lives of the retirees whose pensions he was managing. The message is clear: "Workers want to feel that their labors are meaningful." It is easier for most of us to identify with a cause that is larger than self-interest. That is why purpose will always trump profit when it comes to finding meaning in our lives.

2 Quick review of the model for would–be sustainability leaders

Contouring your corporate purpose is the key first step – it is finding the answer to the all-important question of why you and your company do what you do. Some experience their epiphanies in the desert, others on seeing a homeless person on the street, or after a rude nudge by a non-governmental organization (NGO). I remember a story told by Frank Henke, the sustainability head of Adidas, at one of my Berlin Roundtable meetings. Adidas's then-CEO was attending the 1998 soccer World Cup Final in Paris. He was voicing his pride that the ball for the match between France and Brazil carried the Adidas logo. But suddenly a Greenpeace emissary tapped him on the shoulder to tell him that the ball had been made in a Chinese prison.

The claim turned out to be true. It was symptomatic of the kind of supply chain transgressions consumers have opined, and companies have battled for many years. It forced Adidas to take a hard look at itself and transform its organization, in part by giving it a clear purpose: "Through sports, we have the power to change lives." Today, Adidas works hard on sustainability and even has a shoe made from plastics recovered from the ocean.

Ray Anderson, the former CEO of carpet manufacturer Interface, got his push for purpose another way. In 1994, he was at the height of his success with Interface, a company he had built with grit and determination. But that year, one of his customers asked Anderson a question that would define the rest of his life: "What is your company doing for the environment?" In an effort to discover the answer to that question, Anderson read a book by Paul Hawken, *The Ecology of Commerce*. It made him aware for the first time that Interface was doing much more to harm the environment than it was doing good. Anderson came to describe himself as a "plunderer" and to believe he should go to jail for his deeds.

This "spear in the chest" epiphany led to what Anderson later called his "mid-course correction." He went on a quest to prove that sustainability was not just the right thing to do, but the smart thing to do. His mission led him to deliver his message from shop floors to the White House. He was clear, direct, and demanding. He captivated audiences with his stories about life's lessons. When he was asked how he would go about overcoming the challenges and complexities facing the world, his reply borrowed from the lyrics of a Sunday school hymn he learned while a child – "Brighten the Corner Where You Are." He pushed, prodded, inspired, and chided all who would listen. He challenged the people around him, anyone who would listen, to create a better world for our children. Some of his inspiring videos are on YouTube.

The step of contouring purpose is typically done by the CEO with his leadership team. But there is nothing to stop you from engaging more of your employees at this stage already – they are an integral part of the company after all. But it is not enough to contour and define purpose, it has to be communicated far and wide – both internally and externally. In an interesting study, Claudine Gartenberg, Andrea Prat and George Serafeim looked at the relationship between firm purpose and financial performance. They found that purpose fuels performance only when there is "clarity," when employees know exactly what the firm wants to achieve. Importantly, and contrary to conventional wisdom, the relationship between clarity of purpose and financial performance is strongest for middle management, those responsible for implementing the strategy of the organization. The role of clarity can hardly be overemphasized. A study by PwC found that more than 50 percent of CEOs said their employees did not understand how to translate purpose and values into tangible actions.

Defining concrete sustainability goals is a key starting point for bringing purpose to life in your company. No one company can solve all the world's problems. What is material from a sustainability standpoint differs from company to company, and even within a company, say from region to region. But making goals concrete can reduce the burden of gathering information for those tasked with reaching these targets. Defining goals also allows stakeholders to understand them and how they can be achieved, fostering feelings of ownership. Companies must footprint their value chains to identify hotspots, and they must seek stakeholder input when assessing materiality. Companies that focus on material issues boast sustainability initiatives that are up to 50 percent more profitable than companies that do not.

Armed with a clear corporate purpose and a set of concrete goals, you are ready to launch your sustainability plan to employees and other stakeholders. Job #1 is to entice everyone to assume sustainability ownership – from the boardroom to the mail room, suppliers' representatives, community members, and customers. I hope this sounds familiar by now. We need all hands on deck. When an object or idea is attractive, it is an easier target for ownership. Which is why you shouldn't remind your stakeholders of what they can do for sustainability. You should tell them what sustainability can do for them. Engaging in sustainability can make them feel part of the solution, it can make them feel valued. And it can make them money.

Inova Health System went through this exercise. As Seema Wadhwa, assistant vice president of sustainability and wellness, reported in a *Wharton Magazine* article, employees engage more deeply with their own health and sustainability if everyone can be made "to see not just what effect we are

having on the environment, but what effect the environment is having on us."
When stakeholders ask: "Why should I care about the environment," an effective response would be, "Because it impacts the air you breathe and the food
you eat." There are many ways to have such conversations about sustainability.
Deutsche Telekom, for example, has "sustainable breakfasts," BASF regularly
organizes brown-bag lunches, and Marks & Spencer has informal after-hours
meetings at local pubs. Of course, for new recruits, sustainability sessions during their induction training are a must.

Framing your messaging appropriately to entice stakeholders is crucial.
Today, most of us believe that doing our part for sustainability is the "right
thing to do." However, there are hard-nosed line managers for whom the
financial argument continues to dominate. You need to convince them that
sustainability is the "smart thing to do" and show them the various ways by
which sustainability can reduce costs and increase revenue.

Hybrid appeals that combine propositions for the heart and for the head
are also effective. This is the phase where there should be a lot of buzz and
excitement in the organization about the sustainability agenda. Both the company leadership and sustainability ambassadors should seize the opportunity to
spread the word in the organization. Such tactics can be very effective. As the
chief operations officer of one consumer goods company said about the middle
management in his company:

> They've got there now. I mean, if you talk to people that are in middle
> management, they get it. They understand it, and the ones that might have
> been a little questioning or skeptical in the beginning are not anymore.

Among other benefits, the enticement process discourages that negative inner
voice that so often growls in many of our heads – what difference can I or even
my company make to this huge problem?

Enabling employees and other value-chain stakeholders to integrate sustainability into their day jobs is the surest way to build ownership. It allows stakeholders to gain a deep understanding and invest themselves in relevant issues,
fulfilling their needs for efficacy, identity, and belongingness. Training and the
creative freedom to identify solutions are key, as are lowering the costs and
increasing the benefits of acting sustainably. Management systems with built-in
processes that make it unnecessary to reinvent the wheel are very effective. As
a Marks & Spencer manager said:

> Sustainability is baked into our decision making. When somebody pushes
> the button in our business, within reason, Plan A happens automatically.
> You don't have to think about Plan A at the end of the process, it's built
> into the process.

This is a great example of a context in which the costs of acting sustainably
are low.

For those of you who lead or work for companies that have multiple locations, bear in mind that sharing best practice is another great way to reduce learning costs. As I heard from the sustainability chief of a beverage manufacturer: "Best practices in water use in one factory can be shared with another factory – best practices in terms of waste management absolutely the same. It doesn't need to come through my office." Being able to share is crucial.

Companies should also do whatever they can to increase the incentives to conduct business through the sustainability lens. Such benefits can be financial in nature – tying bonuses to sustainability performance, for example, or promoting those who take leadership in this area. But benefits can also be psychosocial – higher self-esteem, say, or more meaning to a job. A favorable cost-benefit ratio will go a long way in promoting sustainability ownership.

The third and final phase of the model deals with entrenching sustainability ownership so that sustainable behaviors become routine. The main idea is to keep sustainability salient in the organization and create self-investment opportunities for stakeholders.

The first step toward entrenching sustainability ownership is to demystify – or make evident – stakeholders' contributions to achieving sustainability targets. This allows them to feel accomplished and competent. In other words, you must measure and communicate back to stakeholders the progress they have made – this can prompt a joyous feeling if goals have been exceeded or create the resolve to do more and better if they are found lacking. Comparisons across factories, stores, or geographic regions are terrific for stirring constructive competition.

The measures themselves, of course, are idiosyncratic to your business. An executive from the financial services firm Old Mutual told me:

> We're looking at setting bigger, more aspirational targets. How many people will we touch with all our financial education programs? How many people's lives will we change and, in a sense, give them that financial well-being and help them achieve their lifetime financial growth?

In comparison, at BASF I heard that: "Our main concerns are emissions to water [i.e. effluents], energy usage, and [greenhouse gas] GHG emissions." You need to figure out the most important key performance indicators (KPIs) for your company and measure them correctly and continuously. Then you have to cascade the results to every relevant stakeholder. That will help build pride, entrench sustainability ownership, and inspire stakeholders to do more.

The second way to entrench sustainability ownership is to enliven your sustainability program. Pep it up to make your message stay fresh and appear vital at the forefront of stakeholders' thinking. Inspire them to conduct business through the sustainability lens. Co-creation, celebration, and communication – the Three Cs – are the best way to achieve this.

GE provides a great early example of co-creation with the Energy Treasure Hunt. While the main purpose of the Energy Treasure Hunt was to identify opportunities to use resources efficiently, a more important result was the start of a culture change. Employees were encouraged to tackle wasted energy through the exhortation "genchi genbutsu" – loosely translated as "go and see," but what GE refers to as "get your boots on."

While efficiency projects were the direct outcome of that initiative, GE trained more than 3,500 of its employees around the world to think about wasted energy and water in a different and powerful way. Those individuals identified more than 5,000 projects that presented many opportunities to drive energy efficiency, eventually eliminating 700,000 metric tons of greenhouse gas emissions and $111 million in operational cost. And they also understood the link between cost and wasted resources as it applied to their own jobs.

Turning to the uses of celebration, Marks & Spencer has annual sustainability award ceremonies with over 400 nominations worldwide. A "real kind of red carpet event," as one employee told me about these ceremonies.

> We hear some of the most incredible stories of people going the extra mile to do the right thing [the manager said]. It might be for an organization for which they fund-raise or volunteer for, or it might be for them getting their whole store on board with Plan A, in a way that you'd never imagine.

The final step to entrench sustainability ownership is to show your stakeholders that there are supremely good and necessary reasons to expand the company's sense of ownership to other actors – including traditional competitors – to benefit the collective good. As I showed in Chapter 9, collaboration is hard but essential if you want to tackle the tragedies of the commons so abundant today. A food company executive put it this way:

> If we all do it then our industry survives – because if our industry goes down the drain, we can be a good company, but we will also go down the drain. So we need to have a collective approach to this.

As a company collaborates with NGOs, governments, and competitors, and communicates its actions to its value-chain members and beyond, the idea of ownership goes from the company, to the industry it's in, to planet and society. That's what you and your company need to be doing.

That's what Adidas did, for example. At the meeting of my Business Roundtable in Berlin in April 2018, Frank Henke, vice president of sustainability at the sportswear maker, related a fascinating story about the challenges of collaborating with NGOs and competing companies. "In the early years we made the mistake of believing that we can manage everything," he said. "But it doesn't work, particularly something which takes place further upstream in the supply chain."

Adidas realized this the hard way when Greenpeace came knocking to ask, as Henke put it: "Are you doing wastewater testing at your suppliers? How are you formulating or defining your input chemicals for your business partners, so they know that they're using the right formulas?" The company confessed it didn't have a clue. For years, Adidas had tested its products to make sure they met all legal standards. But had not thought of managing chemicals in its supply chain. This was a problem because companies for decades had dumped chemicals and other industrial waste in the natural environment. What if Adidas' suppliers were still doing so?

Greenpeace, for its part, launched its "Detox My Fashion" campaign in July 2011 to address this. It was asking the textile industry to urgently take responsibility for its contribution to the problem, past and present. Hazardous chemicals – including 11 priority groups identified by Greenpeace – are commonly used by many well-known brands to make clothes. These chemicals were found in effluent from their supply chain manufacturers, in their products, and in the environment, despite decades of regulation and corporate responsibility programs.

In response, six global sportswear and fashion brands, including Adidas, Nike, and H&M, formed the Zero Discharge of Hazardous Chemicals (ZDHC) group in 2011. It was a collective industry response to Greenpeace's Detox campaign, and it inspired the companies to make detox commitments shortly after ZDHC's launch. But the going eventually proved tough. The brands were committed in principle but didn't know each other that well. They found they had different communication and decision-making styles, making agreements hard to reach.

"Our industry is heavily characterized by many players who are super self-confident, these are brands, brands with a very strong public exposure," Henke said. "So you can imagine how hard it is to find a common denominator." As a result, some of the meetings between the companies and Greenpeace dragged on for almost 24 hours. No one wanted to make too many concessions – and the problem of reaching agreement only got worse when ZDHC's membership increased.

Remember that I said in Chapter 9 that this last stage of your company's path to sustainability might not be easy. Greenpeace views the ZDHC initiative with ambivalence: The companies involved have still not collectively endorsed or implemented some of the key principles of Detox. But they need to do so if they want to begin a fully credible implementation of eliminating all hazardous substances by 2020. Moreover, the 70-plus brands that have now signed up to Detox represent only 15 percent of global textile production – 85 percent of the textile industry is still doing little to eliminate hazardous chemicals and improve factory conditions.

But remember I also said in Chapter 9 that collaboration was the only way to tackle major issues – or rather, to begin to tackle them. And indeed, after Henke had laid out ZDHC's problems, he suddenly struck an optimistic note.

> Step by step we have been moving on in terms of turning risks into opportunities [he said]. Working with business partners and building a level of joint understanding, commitment in terms of management systems, training, capacity-building, and communication tools that truly help business partners is the only way to move forward.

Collaborations may never entirely get over their teething troubles. But collaboration is a must in certain contexts, however tricky it is. And things often get better over time. For example, the collaboration challenges of ZDHC described above mostly represent the status in the first years of the organization. Since the organization was transformed into a foundation, based in Amsterdam and with a strong team in place, it has turned into a more effective and impactful organization. The ZDHC tools and standards have been more widely adopted by relevant stakeholders thereby contributing to better chemical management in our industry.

Now that we have revisited all the steps of the model, you might ask what that sense of sustainability ownership does for your company. Sustainability journalist and Greenbiz CEO Joel Makower relates how after spending a day with the head of sustainability at a large, Midwestern printing company, seeing the impressive work they were doing to reduce waste and cut costs, he asked his host how big the company was. "Sixty-eight hundred people," his host said. "And how many are working on these environmental initiatives?" Makower asked. Without hesitation, the manager responded: "Sixty-eight hundred." The perfect answer, Makower thought.

This book has that ambition for every company – to have all hands on deck of the good ship Sustainability. How can your company accomplish this? By making conducting business through the sustainability lens second nature. There is a yearning among your stakeholders for a better world – remember I said they are "uncomfortably numb." Your job is to use the steps outlined to shine a light and to illuminate the way forward. As one CEO who has worked tirelessly to transform his company to a sustainable business model said about his employees: "They are always looking for things they can do to save money, reduce energy, reduce water, increase recycling." At this point, sustainability becomes an extension of every employee's self. Their desire to maintain, protect, and enhance that identity results in higher productivity and greater responsibility to protect, nurture, and improve environment and society.

3 Sustainability leaders continuously collect feedback and refine strategy

If you follow the steps I have described in this book, you will make a difference not only to your own company, but to your industry and to the planet and people as well. But as I have emphasized, you cannot take a scripted or formulaic approach to this journey. There will be context-specific twists and turns you will have to navigate. To fully leverage your investment, you'll need to empirically assess what works best for your employees and other stakeholders.

How many people are aware of your purpose? To what extent do they identify with it? Which framing – the right thing vs. the smart thing – resonates better? How does this differ across employee levels? Do employees feel they are empowered by the company to identify solutions? There will be many more questions, depending on those twists and turns and the model you come to implement. Never forget to ask to what extent employees perceive a sense of sustainability ownership. Most importantly, always ask whether and how are they integrating sustainability into their daily decision making? Collecting and analyzing this data will make you see what works and what doesn't. This will enable you to revise your strategy continuously. I would recommend doing this exercise once this year – a bit like an annual medical check.

Together with my colleagues Sankar Sen and Laura Marie Schons, I recently started a small, preliminary data collection exercise, what we in the research world call a "pretest." We are collecting data from a cross-section of employees working in different companies. The respondents and their companies are anonymous unless participants choose to disclose names. The good news is that a third of the respondents think their company has a purpose that goes beyond profit and can articulate it in plain English. Here are a couple of examples of stated purpose: "To provide care for underprivileged families with a need," or "to help people love where they live (i.e. fixing up the house, the lawn, the garden, etc.)." The slightly less good news is that there is clearly a need to do more in this regard. Some respondents said their company's purpose was "to sell as many watches as possible" or "making more money." The companies these participants work for desperately need a shift in mindset.

The pretest has also delivered preliminary evidence of employees voluntarily engaging in sustainable conduct at work. Here are three examples: "I turn off the lights of the computer labs that are not in use," "fitting more packages into a trailer," and "making suggestions on how to use less chemicals." You may not think that these actions amount to much, but remember, small actions multiplied by many people equal a big difference. I also want to highlight one other interesting response: "I work for a sustainable company, but the duties of my position do not allow me to make sustainability decisions." This is a cry for help on the part of the employee. They sound all too willing to help – a missed opportunity for the organization. This company needs to show its employee how they can contribute.

Going forward, my colleagues and I are going to collect data from many more individuals working in different companies. We aim to empirically test the drivers and facilitators of sustainability ownership. Then we want to look at the link between such ownership and actual decisions made on the job. We expect this hard data to be illuminating.

4 Your sustainability is unsustainable if it fails to reach other stakeholders

As I have emphasized throughout the book, the ultimate goal is to make each and every one of us owners – and then champions – of sustainability. Employees, supply chain managers, community members are typically the first targets of any company setting out on the path to sustainability. But remember that no one can afford to ignore their customers for long.

When I asked Mike Barry of Marks & Spencer to describe one big challenge he was facing, he said without hesitation:

> I think it all leads back to our ability to connect with our customer. Thirty-one million people visit our shops and our websites every week. But I don't think we've yet managed to land Plan A properly as a customer proposition.

I probed a bit more, asking him what he would like to see happen. He replied:

> What I'm looking for is a sense of "together we're stronger." If all of us just don't take one new carry bag every week, if we recycle our packaging, wash at low temperatures, recycle our clothing. That might be quite easy individually. Across 31 million people it's harder but makes a much bigger difference. That's customers.

Customers can become the big multiplier for your company's sustainability initiatives. Unilever touches the lives of 2.5 billion customers every day. As you read before, most of Unilever's footprint is from the consumer use and disposal phase and that's obviously where the company has the biggest challenge to get traction. Customers are undoubtedly an extremely important group and companies need to encourage them to behave more sustainably in their daily lives. The question is, how best to reach them?

In the business-to-business context, employees of, say, a manufacturing company are the most effective channel. They are in constant contact with their clients and best understand the nuances of sustainability in the products and services they offer. This is also a reasonable strategy in the retailing world, where employees often interact with customers, and have the chance to educate them. As a retailing executive told me:

> Change can come from our store personnel talking to customers, like, look at this organic product or look at this product where we reduced the packaging. Those are the kind of conversations that are going to bring about systemic change.

This is not a foolproof strategy as many customers may dash in and out of stores, and not have any interest in speaking to company representatives. But it's a start.

But the business-to-consumer context will remain the trickiest. We buy so many things in supermarkets, shopping malls, and online without ever interacting with another person. Few consumers take the time to find out sustainability information by looking at product features, usage, or disposal options. And few companies are as bold as outdoor clothing manufacturer Patagonia, which urges its consumers to lessen their footprint through provocative communication, even exhortation: "Don't Buy this Jacket."

This advertisement first ran on the day after Thanksgiving in the USA in 2011 – a day also known as Black Friday as it is traditionally the biggest shopping day of the year. The company plainly stated: "We ask you to buy less and to reflect before you spend a dime on this jacket or anything else." Most of us in the developed world consume way too much. As Annie Leonard points out in "The Story of Stuff," per capita consumption in the USA has doubled in the last 50 years. An even more telling statistic is that 99 percent of the "stuff" bought in the USA is thrown away within six months of purchase. We desperately need responsible consumerism.

Consumers must demand that sustainability information be made available front and center – as boldly as price and quality. Dinner-table conversations are a good forum for raising sustainability awareness. But education is the real key, school has to be the starting point. By that, I mean sustainability has to become an integral part of school and college curricula – by the time I get my MBA or executive education students to play the fishing game, it's too late.

Thanks to the huge power of advertising, all the modern consumer sees of the whole product life cycle is usually the consumption phase. Most of us don't know where our products come from or where they go after we use them. The stages of extraction, manufacturing, delivery, and disposal aren't visible to us – and they're certainly not advertised by companies.

This has to change. Young people who are taking to the streets to protest about climate change are ready to learn about the conditions in the mines and fields, in the factories and in the garbage dumps and oceans. They are ready to learn about the role of consumption in creating our footprint. I regularly teach 30-year-olds and they have a hard time relating emissions and our footprint to our consumption habits. Why? Is this knowledge any less important today than the chemistry formulas my 16-year-old has to learn? The state of planet and people has to be part of school curricula worldwide, starting in elementary school.

Regulation is also an incredibly important part of the equation as it has the power to steer both companies and consumers. If we compare quality of life and ecological footprints in the European Union and the United States, some differences become apparent. According to the United Nations Development Program, both regions are equally developed in terms of the parameters of human development – per capita income, education, life expectancy. But the average EU citizen has a far smaller ecological footprint than the average American citizen.

The difference is partly attributable to the stricter regulatory environment in the EU. And partly down to the culture of individual European countries, which, over time, has conditioned its citizens to behave more sustainably. I lived in Berlin for eight years and noticed how recycling was a serious activity in the German capital – to the point of putting different colored bottles in different recycling bins. In Pittsburgh, Pennsylvania, where I currently live, we don't sort recycling items ahead of time – we're told (and we trust) they're sorted later. Recently, the EU passed legislation to ban single-use plastics such as cutlery and straws by 2021 – it is difficult to envision anything similar happening in the USA or other big countries anytime soon.

The huge populations of China and India are just beginning the mass consumption of convenience and fast foods, and although there are isolated pockets of regulatory excellence in both countries, the likelihood of a complete ban on plastics – or, for that matter, palm oil or fossil fuels – any time soon is rather dim. But during a recent visit to General Motors in China, I was heartened to learn that the Chinese government encourages the purchase of electric and hybrid vehicles by imposing a far lower tax of about 5 percent of the purchase price relative to the whopping 30 percent charged on conventional gasoline vehicles, not to mention that there is no wait for the license plates for the former compared to the uncertain lottery system used to allocate plates for the latter. Many more of such regulatory moves are absolutely essential.

In the same vein, there are plenty of good ideas around in the USA as well – the "Green New Deal," proposed by young Democrats in the US House of Representatives, for example, or the "Accountable Capitalism Act," tabled by Senator Elizabeth Warren, who is running for president in 2020. But the road to these ideas being implemented even in the United States is rather rocky, to put it politely.

Which brings us back to starting with companies as the focal point of sustainability transformation. If you can recognize the warning signs, you don't need to wait for legislation to change your company's ways, you can start to transform its business model today. No one knows how the future will unfold. But doing nothing for sustainability today will prove suicidal for business as we know it. To repeat from Chapter 4 what one executive told me:

> I can't exactly say how the world's going to unfold over the next 10–20 years, with climate change, with inequality, with issues to do with business behavior. But I do know that what's expected of business will be dramatically different than today. We're trying to create in the organization the ability to respond and adapt to whatever the world throws at us.

I call this working within our spheres of influence. This is ultimately all we can do. I can write, I can teach, I can help companies with my expertise. But I cannot single-handedly solve any of our mega-challenges. None of us can. Perhaps you are running a small company or a restaurant. Or perhaps you are working for a big company and aspiring to be its CEO one day. Or you are preparing for a job interview. Or perhaps you are a department or business-unit head. Whoever you are, whatever you do, I hope that this book has proved valuable. If it did, you now need to join the movement and put your knowledge to work. My writing this book was a small action. But our collectively acting upon it could make a big difference.

Bibliography

M. Taylor, S. Laville, A. Walker, P. Noor, and J. Henley (2019). School pupils call for radical climate action in UK-wide strike, *The Guardian*.

C. Duhigg (February 24, 2019). The future of work: Wealthy, successful, and miserable. *New York Times Magazine*.

D. Kiron, G. Unruh, N. Kruschwitz, M. Reeves, H. Rubel, A. Meyer Zum Feld (2017). *Corporate Sustainability at a Crossroads: Progress Toward Our Common Future in Uncertain Times*. MIT Sloan Management Review, Boston Consulting Group.

Global Environmental Leadership & Knowledge at Wharton (2015). *Employees Can Be a Powerful Force in Sustainability. Initiative for Global Environmental Leadership*. IGEL, Wharton, University of Pennsylvania.

C. Gartenberg, A. Prat, and G. Serafeim (2019). Corporate purpose and financial performance, *Organization Science*, 30(1), 1–18.

G. Hancock (2009). *How GE's 'Treasure Hunts' Discovered More Than $110M in Energy Savings*. Greenbiz.com.

PricewaterhouseCoopers (PwC) (2017). *Connecting the Dots: How Purpose Can Join Up Your Business*. PWC.

A. Leonard, L. Fox, and J. Sachs (2007). *The Story of Stuff*. Directed by Louis Fox and produced by Free Range Studios. Executive Producers included Tides Foundation and the Funders Workgroup for Sustainable Production and Consumption.

T. Nudd (November 28, 2011). Ad of the day: Patagonia…, Ad of the day: Patagonia – The Brand Declares War on Consumerism Gone Berserk, and admits its own environmental failings. *Adweek*.

United Nations (2018). *Human Development Reports*. United Nations Development Programme. Available at: http://hdr.undp.org/en/2018.

Index

Page numbers in **bold** reference tables; Page numbers in *italics* reference figures.